DRAFTING COMMERCIAL AGREEM

Drafting Commercial Agreements

A G J Berg, BA (OXON)
Solicitor

Butterworths
London, Dublin, Edinburgh
1991

United Kingdom	Butterworth & Co (Publishers) Ltd, 88 Kingsway, London WC2B 6AB and 4 Hill Street, Edinburgh EH2 3JZ
Australia	Butterworths Pty Ltd, Sydney, Melbourne, Brisbane, Adelaide, Perth, Canberra and Hobart
Belgium	Butterworth & Co (Publishers) Ltd, Brussels
Canada	Butterworths Canada Ltd, Toronto and Vancouver
Ireland	Butterworths (Ireland) Ltd, Dublin
Malaysia	Malayan Law Journal Sdn Bhd, Kuala Lumpur
New Zealand	Butterworths of New Zealand Ltd, Wellington and Auckland
Puerto Rico	Equity de Puerto Rico, Inc, Hato Rey
Singapore	Butterworths Asia, Singapore
USA	Butterworth Legal Publishers, Austin, Texas; Boston, Massachusetts; Clearwater, Florida (D & S Publishers); Orford, New Hampshire (Equity Publishing); St Paul, Minnesota; and Seattle, Washington

Reprinted 1992

A CIP Catalogue record for this book is available from the British Library.

ISBN 0 406 00142 1

Typeset by Kerrypress Ltd, Luton, Bedfordshire
Printed and bound in Great Britain by Dotesios Ltd, Trowbridge, Wiltshire.

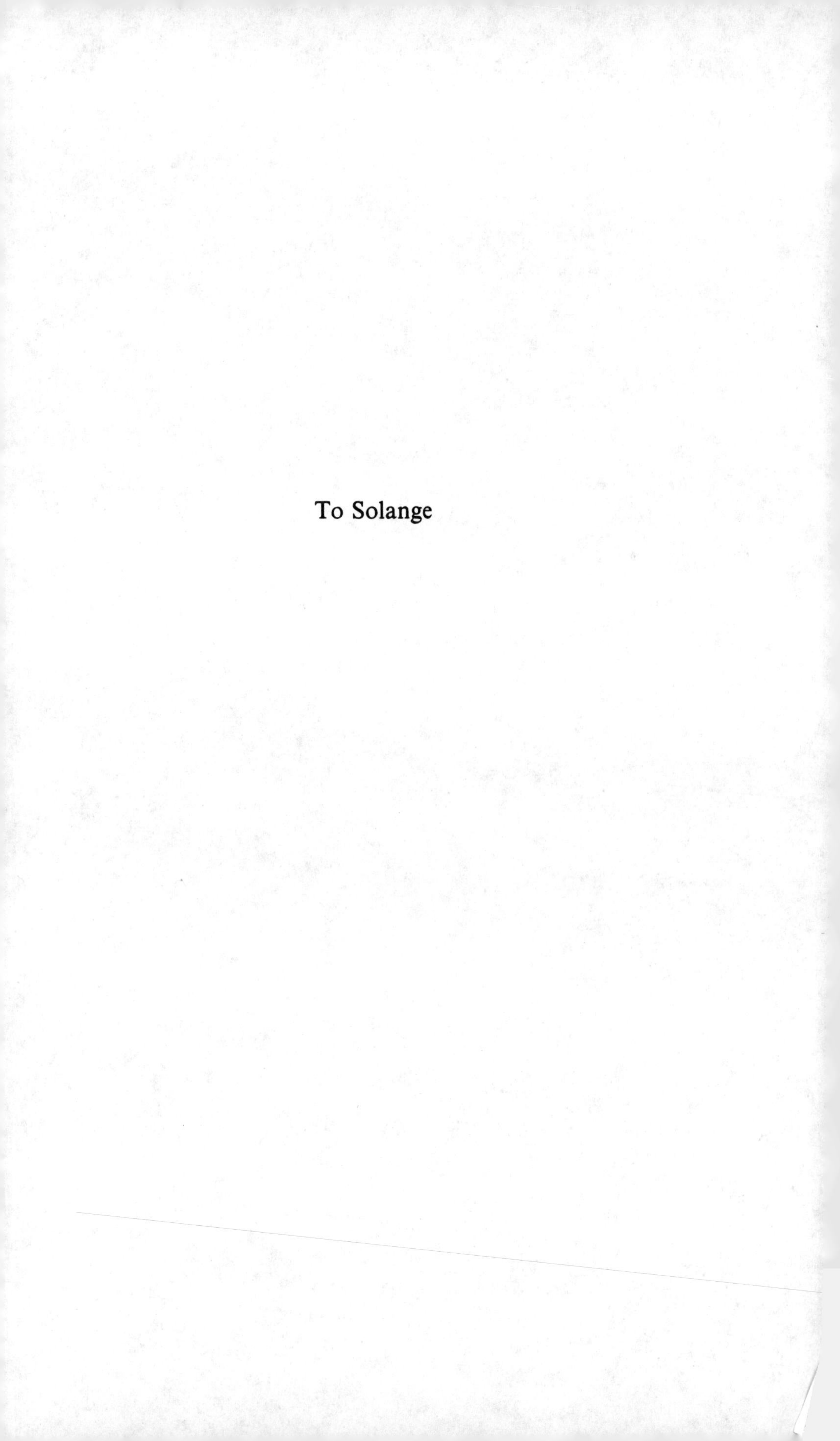

To Solange

PREFACE

Drafting is an important part of lawyers' non-contentious work, particularly in commercial practices. And for the client, it is no less essential that the contract which he signs should be drafted clearly and correctly than that he should be properly advised on points of law. Moreover, the increasing complexity of commercial transactions calls for correspondingly developed drafting techniques.

The main purpose of this book is to describe modern drafting techniques. It also examines certain points which often arise in drafting a commercial agreement; these include those relating to the Law of Property (Miscellaneous Provisions) Act 1989, the 1968 Brussels Convention on jurisdiction and the enforcement of judgments and the 1980 Rome Convention on the law applicable to contractual obligations.

The drafting methods described are primarily relevant to commercial agreements, but they can be used for family settlements and other non-commercial documents. Most of these methods are those now used in English legislation; these tend to be more advanced than those employed even by the larger law firms. Also, an Act of Parliament may reasonably be taken as an indication of acceptable usage.[1]

This book is mainly intended to assist those starting their careers as lawyers. But it may also be of interest to more experienced practitioners, including lawyers in other European countries who need to prepare contracts in English.

There has been an attempt to reflect the law as at 1 June 1991. However, the Companies Act 1985 is referred to as it is amended by the Companies Act 1989, even though not all the amendments were then in force. Similarly, the 1968 Brussels Convention is referred

1 Modern legislative drafting was pioneered in England by Henry (later Lord) Thring. He drew a vast amount of major legislation, including the second Reform Act of 1867 and Mr Gladstone's Irish Home Rule Bill of 1886. His comparative account of drafting for Mr Gladstone and Mr Disraeli is reproduced in Appendix 3 below.

to in amended form set out in the Civil Jurisdiction and Judgments Act 1982 (Amendment) Order 1990.

The discussion on page 122 of the damages recoverable for misrepresentation should be read in the light of the Court of Appeal's decision in *East v Maurer* [1991] 2 All ER 733, [1991] 1 WLR 461, which was reported after the text went to press. This decision establishes that a person who has purchased a business in reliance on a fraudulent misrepresentation (in that case, a statement of intention) is entitled to damages equal to the profits which he might reasonably be expected to have made had he used the purchase price in buying a hypothetical alternative business in a similar line of trade (as well as to damages for the losses he has incurred in the business that he actually purchased). *Royscot Trust Ltd v Rogerson* indicates that this measure of damages applies under section 2(1) of the Misrepresentation Act 1967.

Mr Lawrence Thacker of Wadham College, Oxford kindly read the book in proof, but any errors remain the author's responsibility. The consideration and patience of the staff of Butterworths is also gratefully acknowledged.

Note to the 1992 reprint

Three particular developments since the original publication date require mentioning. In *Walford v Miles* [1992] 1 All ER 453, the House of Lords approved the statement of Lord Denning MR in *Courtney & Fairbairn Limited v Tolaini Bros* that the law does not recognise a contract to negotiate, but held that a 'lock-out' agreement would be enforceable if made for good consideration and if limited to a specified period; accordingly P, negotiating with V for the purchase of V's property, can obtain an enforceable undertaking from V that, during a specified period, V will not negotiate with anyone else regarding the sale of his property.

In *Kurz v Stella Musical Veranstaltungs GmbH* [1992] 1 All ER 630 Hoffmann J held that a non-exclusive submission to the jurisdiction of the English courts is valid under article 17 of the 1968 Brussels Convention on Jurisdiction and the Enforcement of Civil and Commercial Judgments.

In *Watts v Morrow* [1990] 4 All ER 939, the Court of Appeal reaffirmed the principle that the proper measure of damages for breach of contract is the sum of money which will, so far as possible, put the plaintiff into as good a position as if the contract had been properly performed.

CONTENTS

LIST OF CASES

C

S

CHAPTER 1

STRUCTURE OF THE TYPICAL AGREEMENT

A typical commercial agreement takes the following form.

Commencement

The agreement starts with a formal commencement part, often indicating the nature of the agreement (eg 'This Underwriting Agreement' or 'This Assignment'). The commencement specifies the date on which the agreement is entered into and the parties to it.

Recitals

The formal commencement may or may not be followed by recitals (or preambles). These are paragraphs introduced by the word 'Whereas' which describe, or recite, various background facts against which the agreement should be read. Often recitals also state the purposes for which an agreement is being entered into.

Operative part

Following the recitals, this one-line rubric always appears:

'NOW IT IS HEREBY AGREED as follows:-'

In an agreement without recitals similar words follow the list of parties in the formal commencement. These words signal the beginning of the operative part of the agreement – the provisions which actually create rights and obligations or create or transfer interests in property.

Definitions

In all but the simplest agreements the first operative clause is usually a general definitions clause. This sets out the definitions of terms used throughout the document. Most defined terms are given capital initial letters; for example 'the Security Documents'. Particular Parts or clauses of an agreement may also contain their own definitions provisions covering terms which are used only in the Parts or clauses concerned and not elsewhere in the agreement. Definitions clauses are of great importance. Many defined terms will be key concepts of fundamental importance to how the agreement works.

Sometimes the definitions are put at the end of the agreement. The advantage of this is that the reader does not have to work through what can be a long and legalistic clause before coming to the main business terms.

Conditions precedent

Where the general definitions clause is at the start of the document, it is often followed by a clause stipulating that certain of the agreement's provisions are to come into force only if and when specified conditions are satisfied. These conditions may concern the receipt of certain documents, such as legal opinions about the validity of the agreement. They can also relate to such matters as the receipt of clearances from the Inland Revenue (usually under section 707 of the Income and Corporation Taxes Act 1988 or section 88 of the Capital Gains Tax Act 1979). Common conditions in agreements for the purchase of companies concern receipt of confirmation from the Director-General of Fair Trading that it is not his intention to refer the transaction to the Monopolies and Mergers Commission and the admission to the Official List (ie the granting of a Stock Exchange listing) of any shares which the purchaser will issue to the vendors as the consideration for the acquisition.

These conditions can be crucial because they protect a party against becoming bound by the substantive provisions of the agreement unless and until all the prerequisites which are essential to the deal from his point of view have been satisfied. So, a bank making a loan will require that, before it becomes obliged to advance any money, it must have received a legal opinion that its security will be valid.

The positioning of these clauses about pre-conditions varies, and often they are to be found in the middle of an agreement. But the beginning is usually a more logical place.

Other operative provisions

Once the general definitions and conditions precedent have been set out, the agreement will proceed to describe the rights and obligations to which the parties are to become entitled and subject. The nature of the clauses dealing with this will obviously vary according to the type of transaction which the agreement documents.

But one kind of clause is found in many types of agreement. This is a clause setting out representations and warranties - statements about factual (and sometimes legal) matters which one of the parties requires to be made to him in a legally binding manner. In some agreements, notably those which concern the acquisition of companies or businesses, the clauses on representations and warranties also contain elaborate provisions specifying and limiting the damages recoverable should any of the representations and warranties prove incorrect.

Boiler-plate

The clauses towards the end of an agreement usually contain 'the boiler-plate'. These clauses deal with such matters as whether or not the parties are entitled to assign their rights under the agreement, the way in which notices under the agreement have to be served and the time at which they take effect, who is to pay the legal fees connected with the agreement, and, if an agreement has an international element, its applicable law and also in which countries it can be sued upon.

The applicable law and jurisdiction clauses are normally the last clauses. They are followed by some such formula as:

> AS WITNESS the hands of the duly authorised representatives of the parties to this Agreement the day and year first before written.

Schedules

But that is not always the end. It is increasingly common to use Schedules to set out matters of detail. Banking documents generally contain Schedules showing the addresses and participations of the banks which are parties, and agreements for the sale of companies have Schedules which specify the shareholdings of each of the vendors, the subsidiaries of the company being sold and the land and buildings held by that company and its subsidiaries. In addition, agreements for the sale of companies or businesses normally set out in a Schedule the lengthy representations and warranties about the commercial and financial position of the company or business.

Also, where an agreement provides that another document has to be delivered as a condition precedent to certain clauses of the agreement coming into force, or that a transaction under the agreement has to be carried out by means of a document in a certain form, the invariable practice is to set out the form of the document in a Schedule to the agreement. So an agreement for the sale of a private company will set out in a Schedule the form of the deed of indemnity which the vendors are required to execute as protection against potential tax liabilities, and a loan agreement will set out as a Schedule the form of the legal opinions which the banks require to receive before they become obliged to make advances.

Traditional English practice is that, where an agreement contains Schedules, the parties' signatures appear after the Schedules, right at the end of the document. This probably originates from conveyancing where Schedules often contain material of great importance (notably, details of the property being conveyed or the lease being granted) and the parties' signatures after the Schedules are intended to authenticate the contents of the Schedules as well as the provisions which go before them. However, American practice appears to be to interpose the parties' signatures between the end of the clauses and the start of the Schedules. Sometimes Schedules are described as Exhibits, Appendices or Annexes.

Many of the provisions mentioned in this Chapter will be considered in more detail later on.

Chapter 3 describes the special requirements that apply to deeds.

CHAPTER 2

COMMENCEMENT AND EXECUTION CLAUSES FOR AGREEMENTS

The following examples illustrate how an agreement commences according to whether or not it contains recitals:

THIS AGREEMENT is made on 3rd May 1991

BETWEEN

(1) ADOLPHUS & ELLIS PLC whose registered office is at 3 Cathedral Place, Barchester, Barsetshire BN8 4BL ('the Vendor') and

(2) ENTERPRISES FOJAC SA whose principal office is at 48 rue Albert Thomas, 75010 Paris ('the Purchaser')

WHEREAS the parties wish to amend an agreement between them dated 19th September 1990 ('the Acquisition Agreement') under which the Purchaser has purchased from the Vendor shares representing 60 per cent of the issued shares of T Barnardiston Limited

NOW IT IS HEREBY AGREED as follows:-

AN AGREEMENT made on 3rd May 1991

BETWEEN

(1) ADOLPHUS & ELLIS PLC whose registered office is at 3 Cathedral Place, Barchester, Barsetshire BN8 4BL ('the Vendor') and

(2) ENTERPRISES FOJAC SA whose principal office is at 48 rue Albert Thomas, 75010 Paris ('the Purchaser')

WHEREBY IT IS AGREED as follows:-

Date

Normally, the correct date to insert in an agreement is the date on which it is signed by the last party or, if it is signed in two or more parts intended to be exchanged, the date on which exchange takes place.[1]

If the parties intend their agreement to come into effect on a future date, that should be stated in a commencement clause. Similarly, if they intend that the agreement should be operational from a date earlier than that on which it was signed, a clause to that effect should be inserted. The agreement should not be ante-dated.[2] A clause which provides that an agreement shall be deemed to come into effect on a date prior to the date of signature is only effective as regards the parties to it; it cannot prejudice the position of other persons.

Parties

Traditional practice is to refer to 'AB of the one part and CD of the other part' or, if there are more than two parties, 'AB of the first part, CD of the second part ...'. Modern practice replaces this wording by numbers.

The term 'registered office' is normally confined to companies incorporated in the United Kingdom or in a jurisdiction whose company law is based on the British Companies Acts. Sometimes the registered number of a British company is also given; this might be done if it is in the course of changing its name. However, a mistake in setting out the name of a company party should be immaterial.[3]

For foreign companies, the usual term is 'principal office', although this might be thought to mean a company's management headquarters, rather than the foreign equivalent of a registered office under section 287 of the Companies Act 1985. It would certainly not be wrong to refer to a foreign company's 'registered office'; this is the term used, for example, by Council Directive (EEC) 80/390, the Listing Particulars Directive. An alternative is 'official address', the term used in section 42 of the Civil Jurisdiction and Judgments Act 1982.

The doctrine of privity of contract is relevant to determine which persons need to be made party to an agreement. The doctrine, which is currently under review by the Law Commission, normally prevents a person from enforcing, or relying on, a term in an agreement which does not name him (or otherwise identify him) as a party. For example, X cannot enforce a clause in an agreement between A, B and C which provides for A to indemnify X against certain claims; nor can X defend a negligence action by A on the ground that the

1 *Alan Estates Ltd v WG Stores Ltd* [1981] 3 All ER 481 at 485f. Exchange by a telephone conversation between solicitors was sanctioned in *Domb v Isoz* [1980] Ch 548, [1980] 1 All ER 942.
2 See section 9(1)(g), Forgery and Counterfeiting Act 1981.
3 *F Goldsmith (Sicklesmere) Ltd v Baxter* [1970] Ch 85, [1969] 3 All ER 733.

agreement between A, B and C contained a clause excluding liability on the part of X.

Sometimes it is impossible to join as parties all those whom a clause is intended to benefit or protect. A company being floated might give warranties intended to protect successful applicants for its shares, or it might give indemnities to the directors and employees of the issuing house. In such a case, the relevant undertaking can be made with a person who is a party to the agreement, and he will be stated to take the undertaking as trustee for the persons intended to be benefited – in the previous example, the investors and the issuing house's personnel. The decision of Judge David Smout QC in *Southern Water Authority v Carey*[4] indicates that a party to an agreement cannot take the benefit of an undertaking as agent for persons who cannot be identified on the date on which the agreement is entered into; but see also *New Zealand Shipping Co v Satterthwaite*[5] and *Port Jackson Stevedoring v Salmond & Spraggon*.[6] There is also this statement in *Chitty on Contracts* at paragraph 2521:

> 'It is submitted that an unnamed (but ascertainable) principal can ratify: but a person who was not in existence and contemplated at the time a contract was made eg a person who might in the future come within the particular class, cannot do so, although he can be the beneficiary of a trust.'

A trust is probably effective to confer the benefit of an undertaking on the persons whom it is really intended to benefit, but it can produce several problems for the party who is the trustee. What is his position if a conflict arises between his interests under the agreement and those of the beneficiaries? He should have an express right to resign as trustee at any time and to appoint a successor. Does he have an obligation to the beneficiaries to litigate if that becomes necessary to enforce the undertaking? At a minimum, such an obligation should be made conditional on the trustee's being indemnified for costs to his reasonable satisfaction. Can the trustee agree to an alteration of the undertaking, or of another clause in the agreement which affects the undertaking, without the consent of all the beneficiaries – which it will, of course, be impossible to obtain? The trustee should be expressly authorised to agree to amendments to the undertaking and other relevant provisions of the agreement, and also to enter into compromises and similar arrangements.

Section 2 of the Law of Property (Miscellaneous Provisions) Act 1989, discussed below, is also relevant to the choice of parties.

In the list of parties, a vendor usually appears before a purchaser; a lessor before a lessee; and a lender before a borrower.

Several parties with a common interest are usually grouped together

4 [1985] 2 All ER 1077 at 1085a.
5 [1975] AC 154, [1974] 1 All ER 1015.
6 [1980] 3 All ER 257, [1981] 1 WLR 138.

in the list of parties. For example, an agreement for the sale of a private company might be made between: (1) all shareholders who own shares in the company beneficially; (2) the trustees of the family settlement which holds the rest of the shares; (3) the purchasing company; and (4) the purchasing company's parent company, as guarantor of the purchasing company.

Successors and assigns

In listing the parties the opportunity is often taken to add wording which picks up successors and assigns. For example:

> The Commercial Bank Limited whose registered office is at 3 Lombard Place, London EC2T 1FY ('the Bank', which includes its successors and assigns).

This ensures that all subsequent references to 'the Bank' in provisions of the agreement which create rights are, as it were, directly applicable to an assignee. The effect of the 'successors and assigns' wording can be illustrated as follows: an agreement contains a clause requiring A to indemnify B in respect of certain tax liabilities which might fall on B; B assigns this agreement to C; C incurs a tax liability of the type covered by the clause; but, had B stayed in the transaction, B would not (owing to its different tax position) have incurred the liability at all or would have done so but in a lesser amount than C. Here C should be able to recover under the indemnity (on the basis that the 'successors and assigns' wording makes references to B directly applicable to C), unless the context of the indemnity shows that the 'successors and assigns' wording was not intended to apply in a way which increases the amount A has to pay.

A further illustration of the operation of the 'successors and assigns' wording is provided by the decision in *First National Finance Corpn Ltd v Goodman.*[7] The Court of Appeal held that a provision in a guarantee which defined 'the Bank' to include the bank's assigns had the effect of disapplying the rule that a change in the identity of the creditor revokes a guarantee as to future transactions; the definition extended the guarantee to advances made by a company with which the original bank amalgamated.

It is unclear whether a provision defining a party to include 'its successors and assigns' covers an assignee in provisions which impose obligations. In *Tito v Waddell (No 2)*[8] Sir Robert Megarry V-C considered at length the circumstances in which an assignee of the benefit of a contract must also bear the burden. He concluded that, apart from the conditional benefit cases (where a contract confers a right which is conditional on certain restrictions or obligations

7 [1983] BCLC 203.
8 [1977] Ch 106 at 289.

being observed or performed) and the cases of obligations annexed to property (such as mortgages or easements), there was ample authority for holding that there had become established in the law what he called 'the pure principle of benefit and burden'. Under this, the obligations under a contract can pass to an assignee of the benefit of it, even though the obligations and rights created by the contract are distinct and not interdependent. Sir Robert Megarry V-C stated[9] that the question of whether an assignee of rights under a contract will assume the obligations under it, where those are distinct from the rights,

> 'will prima facie depend upon the circumstances in which he comes into the transaction'.

The Vice-Chancellor gave this example of an assignee assuming obligations:

> '...if the assignee takes as a purported assignee of the whole contract from a company which is on the point of going into liquidation, he undertaking to discharge all the burdens and to indemnify the company, ... I would have thought that ... he was not intended to take the benefit without also assuming the burdens, and that the result would accord with the intention, vis-à-vis not only the company but also the persons entitled to enforce those burdens. No doubt the terms of any relevant document would be of major importance: but I would regard the matter as one which has to be determined from the surrounding circumstances as a whole.'

However, there is little case law to indicate in which types of contract and situation the 'pure principle of burden and obligation' operates. In practical terms, therefore, little reliance is placed on this principle and a novation is normally thought necessary in order to transfer contractual obligations in a way which discharges the original obligor. Under English law, a novation is a transaction by which A releases B from his obligations and C enters into a new contract with A under which C assumes the obligations which were previously binding on B. Any rights which B had can be assigned to C, or they can be released by B, with A conferring corresponding rights on C.[10]

Even in relation to an assignment of rights the scope of the term 'successors and assigns' is uncertain. It is not clear that it would cover a person who only has an equitable assignment: in *Safeguard Industrial Investments Ltd v National Westminster Bank Ltd*[11] the Court

9 [1977] Ch 106 at 302.

10 In *Bradford Old Bank v Sutcliffe* [1918] 2 KB 833, at 849 Scrutton LJ said: 'Novation means this: "that there being a contract in existence, some new contract is substituted for it, either between the same parties ..., or between different parties; the consideration mutually being the discharge of the old contract"; and, I may add, the undertaking of rights and duties by the new party.'

11 [1982] 1 All ER 449 at 455d and e.

of Appeal held that a reference to a 'transfer' of shares in pre-emption provisions in a private company's articles of association was 'wholly inapt to apply to transfers of beneficial interests'. However, it is thought likely that 'assigns' would cover a person taking a mortgage of a contract by means of an absolute assignment complying with section 136 of the Law of Property Act 1925. But it is doubtful whether a reference in contract 2 to A's 'successors and assigns' in respect of contract 1 would cover a person who takes over contract 1 from A by a novation which discharges contract 1, as opposed to an assignment of A's rights under contract 1, unless contract 1 plainly contemplated novations as a method of transfer.

It has been held that 'assigns' only covers a person taking under a voluntary (normally contractual) assignment, and not a person in whom a party's property and rights vest by operation of law; for example, a trustee in bankruptcy in whom the bankrupt's estate vests under section 306 of the Insolvency Act 1986 is not an assign of the bankrupt, but his successor.[12] By contrast, under the Insolvency Act 1986 the property of a company in liquidation or administration remains vested in the company except where, in a winding up by the court, it makes an order directing that the property shall vest in the liquidator. However, a liquidator's acts are treated as those of the company;[13] and it is thought that the same applies to the acts of an administrator who is deemed to act as the company's agent: Insolvency Act 1986, section 14(5). Accordingly, references to a company would cover a liquidator or an administrator without the need for any 'successors and assigns' wording.

It seems likely that 'successors and assigns' would cover another company to which part of a company's property is transferred by an order made under section 427 of the Companies Act 1985 in connection with an amalgamation, reconstruction or division of the latter company.

These considerations suggest that the traditional 'successors and assigns' formula may be inadequate to cover all modern methods of transferring rights or obligations. There could be additional problems if any of the parties is domiciled or incorporated in a country whose succession and insolvency procedures have no English counterparts. A more comprehensive formula is:

> In this Agreement references to the Company include references to a person who for the time being is entitled (by assignment, novation or otherwise) to the Company's rights under this Agreement (or any interest in those rights) or who, as administrator, liquidator or otherwise, is entitled to exercise those rights; and in particular those references include

12 See *Re Cyril Wright (a Bankrupt), ex p Joshua Landau (a Creditor) v the Trustee of the Property of the Bankrupt* [1949] Ch 729, at 736.

13 *Re Farrow's Bank Ltd* [1921] 2 Ch 164. See also *Ayerst v C&K (Construction) Ltd* [1976] AC 167, [1975] 2 All ER 537.

a person to whom those rights (or any interest in those rights) are transferred or pass as a result of a merger, division, reconstruction or other reorganisation involving the Company.

For this purpose, references to the Company's rights under this Agreement include any similar rights to which another person becomes entitled as a result of a novation of this Agreement.

Who should sign?

The general rule is that, although a person must be named (or otherwise identified) as a party to a contract to be able to enforce it or use it as a defence, he only has to sign if he assumes obligations; so a bank does not usually sign a guarantee which it receives.

An important exception is a contract falling within section 2 of the Law of Property (Miscellaneous Provisions) Act 1989:

'2 Contracts for sale etc of land to be made by signed writing

(1) A contract for the sale or other disposition of an interest in land can only be made in writing and only by incorporating all the terms which the parties have expressly agreed in one document or, where contracts are exchanged, in each.

(2) The terms may be incorporated in a document either by being set out in it or by reference to some other document.

(3) The document incorporating the terms or, where contracts are exchanged, one of the documents incorporating them (but not necessarily the same one) must be signed by or on behalf of each party to the contract.

(4) ...

(5) This section does not apply in relation to–

(a) a contract to grant such a lease as is mentioned in section 54(2) of the Law of Property Act 1925 (short leases);
(b) a contract made in the course of a public auction; or
(c) a contract regulated under the Financial Services Act 1986;

and nothing in this section affects the creation or operation of resulting, implied or constructive trusts.

(6) In this section–

'disposition' has the same meaning as in the Law of Property Act 1925;
'interest in land' means any estate, interest or charge in or over land or in or over the proceeds of sale of land.

(7) Nothing in this section shall apply in relation to contracts made before this section comes into force.

(8) Section 40 of the Law of Property Act 1925 (which is superseded by this section) shall cease to have effect.'

Section 2 is based on the Law Commission's Report No 164 about transfer of land and formalities for the sale of land.[14] That Report identified or alleged several deficiencies in the way that section 40 of the Law of Property Act 1925 operated, particularly after the decision of the House of Lords on part performance in *Steadman v Steadman.*[15]

Section 2 imposes a double requirement: all the express terms of the contract have to be contained, or incorporated by reference, in a single document; and all the parties to the contract have to sign that document, except that, where there is an exchange, it is enough for A to sign the copy that goes to B and for B to sign the copy that goes to A. The signature requirement applies even to a party who assumes no obligations under the contract.

A contract which does not comply with either of these requirements is void. This was the result recommended by the Law Commission, and contrasts with mere unenforceability under the old section 40. The doctrine of part performance, which used to save contracts which would otherwise have been unenforceable under the old law, has been abolished.

The scope of section 2 is considerably wider than pure conveyancing contracts for the sale or lease of land, and almost certainly wider than the Law Commission realised. It applies to a contract for the sale 'or other disposition of an interest in land'; by subsection (6) 'disposition' includes a mortgage or charge as well as a disclaimer, release 'and every other assurance of property or an interest therein by any instrument'. And 'interest in land' is extended to include–

> 'any estate, interest or *charge* in or over land or in or over the *proceeds of sale* of land.'

The following are some of the contracts covered by section 2:

(1) an option to buy land, and also an option to sell land; but not a notice exercising the option;[16]

(2) a letter from a borrower to his tenant irrevocably instructing him to pay his rent to a bank which has made advances to the borrower;[17]

(3) an equitable mortgage over land; since the doctrine of part performance has been abolished, an equitable mortgage over land

14 Law Commission Reports should be referred to in construing legislation based on them. In *R v Shivpuri* [1987] AC 1, [1986] 2 All ER 334, in which the House of Lords overruled its decision in the previous year in *Anderton v Ryan*, Lord Bridge regretted that in the previous case the Law Lords did not take due note of a paragraph in the relevant Law Commission Report. Similarly, in *A-G's Reference (No 1 of 1988)* [1989] AC 971, [1989] 2 All ER 1, Lord Lowry drew attention to a paragraph of a White Paper for the purpose of identifying the scope of the mischief of insider dealing.

15 [1976] AC 536, [1974] 2 All ER 977.

16 *Spiro v Glencrown Properties Ltd* [1991] 1 All ER 600.

17 In *Re Whitting, ex p Hall* (1878) 10 Ch D 615.

can no longer be created simply by a deposit of title deeds and section 2 requires the memorandum of deposit which creates the mortgage to be signed by the mortgagee as well as the mortgagor;

(4) a charge over an option to purchase land, since the option creates an equitable interest;[18]

(5) a loan agreement which provides for the borrower to create a charge over land (or its sale proceeds or rent) in certain conditions, for instances, if it breaches specified financial ratios;

(6) a contract for the transfer of a debenture secured by a floating charge[19] unless, it seems, it is entered into by either party in the course of carrying on investment business in the United Kingdom and is so regulated by the Financial Services Act 1986.

However, the section does not apply to a collateral warranty (for example, as to the vendor's title) which gives rise to an independent contract collateral to the main contract for the sale of land.[20] It is unclear whether a charge over, for example, future acquired land or the proceeds of future sales of land is a 'contract' within section 2.[1]

Section 2 probably catches a contract (for example, for the sale of a business or for a banking facility) which covers a number of disparate matters if one of the essential terms provides for the transfer or other disposition of an interest in land: this is so even though the contract would not normally be classified as a 'contract for the sale of land'.[2] *Steadman v Steadman* also suggests that, if a contract for a transaction in land is an essential element of a larger transaction documented by several agreements, it may be impossible to isolate the contract for the land transaction from the rest of documentation; the larger, overall, transaction may be 'the contract' for the purposes of section 2.

Execution clauses

The following applies only to agreements which are not intended to take effect as deeds. The requirements for deeds are described in the next chapter.

Traditionally, 'As Witness' wording is added at the end of the operative clauses, before the Schedules, if any. However, omitting this does not make an agreement invalid. The following example assumes that the vendor is an individual and the purchaser is an English or foreign company:

18 *Pritchard v Briggs* [1980] Ch 338, [1980] 1 All ER 294.
19 *Driver v Broad* [1893] 1 QB 744.
20 *Record v Bell* (1990) Times, 21 December 1990.
1 *Independent Automatic Sales Ltd v Knowles and Foster* [1962] 3 All ER 27 at 36.
2 See *Steadman v Steadman* [1974] QB 161, CA, affd [1976] AC 536 at 540B, 551B and 556G.

AS WITNESS the hands of the Vendor and of a duly authorised officer of the Purchaser the day and year first before written.

The convention is to use 'As Witness' for agreements and 'In Witness' for deeds.

There is no mandatory signing formula, but common forms are:

SIGNED by
John Bernard Bosanquet
[Director] [Authorised officer]
for and on behalf of
BOSANQUET AND PULLER PLC

BOSANQUET AND PULLER PLC
By John Bernard Bosanquet
duly authorised officer

As a matter of practice, a person who is party to an agreement in two capacities normally signs twice (and so on, if he has more than two capacities). However, a single signature is legally effective if it is stated to be in both capacities or there is evidence that the signatory intended it to be a double signature.[3] Also, section 63 of the Law of Property Act 1925 provides that (unless a contrary intention is expressed) a 'conveyance' passes all the interest which the conveying party has in the property conveyed or intended to be conveyed. 'Conveyance' is widely defined in section 205 to include a mortgage, lease 'and every other assurance of property or of any interest therein by an instrument, except a will'. An agreement for the sale of shares in a company would therefore clearly be covered.

There is no fixed practice about witnessing, but this tends to be done for guarantees and more important commercial agreements. Banks taking a personal guarantee often require the guarantor's signature to be witnessed by a solicitor, who signs a declaration on the guarantee that he explained its effect to the guarantor before the latter signed: see *Cornish v Midland Bank plc*[4] and the note by John Cartwright in [1990] LMCLQ 338 on the Court of Appeal's decision in *Lloyds Bank plc v Waterhouse*.[5]

Signing under a power of attorney

If a person will sign under a power of attorney, this should be stated:

SIGNED by
William Pyle Taunton
for and on behalf of
BOSANQUET AND PULLER PLC
under a power of attorney
dated 5th March 1991.

3 *Young v Schuler* (1883) 11 QBD 651.
4 [1985] 3 All ER 513.
5 [1991] Fam Law 23.

There seems no reason why a person who is the attorney of two or more parties should not sign once if it is stated that his signature is for and on behalf of each of those parties. This is subject to the terms of each power of attorney which may, expressly or by implication, require the attorney to sign separately for the principal concerned. But, in the case of a deed, it may be preferable for an attorney to execute or sign separately for each principal.

There is a technical point where an attorney executes. The former rule was that an attorney who executed a deed, and possibly also an agreement under hand, had to sign the name of his principal, not his own name. That rule is modified by section 7(1) of the Powers of Attorney Act 1971 as amended by the Law of Property (Miscellaneous Provisions) Act 1989:

> 'If the donee of a power of attorney is an individual, he may, if he thinks fit–
>
> (a) execute any instrument with his own signature, and
> (b) do any other thing in his own name.'

Section 7(1) seems inapplicable to a power of attorney given to a company, for example, a power of attorney in a debenture or mortgage which authorises the bank to execute further assurances. In such a case, it seems that the officer of the corporate attorney who signs should sign the name of the principal, for example, the company which created the mortgage or debenture. This would also be consistent with subsections (3) and (4) of section 74 of the Law of Property Act 1925. However, these problems do not, of course, arise if a power of attorney expressly authorises the attorney or signing officer to sign in his own name.

Appendix 4 sets out a form of power of attorney. A power of attorney in favour of a company should expressly authorise the company to delegate the power to any of its officers or, if that is intended, to others. Section 74(4) of the Law of Property Act only permits a corporate attorney to delegate to its officers where the power of attorney is to convey any interest in property. Moreover, this section requires the board of directors of the corporate attorney to delegate the power. However, even if a power of attorney in favour of a company does not expressly permit delegation to officers, and section 74(4) is inapplicable, it is thought that, by necessary implication, the company's directors (or other governing body) must have power to pass a resolution authorising a particular officer to execute the relevant document, although they would probably have to approve the terms of the document and little could be left to the individual's discretion.

Board resolutions

The implied authority of an individual ordinary director is limited. Nor has it been extended by the new sections 35 and 35A of the

Companies Act 1985 which abolish the ultra vires rule and disapply as regards a person dealing with the company in good faith any limitation on the directors' powers imposed by the company's constitution. The current position of a director under English law is described in *Gore-Browne on Companies* (edited by Boyle & Sykes):

> 'Individual directors, as such, have almost no usual authority beyond a power to execute documents to clothe a transaction with formal validity which has already been authorised by the board or the managing director.'

However, as this implies, the powers of a managing director or chief executive are considerably wider. A director whose title indicates responsibility in a particular area (for example, a finance director) almost certainly has some measure of implied authority in that area.

Because of the limited extent of implied authority possessed by an ordinary director, and the uncertainty regarding the extent of even a managing director's authority, a person entering into an important transaction with a company will usually require some evidence that the transaction has been authorised by the company's board or an appropriate committee of the board. The 'As Witness' wording can be used to record that a company's entering into an agreement has been authorised by a board resolution:

> AS WITNESS the hands of an authorised officer of the Bank and of a director of the Company duly authorised by a resolution of its directors passed on 16th April 1991.

Additionally, on a major transaction, it would be usual to require a company secretary's certificate as to a board resolution approving the transaction and authorising a named person, or more usually, any director to sign the agreement. The certificate should take the form of a certified extract from the minutes of the meeting of the board (or board committee) at which the relevant resolution was passed. Under section 382 of the Companies Act 1985, minutes of a board meeting which have been signed by the chairman of that, or the next, board meeting are evidence of the proceedings which took place at the meeting; and, once the minutes are entered in the company's minute book, the section creates a prima facie presumption that the meeting was duly held and convened and that all proceedings at it were valid.

Appendix 5 sets out a company secretary's certificate about board resolutions.

If the directors do not have power under the company's memorandum of association to enter into a transaction, section 35(2) of the Companies Act 1985 requires a special resolution for the transaction to be ratified by the company. This would be needed for a transaction outside the scope of the objects clause in the company's memorandum of association. Section 35(2) requires a second, separate, special resolution to relieve the directors from liability to the company for having entered into such a transaction. There are also certain types of transaction with a director (or a person connected with a director) which have to be approved by shareholders under Part X of the Companies Act 1985.

Letter agreements

A straightforward contract between two parties is often drafted as an offer letter from one of them which the other accepts.[6] Examples are a letter from a bank to a company which sets out the terms for underwriting a proposed rights issue or the terms of a loan facility. It is thought preferable for the letter to be addressed to the company rather than its directors since it is the company that is the other party to the contract. The introductory paragraph to such a letter is along the following lines:

> We write to set out the terms and conditions on and subject to which we offer to underwrite the proposed issue by way of rights of 5,697,468 new shares of 25p each in the Company.

There is a concluding paragraph to the following effect:

> To accept this offer, kindly return the enclosed duplicate of this letter, with the form of acceptance duly signed, together with a certified extract from a resolution of your board of directors approving this agreement, so that we receive these documents not later than 1 November 1991.

This paragraph might also make it clear that the offer will lapse if the countersigned duplicate and extract from the board resolution are not received on or before the specified date. The duplicate of the bank's letter will have the following typed at the end of it:

> Accepted and Agreed
> Dated , 1991
> Director
> Duly authorised
> For and on behalf of
> X Y Z Plc.

An agreement in the form of a letter from a bank to a company will provide for the company to give warranties and undertakings by stating that the company is deemed to give these by signing the form of acceptance on the duplicate.

As noted above, section 2(3) of the Law of Property (Miscellaneous Provisions) Act imposes the following requirement in the case of

6 *Gibson v Manchester City Council* [1979] 1 All ER 972, [1979] 1 WLR 294, HL shows the need to phrase the letters as an offer and acceptance.

a contract for the sale of land or any other contract within the section's scope:

> 'The document incorporating the terms or, where contracts are exchanged, one of the documents incorporating them (but not necessarily the same one) must be signed by or on behalf of each party to the contract.'

There has been a suggestion that the usual procedure of a bank sending a facility letter to a company and the latter returning it to the bank with the form of acceptance signed may not be an 'exchange' for this purpose.[7] However, it is not considered that there is any justification for such doubts; the judgment of Hoffmann J in *Spiro v Glencrown Properties Ltd*[8] indicates that the courts will adopt a robust and non-technical approach to section 2.

7 Note by Gregory Hill in [1990] LQR 396.
8 [1991] 1 All ER 600.

CHAPTER 3

DEEDS

The main types of document which have to be executed as deeds are: documents which convey or create a legal estate in land (section 52, Law of Property Act 1925); powers of attorney, including documents which contain powers of attorney as well as other provisions (section 1, Powers of Attorney Act 1971); any mortgage or charge, whether of land or other property, if the mortgagee or chargee is to have the statutory power of sale and consequently, under section 104 of the Law of Property Act 1925, the important power to overreach subsequent charges; and a document executed under section 40 of the Trustee Act 1925 to appoint a new trustee if there is not to be a separate transfer of the trust property into the names of the new trustees. In England, a gift of chattels which are not delivered to the donee must be by deed, unless the donor declares himself a trustee of the chattels.[1]

Even where the general law does not make a deed obligatory, it is not uncommon for a document to require a deed for certain purposes. Family settlements normally require the trustees to exercise a power of appointment by deed. However, a deed is not necessary for the appointment of a receiver under a debenture, unless the debenture expressly requires this.[2]

A deed is often used where there is doubt about whether the party (or each of the parties) which a document is intended to benefit or protect is providing valid consideration for it. A purchaser of a company will require the vendors to execute a deed in which they covenant with the company to indemnify it against certain tax liabilities. A bank will normally require a guarantee of amounts which it has previously advanced to be given by deed, unless it is clear that the bank is providing consideration, for instance, by refraining from exercising a right to call in the overdraft. Normally a deed

1 *Cochrane v Moore* (1890) 25 QBD 57; see also Bills of Sale Act 1878.
2 *Phoenix Properties Ltd v Wimpole Street Nominees Ltd* [1989] EGCS 167.

is used for the release of security. A deed is often used to amend a previous contract if the amendments are to the advantage of only one of the parties, although a deed is not normally required to vary another deed.[3]

Deeds *inter partes* and deeds poll

A deed *inter partes* starts 'This Deed is made the ... day of ... 1991 Between' and then lists the persons who are party to it. A deed poll now normally starts 'This Deed is made the ... day of ... 1991 By' and specifies only a single 'party', namely, the person who executes the deed.

The distinction between a deed *inter partes* and a deed poll is as follows. Subject to section 56 of the Law of Property Act 1925 (which was considered by the House of Lords in *Beswick v Beswick*[4]), a deed *inter partes* cannot transfer property or give a right to a person who is not a party to it. However, this rule has never applied to a deed poll which can always be sued on by any person with whom the covenant in issue was made. The basis of this distinction was explained by Vaisey J in *Chelsea and Walham Green Building Society v Armstrong*:[5]

> 'Normally speaking, a deed between parties is contemplated as a contract, or as carrying out a contract made, so to speak, indoors, round the table by the family, as a matter done not in public but in private. On the other hand, a deed poll is clearly addressed to everybody – "Know all men by these presents" – or is addressed to "All to whom these presents shall come".'

However, the 'Know all men by these presents' wording is seldom used today. In *Chelsea & Walham Green Building Society v Armstrong*, Vaisey J held that, although a Land Registry transfer is not strictly a deed poll, it is not a deed *inter partes*, so that a building society could enforce a covenant with it that was contained in the transfer, although the society was not a party to the transfer. The most common type of deed poll is a power of attorney; although the attorney is not a party to the power of attorney, it is, of course, effective to confer authorities on him and he can sue on any covenants with him which it contains, for example, a covenant for ratification or indemnity.

One qualification is necessary about the enforceability of a deed poll. There is a principle that a covenant cannot be made with a person who does not exist or cannot be identified when the deed

3 *Plymouth Corpn v Harvey* [1971] 1 All ER 623, [1971] 1 WLR 549; *Mitas v Hyams* [1951] 2 TLR 1215, CA.
4 [1968] AC 58, [1987] 2 All ER 1197.
5 [1951] Ch 853 at 857.

containing the covenant is executed.[6] There is no clear authority excluding deeds poll from this principle. It therefore seems to be an open point whether, for example, a guarantee of Eurobonds which is given by a deed poll could be enforced by a company formed after the deed poll is executed or, indeed, by future holders of the bonds generally (because they were not capable of being identified when the deed poll was executed). Beyond doubt, however, a holder who was aware of the guarantee when he purchased his bonds could enforce it as a unilateral contract of the type which featured in *Carlill v Carbolic Smoke Ball Co.*[7]

The 1989 legislation[7a]

The law about deeds is a combination of ancient common law and recent legislation. The primary legislation is section 1 of the Law of Property (Miscellaneous Provisions) Act 1989 and section 36A of the Companies Act 1985 (which was inserted by section 130 of the 1989 Act). Deeds executed by companies incorporated outside Great Britain will be governed by regulations made under section 130(6) of the Companies Act 1989. At present, such a company has to execute a deed under seal, but a red wafer can be used, an official seal being unnecessary. Section 1 was introduced to give effect to the Law Commission's Report (No 163) about Deeds and Escrows. The legislation makes it possible, subject to three new requirements, to execute a deed without sealing it. The new methods of executing deeds do not replace, but are alternative options to, the traditional methods of executing under seal; except that the Land Registration (Execution of Deeds) Rules 1990 (SI 1990/1010) make the new non-sealing method mandatory for an individual (but not a company) who executes a deed concerning registered land.[8]

In the case of individuals, section 1(1) of the Law of Property (Miscellaneous Provisions) Act simply abolishes 'any rule of law which ... requires a seal for the valid execution of an instrument as a deed by an individual'. In the case of a British company, however, section 36A(4) of the Companies Act requires an unsealed document to meet certain requirements before it has the same effect as if the company's common seal had been affixed:

> 'A document signed by a director and the secretary of a company, or by two directors of a company, and expressed (in whatever form of

6 *Kelsey v Dodd* (1881) 52 LJ Ch 34 at 39 and *Forster v Elvet Colliery Co Ltd* [1908] 1 KB 629, on other points, in *Dyson v Forster* [1909] AC 98.

7 [1893] 1 QB 256, CA; see also *Re Agra and Masterman's Bank, ex p Asiatic Banking Corpn* (1867) 2 Ch App 391.

7a See article by G Virgo and C Harpum in [1991] 2 LM CLQ 209.

8 See also the Land Registry's Practice Note of July 1990 about Form and Execution of Deeds.

> words) to be executed by the company has the same effect as if executed under the common seal of the company.'

The requirement that the document has to be 'expressed (in whatever form of words) to be executed by the company' will be satisfied as a matter of course in all but the most exceptional cases. However, the reference to 'the secretary' of a company creates a potential technical problem. Many British companies' articles of association define 'the Secretary' to include 'any other person appointed to perform the duties of the secretary of the company, including a joint, assistant or deputy secretary'.[9] By contrast, the effect of section 283(3) of the Companies Act 1985 is that an assistant or deputy secretary is only treated as 'the secretary' for the purposes of that Act, including, of course, section 36A, if the office of the secretary is vacant 'or there is for any other reason no secretary capable of acting'. Similarly, an officer of the company, other than an assistant or deputy secretary is only treated by the Act as 'the secretary' if 'there is no assistant or deputy secretary capable of acting'. It follows that a deed signed by a director and the assistant or deputy secretary is not validly executed under section 36A if the circumstances were such that the secretary could have signed it himself.

Section 36A of the Companies Act 1985 now makes it optional, but not mandatory, for a British company to have a common seal.

The three new requirements

But three new requirements are imposed.

Section 1(2)(a) of the Law of Property (Miscellaneous Provisions) Act 1989 provides that an instrument shall not be a deed unless

> '...it makes it clear on its face that it is intended to be a deed by the parties making it, or as the case may be, by the parties to it (whether by describing itself as a deed or expressing itself to be executed or signed as a deed or otherwise).'

This applies to all deeds, whether executed by individuals or companies, and whether executed under seal or by the new methods without a seal. The corresponding provision (in positive form) in the Companies Act, section 36A(5), only applies to a document executed by a British company, but probably applies to a document to which such a company affixes its common seal, as well as one which it executes by the new method without a seal:

> 'A document executed by a company which makes it clear on its face that it is intended by the person or persons making it to be a deed has effect, upon delivery, as a deed.'

Often a document will, in the ordinary course of events, make it clear on its face that it is intended to be a deed. For example, it

9 See regulation 1 of Table A in the Companies (Tables A to F) Regulations 1985.

might commence 'This Deed of Indemnity'. Or it might end 'In Witness whereof the parties have executed this mortgage as a deed ...'. Or, if executed by an individual under the new method, it will probably state 'Signed as a deed by ...'.

On the other hand, a document executed in the traditional way with a seal might nowhere describe itself as a deed (for example, 'This Power of Attorney') nor state that it is executed as a deed ('In Witness whereof the Company has caused its common seal to be hereunto affixed'). In these cases, section 1(2) means that the document is not valid as a deed, unless the mere presence of a seal, without any mention at all of the word 'deed' satisfies the requirement for a document to make it clear 'on its face' that it is intended to be a deed.

The second new requirement is imposed by section 1(3) of the Law of Property (Miscellaneous Provisions) Act:

> 'An instrument is validly executed as a deed by an individual if, and only if–
>
> (a) it is signed–
>
> (i) by him in the presence of a witness who attests the signature; or
>
> (ii) at his direction and in his presence and the presence of two witnesses who each attest the signature; and
>
> (b) it is delivered as a deed by him or a person authorised to do so on his behalf.'

Previously, the normal practice was that a deed would be witnessed; this is now mandatory in the case of a deed executed by any individual. But section 1(3) does not apply to companies; so that if, under the new procedure, two directors or a director and the secretary sign, their signatures do not have to be witnessed. Nor do their signatures have to be witnessed if under the old procedure they sign an instrument to which the company's common seal is affixed: see regulation 101 in the Companies (Tables A to E) Regulations 1985 (SI 1985 No 805) or regulation 113 of Table A in the Companies Act 1948.

Read literally, section 1(3) applies where a document is 'executed as a deed by an individual' as the attorney of a company, but it is thought that this interpretation is incorrect since the deed is that of the company/principal not the individual/attorney. But the point is academic since in practice a deed executed by an individual as an attorney for a company is always witnessed.

A party to a transaction cannot be an attesting witness; for example, a person cannot sign as witness to a power of attorney in his favour.[10] Subject to that, it appears that there is no rule against a spouse

10 *Re Parrott, ex p Cullen* [1891] 2 QB 151.

witnessing: see Halsbury's Laws of England, Volume 12, paragraph 1331.

The third new requirement arises from section 1(2)(b) of the Law of Property (Miscellaneous Provisions) Act. This provides that an instrument is not a deed unless 'it is validly executed as a deed' by the person making it or, as the case may be, by one or more of the parties to it. It is unclear whether this permits a document to be executed by one party as a deed and by another party as an ordinary agreement; for example, where the mortgagor has to execute an equitable mortgage as a deed because it contains a power of attorney but it is sufficient for the bank to sign in order to satisfy section 2 of the Law of Property (Miscellaneous Provisions) Act (see Chapter 2). Section 1(2) is (apart from one minor drafting modification) in the same terms as the corresponding provision of the draft Bill set out in the Law Commission's Report No 163 on Deeds and Escrows. The impression which paragraph 2.16 of that Report gives is that the Law Commission thought that their draft Bill would make it no longer possible for a document to be a deed as regards one party but not another. Moreover, section 36A(5) of the Companies Act–

> 'A document executed by a company which makes it clear on its face that it is intended by the person or persons making it to be a deed has effect, upon delivery, as a deed.'

seems to imply that a document can take effect as a deed only as regards all 'the persons making it', and not as regards some of them.

However, neither section 1 of the Law of Property (Miscellaneous Provisions) Act nor section 36A of the Companies Act invalidates a deed which is executed only by one or some of the parties; for example, a deed of indemnity which is executed by the party giving the indemnity but not by the party indemnified, because he does not assume any obligations.

Date of execution for companies

Section 36A of the Companies Act 1985 lays down a number of rules about when a deed is to be regarded as having been 'executed' by a British company. These rules have considerable practical importance, particularly in relation to the term of a lease[11] and the provisions of the Companies Act which require certain charges created by a company to be registered within 21 days after the date on which they are created. The rules can be summarised as follows:

(1) A document executed by a company which is intended to be a deed only takes effect as a deed 'upon delivery'.

11 *Brikom Investments Ltd v Seaford* [1981] 2 All ER 783, [1981] 1 WLR 863.

(2) There is a presumption 'unless a contrary intention is proved' that delivery takes place on execution.
(3) In favour of a purchaser (including a lessee or mortgagee) a document is 'deemed to have been duly executed' by a company if it purports to be signed by a director and the secretary or by two directors.
(4) In favour of a purchaser (including a lessee or mortgagee) such a document, if it makes it clear on its face that it is intended to be a deed, is deemed 'to have been delivered upon its being executed'.

It is not clear that the 'deemed delivery upon execution' described in (4) applies where a company executes a deed under its common seal; but in *Longman v Viscount Chelsea*, the Court of Appeal held that at common law there is a rebuttable presumption that sealing by a corporation imports delivery.[12]

An important point is that the 'deemed due execution' described in (3) applies to documents which are not intended to be deeds as well as those which are. But only a purchaser, lessee, mortgagee or other person who for valuable consideration acquires an interest in property is protected by this 'deemed due execution'. It does not protect, for example, a bank to which a company issues a guarantee.

The 'deemed delivery upon execution' described in (4) may produce adverse results. For example:

1 March	A plc executes a mortgage.
6 March	Closing, with execution by the bank and 6 March being filled in as the date of the mortgage.
25 March	Mortgage delivered for registration under section 395 of the Companies Act 1985.

The effect of section 36A(5) is not entirely clear, but it may well result in the mortgage being 'created' for the purposes of section 395 on 1 March, not 6 March. If that is the case, the mortgage will have been delivered for registration out of time. This would have been the case under the previous law; and the date of creation could not be postponed by leaving the date of the mortgage blank until it had been executed by the other parties as well as the mortgagor company: *Buckley on the Companies Acts*, Volume 1, page 248.

Where there is a risk that delivery for registration might occur more than 21 days after actual sealing (or signing), a clause to the following effect may be of assistance.

The security interests provided for by this Deed shall come into effect–

(a) on the date on which this Deed is received by the Bank or its solicitors; or

12 (1989) 58 P & CR 189. See also the Court of Appeal's decision in *Vincent v Premo Enterprises (Voucher Sales) Ltd* [1969] 2 QB 609, [1969] 2 All ER 941.

(b) if the Bank or its solicitors receive this Deed subject to a requirement to hold it to the order of the Company or a third party, on the date on which the requirement ceases to apply;

and a certificate which is signed by two managers of the Bank and specifies the date applicable under paragraph (a) or (b) above shall be conclusive.

Delivery

The 1989 legislation has not abolished the requirement for a deed to be delivered.[13]

It used to be a rule of common law that authority to deliver a deed had to be given by a document which was itself a deed. This rule, which was always ignored at completions and closings, is abolished by section 1(1)(c) of the Law of Property (Miscellaneous Provisions) Act. In fact four months before the Act was passed, the rule had been ended by the Court of Appeal in *Longman v Viscount Chelsea*.[14]

The Act also provides that, where, 'in the course of or in connection with a transaction involving the disposition or creation of an interest in land', a solicitor or a solicitor's employee purports to deliver a deed on behalf of a party to the deed, he is conclusively presumed in favour of a 'purchaser' to be authorised to do so. 'Purchaser' includes a mortgagee or lessee.

However, it remains the law that a deed is required to authorise a person to make a material alteration to a deed which has already been executed.[15] A deed or other instrument is rendered void by a material alteration which the parties have not approved.[16]

Other aspects

In a deed, the formula which appears after the recitals is:

NOW THIS DEED WITNESSETH as follows:-.

or

NOW THIS DEED WITNESSETH that it is hereby agreed as follows:-

A deed without recitals reads:

This Mortgage made on .... 1990 Between ....
WITNESSETH as follows:-.

13 'In England, as elsewhere, it is probable that there was a combination of ideas new and old. The delivery of the writing was allowed to stand in the place of the delivery of those rings or rods or knives by means of which seisin had formerly been delivered ... To this day a deed takes effect from its delivery.' W S Holdsworth *A History of English Law* Volume III, page 223 (3rd).

14 (1989) 58 P & CR 189.

15 *Powell v London and Provincial Bank* [1893] 2 Ch 555.

16 *Lombard Finance Ltd v Brookplain Trading Ltd* [1991] 1 WLR 271.

An undertaking contained in a deed is termed a 'covenant'. For example, 'A and B jointly and severally covenant with C to indemnify C in respect of all claims . . .'. However, although the primary meaning of 'covenant' is a promise by deed, as a secondary meaning the word may be applied to any promise or stipulation, whether under seal or not.[17]

The 'In Witness' formula, which appears at the end of a deed but before any Schedules, is:

> IN WITNESS WHEREOF the parties have executed this Deed [or: this Mortgage as a deed] the day and year first before written.

The following are the normal execution formulae for individuals and British companies:-

Old style – with seal
Signed Sealed and Delivered as a deed by John Leycester Adolphus in the presence of:

....
Witness

The Common Seal of Adolphus and Ellis Limited was affixed to this deed in the presence of:

Director
Director/Secretary

New style – without seal
Signed as a deed by John Leycester Adolphus in the presence of:

....
Witness

Signed as a deed by Adolphus and Ellis Limited Acting by

[a director and its secretary]
[two directors]

It seems possible that a formula such as 'Signed as deed' may preclude the person who signs from denying that the document was validly executed by him as a deed.[18] Moreover, there have been many instances in which an unsealed document, although ineffective under section 52 of the Law of Property Act 1925 to create or transfer a legal estate in land, has created an enforceable equitable interest: see 27 Halsbury's Laws at 102.[19]

17 Lord Wilberforce in *Rank Xerox Ltd v Lane* [1979] 3 All ER 657 at 659j.

18 See *TCB Ltd v Gray* [1986] Ch 621, [1986] 1 All ER 587, but see also the decision of Judge Fox-Andrews QC (as Official Referee) in *Whittal Builders Co Ltd v Chester-Le-Street District Council* (1987) 40 BLR 82.

19 In *Mason v Clarke* [1955] AC 778, [1955] 1 All ER 914, the House of Lords upheld an oral grant of rabbiting rights to a rabbit catcher for which the latter had paid £100.

CHAPTER 4

STYLE

A contract should be as easy for the lay client to read and understand as is consistent with precision and certainty. Brevity is valuable. In general, legal usages should only be introduced where necessary to avoid uncertainty. The following are some legal usages which can be avoided with safety.

The future tense

It used to be the practice to state in the future tense, using the word 'shall', conditions which would occur (if at all) in the future. For example:

> If, within one year after the date of this Agreement, the Vendor shall notify the Purchaser in writing...

If the condition was a condition precedent to something else occurring, it would be drafted in the future perfect:

> If the period of 12 months from the date of this Agreement shall have expired without the Vendor having given notice to the Purchaser...

This use of future and future perfect tenses is incorrect.[1] The proper usage is the present tense or, in the case of precondition, the perfect tense, as shown by the following examples:

> 'If the auditors fail to obtain all the information and explanations which, to the best of their knowledge and belief, are necessary for the purposes of their audit, they shall state that fact in their report.'[2]

1 'An Act of Parliament should be deemed to be always speaking, and therefore the present or past tense should be adopted, and "shall" should be used as an imperative only, and not as a future. "If" should be followed by the indicative where it suggests a case; for example, "If any person commits, &c, he shall be punished as follows."' Lord Thring, *Practical Legislation:* see also *Re D (a minor)* [1987] AC 317, [1986] 3 WLR 1080.

2 Companies Act 1985, s 237(4).

'If at the end of any financial year of the Board the amount standing to the credit of the Fund is less than £3 million the Board may, with the approval of the Treasury, levy further contributions from contributory institutions so as to restore the amount standing to the credit of the Fund to a minimum of £5 million and a maximum of £6 million.'[3]

'Subject to subsection (2) below, when a person has been convicted of a criminal offence and when subsequently his conviction has been reversed or he has been pardoned on the ground that a new or newly discovered fact shows beyond reasonable doubt that there has been a miscarriage of justice, the Secretary of State shall pay compensation for the miscarriage of justice to the person who has suffered punishment as a result of such conviction ... unless the non-disclosure of the unknown fact was wholly or partly attributable to the person convicted.'[4]

'If the bailee–

(a) has ... given notice to the bailor of his intention to sell the goods under this subsection, or

(b) has failed to trace or communicate with the bailor with a view to giving him such a notice, after having taken reasonable steps for the purpose,

and is reasonably satisfied that the bailor owns the goods, he shall be entitled, as against the bailor, to sell the goods.'[5]

Normally, the future tense, with the word 'shall', should be confined to imposing obligations. Where 'shall' imposes a procedural requirement or time limit, it should be made clear whether this is mandatory (in the sense that non-compliance will cause invalidity) or merely directory.

The proviso

Provisos are archaic. The original and proper function of a proviso is to introduce an exception to the provision which precedes it. However, provisos are now used to tack on additional provisions without creating new subclauses and so having to alter numbering and cross-references. This misuse of the proviso should be avoided. It gives rise to problems of interpretation where the scope of the proviso, on a literal interpretation, is wider than that of the provision to which it relates. The court can restrict the meaning of general words in a proviso to the subject matter of the main provision.[6]

3 Banking Act 1987, s 54(1).
4 Criminal Justice Act 1988, s 133.
5 Torts (Interference with Goods) Act 1977, s 12(3).
6 See *Thompson v Dibdin* [1912] AC 533, but this is not always done: *Comr of Stamp Duties v Atwill* [1973] AC 558, [1973] 1 All ER 576.

Even using a proviso to state an exception can create the problem of whether a reference elsewhere in the document to the clause to which the proviso is added covers the proviso or just the main provision. When this question arose about section 42 of the Income and Corporation Taxes Act 1970, Vinelott J and a majority of the Court of Appeal thought that the proviso was not covered, but the House of Lords held that it was, although Lord Scarman dissented.[7]

Where it is necessary to set out an exception of any length, two subclauses should be used: the first for the main provision, which should be expressed to be 'subject to' the second, which states the exception. Section 7(3) and (4) of the Banking Act 1979 (which concerns the Bank of England's power to revoke a recognition or licence granted under that Act) provides a good example:

'(3) Subject to subsection (4) below, where the Bank proposes to act under subsection (1) or subsection (2) above,–

(a) the Bank shall give the institution concerned notice in writing of its intention specifying the reasons why it proposes to act; and
(b) the provisions of Part I of Schedule 4 to this Act shall apply.

(4) In any case where–

(a) the powers of the Bank under this section have become exercisable with respect to an institution, and
(b) the Bank considers that urgent action is necessary,

the Bank may, without prior notice under subsection (3) above, by notice in writing given to the institution concerned exercise its powers under paragraph (b) of subsection (1) above.'

Similarly section 1(1) and (2) of the Diplomatic and Consular Premises Act 1987:

'1(1) Subject to subsection (2) below, where a State desires that land shall be diplomatic or consular premises, it shall apply to the Secretary of State for his consent to the land being such premises.

(2) A State need not make such an application in relation to land if the Secretary of State accepted it as diplomatic or consular premises immediately before the coming into force of this section.'

Cumulative negatives

Particularly if a provision will need qualifying by exceptions and restrictions, it is better to draft it as a positive statement than in terms of a double negative. This is because where a general principle has been stated in the form of a double negative, any exception

7 *Gubay v Kington* [1984] 1 All ER 513, [1984] 1 WLR 163.

or qualification will normally require the addition of a third negative; and a provision can get out of control if an exception is whittled down during negotiations, so necessitating a fourth negative.

'Such'

It is often thought that, if a provision refers to an item which has been mentioned previously, the second reference must be preceded by the word 'such'. The belief is that this is necessary to make it clear that the second reference is indeed to the item which the provision has previously mentioned. The following is an example of the drafting which results:

> Notwithstanding that a Loan is to be denominated in an Optional Currency for an Interest Period, if prior to 10.00 a.m. (London time) on the first day of such Interest Period the Agent receives notice from Banks participating in not less than 50 per cent. of such Loan that it is impracticable for such Banks to fund their participations for such Loan in such Optional Currency during such Interest Period...

Usually 'such' is unnecessary. 'The' can usually be used instead with no less certainty and more fluency, as section 13(2) of the Sale of Goods Act 1979 demonstrates:

> 'If the sale is by sample as well as by description it is not sufficient that the bulk of the goods corresponds with the sample if the goods do not also correspond with the description.'

Alternatively, a simple pronoun can be equally effective (section 34(1), Sale of Goods Act):

> 'Where goods are delivered to the buyer, and he has not previously examined them, he is not deemed to have accepted them until he has had a reasonable opportunity of examining them for the purpose of ascertaining whether they are in conformity with the contract.'

Generally speaking, the word 'such' should be used only where its meaning is 'of that type':

> The Purchaser shall–
>
> (a) pay any stamp, registration or other documentary tax or charge which is payable under French law in connection with this Agreement; and
> (b) indemnify the Vendor against any liability which it may incur for such a tax or charge.

Where it is necessary to make it clear that a reference is to an item or person previously mentioned, this can be done by 'that' or 'those'.

Where a provision contains a number of references to a particular person, or two particular persons, it is helpful to identify him or them by a 'nickname' which can be added after the first reference.

For example:

'(1) Subject to the provisions of this section, where–

(a) an individual ("the worker") renders or is under an obligation to render personal services to another person ("the client") and is subject to, or to the right of, supervision, direction or control as to the manner in which he renders those services; and
(b) the worker is supplied to the client by or through a third person ("the agency") and renders or is under an obligation to render those services under the terms of a contract between the worker and the agency ("the relevant contract"); and
(c) remuneration receivable under or in consequence of that contract would not, apart from this section, be chargeable to income tax under Schedule E,

then, for all the purposes of the Income Tax Acts, the services which the worker renders or is under an obligation to render to the client under the contract shall be treated as if they were the duties of an office or employment held by the worker, and all remuneration receivable under or in consequence of that contract shall be treated as emoluments of that office or employment and shall be assessable to income tax under Schedule E accordingly.'[8]

However, sometimes a person can be identified just by calling him 'A':

'... if a person enters into or is otherwise concerned in an arrangement whereby–

(a) the retention or control by or on behalf of another (call him "A") of A's proceeds of drug trafficking is facilitated (whether by concealment, removal from the jurisdiction, transfer to nominees or otherwise), or
(b) A's proceeds of drug trafficking–

(i) are used to secure that funds are placed at A's disposal, or
(ii) are used for A's benefit to acquire property by way of investment,

knowing or suspecting that A is a person who carries on or has carried on drug trafficking or has benefited from drug trafficking, he is guilty of an offence.'[9]

Similarly:

'(1) Subject to subsections (3) and (4) below, subsection (2) below applies for the purposes of corporation tax on chargeable gains where–

(a) there is a scheme for the transfer by a company ("company A")–

(i) which is not resident in the United Kingdom, but

8 Income and Corporation Taxes Act 1988, s 134(1).
9 Drug Trafficking Offences Act 1986, s 24(1).

(ii) which carries on a trade in the United Kingdom through a branch or agency,

of the whole or part of the trade to a company resident in the United Kingdom ("company B"),

(b) company A disposes of an asset to company B in accordance with the scheme at a time when the two companies are members of the same group, and

(c) a claim in relation to the asset is made by the two companies within two years after the end of the accounting period of company B during which the disposal is made.'[10]

'Hereof' and 'hereunder'

It is widely assumed that a cross-reference to another clause of the same agreement has to be qualified by the word 'hereof' to make it clear that the clause referred to is the clause of the agreement concerned that bears the relevant number. In most cases, the context makes this clear, but if it is thought appropriate to qualify cross-references in this way, the modern practice is to use the words 'above' and 'below'.

In some contexts 'hereof' can also be ambiguous. For example, if a subclause starts with the words 'Subject to the provisions hereof', it will often be impossible to say whether it takes effect subject only to other provisions of the clause in which it appears or to all the provisions of the contract, whether contained in that clause or elsewhere. The wording should therefore be–

> Subject to the following provisions of this clause

or

> Subject to the provisions of this Agreement.

Similar considerations apply to 'hereunder'. In addition, this word is often unnecessary as in–

> If a Bank is unable to make any Loan hereunder.

Loan (having a capitalised initial letter) will be defined as a loan under the agreement concerned so that 'hereunder' is superfluous. If it is necessary to make a reference to the agreement concerned, the better usage is 'under this Agreement'.

'Hereinafter'

'Hereinafter referred to as' is a very common formula. Section 1(1) of the Insolvency Act 1986 illustrates a modern alternative:

10 Income and Corporation Taxes Act 1970, s 273A.

'The directors of a company ... may make a proposal ... to the company and to its creditors for a composition in satisfaction of its debts or a scheme of arrangement of its affairs (from here on referred to, in either case, as a "voluntary arrangement").'

'Hereby agrees with'

There is usually no need to start a provision with 'A hereby agrees with B' or 'A hereby covenants with B'. In the first place, the operative provisions of the agreement or deed will have been introduced by wording such as 'IT IS HEREBY AGREED as follows:–'. Second, if an agreement signed by a person states that he shall do something, that is enough to impose on him a legal obligation to do it, without its being necessary to state expressly that he agrees to do it.[11]

Normally, there are only two cases in which words such as 'A agrees with B' serve any purpose. The first is where there are three or more parties to an agreement and it is necessary to make it clear whether A's obligations can be enforced by each of the other parties or by only some of them and, in latter case, by whom.

The second is where two or more persons enter into the same undertaking and it is necessary to make it clear whether–

they undertake jointly, or jointly and severally, or severally

or

each of them undertakes only in relation to himself.

Other archaic language

Other words to avoid are 'the same' (which can normally be replaced by 'it' or 'them') and 'thereof', 'thereto', etc. 'In the event that' just means 'if'.

'Pursuant to' probably means the same as 'in pursuance of', an expression to which the House of Lords gave a narrow meaning in *Hampson v Department of Education and Science*.[12] That case concerned an exception from the Race Relations Act 1976 which exempted discrimination done 'in pursuance of any instrument made under any enactment by a Minister of the Crown'. The House of Lords, reversing the Court of Appeal, held that policy reasons required that in that particular context the phrase 'in pursuance of any instrument' had to be limited to acts done in the necessary performance of an express obligation in an instrument and did not

11 See the observations of Sir George Jessel MR in *Dawes v Tredwell* (1881) 18 Ch D 354 at 359.

12 [1991] 1 AC 171, [1990] 2 All ER 513.

extend to acts done in the exercise of a power or discretion conferred by an instrument. In a different context, however, the phrase could cover the latter category of act. In *Mobil North Sea Ltd v IRC*[13] the House of Lords held that, as a matter of language, money paid by Mobil to an engineering contractor in implementation of an agreement between them and then paid by the contractor to a manufacturer in implementation of a contract which the contractor made as Mobil's agent and in implementation of its contract with Mobil could be said to be paid 'in pursuance of' either the contract between Mobil and the engineering contractor or the contract between the engineering contractor and the manufacturer.

Drafting in the singular

A provision is often easier to draft if expressed in the singular. For example–

> No Bank shall commence proceedings against the Borrower unless it has given the Facility Agent seven days' prior notice of its intention to do so

could not be drafted as

> the Banks shall not commence proceedings against the Borrower unless they have given the Facility Agent seven days' prior notice of their intention to do so.

The same applies to–

> This clause applies to any tax which is payable in a country in which any Vendor is incorporated or carries on or has carried on any business.

Consistent language

The same terms should be used throughout an agreement. A change in language can be taken to imply a change of meaning where none is intended. However, in *Payne v Barratt Developments (Luton) Ltd*[14] the House of Lords stated that the rule that the same word occuring more than once in an enactment should be given the same meaning wherever it occurs is a guide, which must yield to indications of contrary intention. Nevertheless, consistency is preferable. For example, if an agreement refers in some places to 'debts' and in others to 'liabilities', that could be taken to mean that 'debts' is being used to exclude contingent items such as amounts payable under guarantees.[15] Similar problems can arise if an agreement refers

13 [1987] 1 WLR 1065.
14 [1985] 1 All ER 257, [1985] 1 WLR 1.
15 *Re Pinto Leite & Nephews* [1929] 1 Ch 221 at 235; *Marren v Ingles* [1980] 1 WLR 983 at 990, HL.

in some places to 'assets', and elsewhere to 'property'; or to some amounts as 'due' and others as 'owing'. Likewise, if the clause on notices specifies how a notice is to be 'served' and at what time it is deemed to have been 'served', other provisions of the agreement should refer to notices being 'served' and not to their being 'given' or 'sent'.

CHAPTER 5

CLAUSES AND THEIR SUB-DIVISIONS

The basic unit of an agreement is the clause. This corresponds to a section in an Act of Parliament. Clauses are numbered 1, 2, and so on. They usually have headings indicating their subject matter.

Clauses are generally divided into subclauses – corresponding to subsections in an Act. Subclauses are numbered (1), (2), and so on.

Clauses and subclauses are often broken down into paragraphs. Paragraphs are indented and designated (a), (b), and so on. A paragraph never forms a provision in itself, but is always preceded by, and has to be read with, introductory wording which ends with a dash (–) just before the indented paragraphs.

Paragraphs can be divided into sub-paragraphs; these are numbered (i), (ii), and so on. Further sub-divisions are designated (aa), (bb), and so on.

The clause 6 which follows contains three subclauses; in subclause (3), (a) and (b) are paragraphs; and in paragraph (a), (i) and (ii) are sub-paragraphs.

6(1) Any director may call a meeting of the full board; and the secretary shall do so at the request of a director.

(2) Notice of a meeting of the full board may be given in writing or orally.

(3) It is unnecessary to give notice to–

(a) a director who is outside the United Kingdom on the date on which notice is given to the other directors unless–

(i) he is due to return to the United Kingdom before the meeting; or

(ii) he has requested that notice of meetings of the full board should be sent to him at a specified address outside the United Kingdom and it is considered that this will not involve a risk to confidentiality; or

(b) a director who is likely to be prevented from attending the meeting by serious illness; or

(c) a director who has waived his right to receive notice of that meeting or of any meetings of the full board which may be held during a period within which that meeting will be held.

Where a subclause is referred to in another subclause of the same clause, the references is to 'subclause (2)' or 'subclause (3)'. If the cross-reference appears in a different clause, the reference is to 'clause 6(2)' or 'clause 6(3)'. If it were necessary in, say, clause 4 to refer to both subclauses (2) and (3) of clause 6, the reference would be to 'clause 6(2) and (3)'.

Cross-references to paragraphs and sub-paragraphs follow a similar pattern. A reference in subclause (1) of clause 6 to paragraph (a) of the same subclause would be to 'paragraph (a)'. On the other hand, a reference to that paragraph which appeared in subclause (4) of clause 6 would be to 'subclause (1)(a)', and a reference appearing in clause 4 would be to 'clause 6(1)(a)'.

Where a provision refers to itself, it is not normally necessary to supplement the reference with the provision's number. For example, 'under this clause' or 'under this subclause' is sufficient, and 'under this clause 1' or 'under this subclause (2)' is unnecessary and creates additional renumbering work if changes are made.

By convention, a provision which appears in a Schedule is called a paragraph instead of a clause; and provisions in Schedules are divided into sub-paragraphs, not subclauses. There is no further subdivision of provisions in Schedules. So, if the example above had appeared in a Schedule, (3), as well as (a), (b), (c) and (i) and (ii), would all have been termed sub-paragraphs.

Schedules used to be designated 'the First Schedule' etc. Now they are numbered.

The numbering system described above is based on that used for Acts of Parliament. There is an alternative system under which the number of a subclause includes the number of the clause of which it is a part. So the subclauses in the example given above would be designated 6.01 and 6.02, not merely (1) and (2).

This alternative system has the disadvantage of creating additional renumbering work if negotiations on a draft agreement result in a clause being deleted or an additional one being inserted. If a draft agreement has 20 clauses, each of which contains, on average, four subclauses, and a new clause has to be inserted after clause 6, the alternative numbering system would mean that 56 units instead of 14 would have to be renumbered.

CHAPTER 6

CLAUSE STRUCTURE

Scope of a clause

The scope of a clause should be restricted to a specific matter. It is all too easy to lose control of a wide-ranging clause. A broad subject should be divided into particular topics each of which should be dealt with by a separate clause. Here is how the Companies Act 1985 divides up the subject of registration of company charges:

Section 395	Introductory provisions
Section 396	Charges requiring registration
Section 397	The companies charges register
Section 398	Company's duty to deliver particulars of charge for registration
Section 399	Effect of failure to deliver particulars for registration
Section 400	Late delivery of particulars
Section 401	Delivery of further particulars
Section 402	Effect of omissions and errors in registered particulars
Section 403	Memorandum of charge ceasing to affect company's property
Section 404	Exclusion of voidness as against unregistered charges
Section 405	Restrictions on voidness by virtue of this Part
Section 406	Effect of exercise of power of sale
Section 407	Effect of voidness on obligation secured

If this approach creates a large number of clauses, an agreement can be given greater coherence by grouping together in Parts those clauses which deal with different aspects of the same subject or with different but similar matters.

Subclauses

Some provisions can be expressed in two or three lines. Examples are those dealing with costs and those declaring time to be of the essence. But most clauses are more complicated. The key to drafting a complicated clause is to break it down into simple component propositions, and to set out these out as subclauses following a logical order. This technique converts a task of drafting a single complex provision into that of drafting a series of more straightforward ones.

This 'building blocks' method is illustrated by section 110 of the Insolvency Act 1986 which re-enacts (with an extension to a creditors' voluntary winding up) what used to be section 287 of the Companies Act 1948. The new section uses four subsections to set out the material previously contained in the first subsection of the old section:

> '**287**(1) Where a company is proposed to be, or is in course of being, wound up altogether voluntarily, and the whole or part of its business or property is proposed to be transferred or sold to another company, whether a company within the meaning of this Act or not (in this section called "the transferee company"), the liquidator of the first-mentioned company (in this section called "the transferor company") may, with the sanction of a special resolution of that company, conferring either a general authority on the liquidator or an authority in respect of any particular arrangement, receive, in compensation or part compensation for the transfer or sale, shares, policies or other like interests in the transferee company for distribution among the members of the transferor company, or may enter into any other arrangement whereby the members of the transferor company may, in lieu of receiving cash, shares, policies or other like interests, or in addition thereto, participate in the profits of or receive any other benefit from the transferee company.'

Which becomes:

> '**110**(1) This section applies, in the case of a company proposed to be, or being, wound up voluntarily, where the whole or part of the company's business or property is proposed to be transferred or sold to another company ("the transferee company"), whether or not the latter is a company within the meaning of the Companies Act.
>
> (2) With the requisite sanction, the liquidator of the company being, or proposed to be, wound up ("the transferor company") may receive, in compensation or part compensation for the transfer or sale, shares, policies or other like interests in the transferee company for distribution among the members of the transferor company.

(3) The sanction requisite under subsection (2) is–

(a) in the case of a members' voluntary winding up, that of a special resolution of the company, conferring either a general authority on the liquidator or an authority in respect of any particular arrangement, and
(b) in the case of a creditors' voluntary winding up, that of either the court or the liquidation committee.

(4) Alternatively to subsection (2), the liquidator may (with that sanction) enter into any other arrangement whereby the members of the transferor company may, in lieu of receiving cash, shares, policies or other like interests (or in addition thereto), participate in the profits of, or receive any other benefit from, the transferee company.'

Applying this technique, a typical clause might be broken down into the following subclauses:

(1) Statement of the circumstances in which the clause applies or of its general subject matter.

(2) The basic rule laid down by the clause.

(3) First exception to the basic rule.

(4) Second exception to the basic rule.

(5) A restriction on the scope of the second exception.

(6) Definitions of terms used only or mainly in the clause.

Section 103 of the Companies Act 1985 illustrates this technique.

'**103** *Non-cash consideration to be valued before allotment*

(1) A public company shall not allot shares as fully or partly paid up (as to their nominal value or any premium on them) otherwise than in cash unless–

(a) the consideration for the allotment has been independently valued under section 108; and
(b) a report with respect to its value has been made to the company by a person appointed by the company (in accordance with that section) during the 6 months immediately preceding the allotment of the shares; and
(c) a copy of the report has been sent to the proposed allottee.

(2) Where an amount standing to the credit of any of a company's reserve accounts, or of its profit and loss account, is applied in paying up (to any extent) any shares allotted to members of the company or any premiums on shares so allotted, the amount applied does not count as consideration for the allotment, and accordingly subsection (1) does not apply in that case.

(3) Subsection (1) does not apply to the allotment of shares by a company in connection with an arrangement providing for the allotment

of shares in that company on terms that the whole or part of the consideration for the shares allotted is to be provided by the transfer to that company (or the cancellation) of all or some of the shares, or of all or some of the shares of a particular class, in another company (with or without the issue to that company of shares, or of shares of any particular class, in that other company).

(4) But subsection (3) does not exclude the application of subsection (1) unless under the arrangement it is open to all the holders of the shares in the other company in question (or, where the arrangement applies only to shares of a particular class, to all the holders of the shares in that other company, being holders of shares of that class) to take part in the arrangement.

In determining whether that is the case, shares held by or by a nominee of the company proposing to allot the shares in connection with the arrangement, or by or by a nominee of a company which is that company's holding company or subsidiary or a company which is a subsidiary of its holding company, shall be disregarded.

(5) Subsection (1) also does not apply to the allotment of shares by a company in connection with its proposed merger with another company; that is, where one of the companies proposes to acquire all the assets and liabilities of the other in exchange for the issue of shares or other securities of that one to shareholders of the other, with or without any cash payment to shareholders.

(6) If a company allots shares in contravention of subsection (1) and either–

(a) the allottee has not received the valuer's report required by that subsection to be sent to him; or
(b) there has been some other contravention of this section or section 108 which the allottee knew or ought to have known amounted to a contravention,

the allottee is liable to pay the company an amount equal to the aggregate of the nominal value of the shares and the whole of any premium (or, if the case so requires, so much of that aggregate as is treated as paid up by the consideration), with interest at the appropriate rate.

(7) In this section–

(a) "arrangement" means any agreement, scheme or arrangement (including an arrangement sanctioned in accordance with section 425 (company compromise with creditors and members) or section 110 of the Insolvency Act (liquidator in winding up accepting shares as consideration for sale of company property)), and
(b) any reference to a company, except where it is or is to be construed as a reference to a public company, includes any body corporate and any body to which letters patent have been issued under the Chartered Companies Act 1837.'

Subsection (1) sets out the general rule that non-cash consideration has to be independently valued before shares are allotted. Subsections (2), (3) and (5) then provide three exceptions, with subsection (4) imposing a condition for the availability of the exception in subsection (3).

Another example is section 178 of the Insolvency Act 1986:

'**178**(1) This and the next two sections apply to a company that is being wound up in England and Wales.

(2) Subject as follows, the liquidator may, by the giving of the prescribed notice, disclaim any onerous property and may do so notwithstanding that he has taken possession of it, endeavoured to sell it, or otherwise exercised rights of ownership in relation to it.

(3) The following is onerous property for the purposes of this section–

(a) any unprofitable contract, and
(b) any other property of the company which is unsaleable or not readily saleable or is such that it may give rise to a liability to pay money or perform any other onerous act.

(4) A disclaimer under this section–

(a) operates so as to determine, as from the date of the disclaimer, the rights, interests and liabilities of the company in or in respect of the property disclaimed; but
(b) does not, except so far as is necessary for the purpose of releasing the company from any liability, affect the rights or liabilities of any other person.

(5) A notice of disclaimer shall not be given under this section in respect of any property if–

(a) a person interested in the property has applied in writing to the liquidator or one of his predecessors as liquidator requiring the liquidator or that predecessor to decide whether he will disclaim or not, and
(b) the period of 28 days beginning with the day on which that application was made, or such longer period as the court may allow, has expired without a notice of disclaimer having been given under this section in respect of that property.

(6) Any person sustaining loss or damage in consequence of the operation of a disclaimer under this section is deemed a creditor of the company to the extent of the loss or damage and accordingly may prove for the loss or damage in the winding up.'

Subsection (1) states the situation in which the section applies. The general rule is set out in subsection (2), followed in subsection (3) by a definition of the key term 'onerous property'. The effect of a disclaimer is described in subsection (4). Subsection (5) contains a restriction on the liquidator's right to disclaim, and subsection

(6) gives a creditor the right to prove for a loss caused by a disclaimer.

Statement of subject matter

Subsection (1) of section 178 illustrates the increasingly common practice of using the first subsection or subclause of a provision to set out the circumstances in which the provision applies or the subject matter with which it is concerned. Other instances are sections 385(1) and 385A(1) of the Companies Act 1985:

> '**385**(1) This section applies to every public company and to a private company which has not elected to dispense with the laying of accounts.
>
> **385A**(1) This section applies to a private company which has elected in accordance with section 252 to dispense with the laying of accounts before the company in general meeting.'

Similarly section 392A, which sets out the right of an auditor who resigns to have the company circulate a written statement of the circumstances connected with his resignation:

> '**392A**(1) This section applies where an auditor's notice of resignation is accompanied by a statement of circumstances which he considers should be brought to the attention of members or creditors of the company.'

Often a section will start with a description of the subject which it covers, eg subsection (1) of section 125 of the Companies Act 1985:

> 'This section is concerned with the variation of the rights attached to any class of shares in a company whose share capital is divided into shares of different classes'

and section 171(1) of the Insolvency Act 1986:

> 'This section applies with respect to the removal from office and vacation of office of the liquidator of a company which is being wound up voluntarily.'

Conditions

A common structure is for the first subsection to set out the main provision and subsequent subsections to set out the triggering conditions; for example, the new section 13A of the Arbitration Act 1950 (as inserted by the Courts and Legal Services Act 1990):

> '**13A**(1) Unless a contrary intention is expressed in the arbitration agreement, the arbitrator or umpire shall have power to make an award

dismissing any claim in a dispute referred to him if it appears to him that the conditions mentioned in subsection (2) are satisfied.

(2) The conditions are–

(a) that there has been inordinate and inexcusable delay on the part of the claimant in pursuing the claim; and
(b) that the delay–

(i) will give rise to a substantial risk that it is not possible to have a fair resolution of the issues in that claim; or
(ii) has caused, or is likely to cause or to have caused, serious prejudice to the respondent.'

Similarly section 31 of the Public Order Act 1986:

'**31**(1) This section applies to any offence which fulfils one or more of the following three conditions.

(2) The first condition is that the offence was committed during any period relevant to a prescribed football match ..., while the accused was at, or was entering or leaving or trying to enter or leave, the football ground concerned.

(3) The second condition is that the offence–

(a) involved the use or threat of violence by the accused towards another person and was committed while one or each of them was on a journey to or from an association football match,
(b) involved the use or threat of violence towards property and was committed while the accused was on such a journey, or
(c) was committed under section 5 or Part III while the accused was on such a journey.

(4) The third condition is that the offence was committed under section 1(3) or (4) or 1A(3) or (4) of the Sporting Events (Control of Alcohol etc) Act 1985 (alcohol on journeys to or from certain sporting events) and the designated sporting event concerned was an association football match.'

This technique is particularly helpful if the conditions themselves have several elements, for example the conditions for stamp duty relief under section 75 of the Finance Act 1986:

'**75**(1) This section applies where a company (the acquiring company) acquires the whole or part of an undertaking of another company (the target company) in pursuance of a scheme for the reconstruction of the target company.

(2) If the first and second conditions (as defined below) are fulfilled, stamp duty under the heading "Conveyance or Transfer on Sale" in Schedule 1 to the Stamp Act 1891 shall not be chargeable on an instrument executed for the purposes of or in connection with the transfer of the undertaking or part.

(3) ...

(4) The first condition is that the registered office of the acquiring company is in the United Kingdom and that the consideration for the acquisition–

(a) consists of or includes the issue of shares in the acquiring company to all the shareholders of the target company;
(b) includes nothing else (if anything) but the assumption or discharge by the acquiring company of liabilities of the target company.

(5) The second condition is that–

(a) the acquisition is effected for bona fide commercial reasons and does not form part of a scheme or arrangement of which the main purpose, or one of the main purposes, is avoidance of liability to stamp duty, income tax, corporation tax or capital gains tax,
(b) after the acquisition has been made, each shareholder of each of the companies is a shareholder of the other, and
(c) after the acquisition has been made, the proportion of shares of one of the companies held by any shareholder is the same as the proportion of shares of the other company held by that shareholder.'

Statement of purpose

Occasionally, a provision starts with a statement of its purpose. This is designed to ensure that the provision will be interpreted in a manner which gives effect to its purpose, rather than in a literal manner which does not. An interesting illustration is subsection (1) of section 739 of the Taxes Act 1988 which states that the purpose of the section is to prevent individuals ordinarily resident in the United Kingdom avoiding liability to income tax by transfers of assets as a result of which income becomes payable to persons resident or domiciled out of the United Kingdom. The predecessors of section 739 also contained that statement of purpose in the form of a recital, but that did not prevent the House of Lords in *Vestey v IRC*[1] from reversing the interpretation which it had given unanimously (and affirming the Court of Appeal) in *Congreve v IRC*.[2]

A statement of purpose introducing a set of complicated provisions prevents the underlying policy objective from becoming obscured. Part VII of the Companies Act 1989, Financial Markets and Insolvency, is introduced by the following statement in section 154:

'This Part has effect for the purposes of safeguarding the operation of certain financial markets by provisions with respect to–

1 [1980] AC 1148, [1979] 3 All ER 976.
2 [1948] 1 All ER 948.

(a) the insolvency, winding up or default of a person party to transactions in the market (sections 155 to 172),
(b) the effectiveness or enforcement of certain charges given to secure obligations in connection with such transactions (sections 173 to 176), and
(c) rights and remedies in relation to certain property provided as cover for margin in relation to such transactions or subject to such a charge (sections 177 to 181).'

Part II of the Courts and Legal Services Act 1990 starts with a statement of what it describes as 'the statutory objective':

'The general objective of this Part is the development of legal services in England and Wales ... by making provision for new or better ways of providing such services and a wider choice of persons providing them, while maintaining the efficient administration of justice.'

It then provides that any person who exercises functions conferred by that Part with regard to the granting of rights of audience or rights to conduct litigation shall–

'(a) so far as it is possible to do so in the circumstances of the case, act to further the statutory objective; and
(b) not act in any way which would be incompatible with the statutory objective.'

Although imposing an obligation to further a defined objective is primarily appropriate for a broad policy aim, this technique may have some use to prevent an underlying commercial objective becoming obscured by detailed provisions.

The one-sentence rule

As a general rule, a subsection or subclause should contain only a single sentence. If a subclause has more than one sentence, the likelihood is that it has become too long or complicated and it should be split up. But this is not always so. Section 235(3) of the Companies Act 1985 shows how two short sentences can be included in a single subclause:

'(3) The auditors shall consider whether the information given in the directors' report for the financial year for which the annual accounts are prepared is consistent with those accounts; and if they are of the opinion that it is not they shall state that fact in their report.'

CHAPTER 7

PARAGRAPHING

Until about 100 years ago, provisions of Acts of Parliament were set out in long sentences, often continuing for 15 lines or more. However, it began to be realised that provisions could be made easier to draft and understand by dividing them into logical components and setting these out in separate paragraphs. An early example of paragraphing, the most important technique in modern legislation, is section 88 of the Bills of Exchange Act 1882:

> 'The maker of a promissory note by making it–
>
> (1) Engages that he will pay it according to its tenour;
>
> (2) Is precluded from denying to a holder in due course the existence of the payee and his then capacity to indorse.'

Paragraphing is particularly helpful where there are several conditions all or any of which have to be satisfied. For example, section 8(1) of the Insolvency Act 1986 imposes two conditions for the making of an administration order:

> '(1) Subject to this section, if the court–
>
> (a) is satisfied that a company is or is likely to become unable to pay its debts (within the meaning given to that expression by section 123 of this Act), and
>
> (b) considers that the making of an order under this section would be likely to achieve one or more of the purposes mentioned below,
>
> the court may make an administration order in relation to the company.'

Similarly, section 153(1) of the Companies Act 1985 requires two conditions to be satisfied for a transaction to be exempted from the prohibition in section 151:

> '(1) Section 151(1) does not prohibit a company from giving financial assistance for the purpose of an acquisition of shares in it or its holding company if–

(a) the company's principal purpose in giving that assistance is not to give it for the purpose of any such acquisition, or the giving of the assistance for that purpose is but an incidental part of some larger purpose of the company, and
(b) the assistance is given in good faith in the interests of the company.'

The requirements for a valid will are separately paragraphed in the new version of section 9 of the Wills Act 1837, introduced by the Administration of Justice Act 1982:

'No will shall be valid unless–

(a) it is in writing, and signed by the testator, or by some other person in his presence and by his direction; and
(b) it appears that the testator intended by his signature to give effect to the will; and
(c) the signature is made or acknowledged by the testator in the presence of two or more witnesses present at the same time; and
(d) each witness either–

    (i) attests and signs the will; or
    (ii) acknowledges his signature

    in the presence of the testator (but not necessarily in the presence of any other witness),

but no form of attestation shall be necessary.'

Paragraphing is also helpful where there are alternative conditions. For example, section 736(1) of the Companies Act:

'(1) A company is a 'subsidiary' of another company, its 'holding company', if that other company–

(a) holds a majority of the voting rights in it, or
(b) is a member of it and has the right to appoint or remove a majority of its board of directors, or
(c) is a member of it and controls alone, pursuant to an agreement with other shareholders or members, a majority of the voting rights in it,

or if it is a subsidiary of a company which is itself a subsidiary of that other company.'

Section 9 of the Wills Act (set out above) shows how paragraphing can set out two or more conditions, one of which consists of alternative sub-conditions. Another example is section 19(4) of the Police and Criminal Evidence Act 1984:

'(4) The constable may require any information which is contained in a computer and is accessible from the premises to be produced in a form in which it can be taken away and in which it is visible and legible if he has reasonable grounds for believing–

(a) that–

(i) it is evidence in relation to an offence which he is investigating or any other offence; or
(ii) it has been obtained in consequence of the commission of an offence; and

(b) that it is necessary to do so in order to prevent it being concealed, lost, tampered with or destroyed.'

In section 4(1) of the Powers of Attorney Act 1971 the first set of paragraphs describe the conditions and the second the consequences:

'**4** (1) Where a power of attorney is expressed to be irrevocable and is given to secure–

(a) a proprietary interest of the donee of the power; or
(b) the performance of an obligation owed to the donee,

then, so long as the donee has that interest or the obligation remains undischarged, the power shall not be revoked–

(i) by the donor without the consent of the donee; or
(ii) by the death, incapacity or bankruptcy of the donor or, if the donor is a body corporate, by its winding up or dissolution.'

Section 2(1) and (2) of the Police and Criminal Evidence Act 1984 also show two separate sequences of paragraphs. The first set of (i) and (ii) are positioned differently from the second set because the former are sub-paragraphs within paragraph (b), while the latter are complete paragraphs:

'(1) A constable who details a person or vehicle in the exercise–

(a) of the power conferred by section 1 above; or
(b) of any other power–

(i) to search a person without first arresting him; or
(ii) to search a vehicle without making an arrest,

need not conduct a search if it appears to him subsequently–

(i) that no search is required; or
(ii) that a search is impracticable.

(2) If a constable contemplates a search, other than a search for an unattended vehicle, in the exercise–

(a) of the power conferred by section 1 above; or
(b) of any other power, except the power conferred by section 6 below and the power conferred by section 27(2) of the Aviation Security Act 1982–

(i) to search a person without first arresting him; or
(ii) to search a vehicle without making an arrest,

it shall be his duty, subject to subsection (4) below, to take reasonable steps before he commences the search to bring to the attention of the appropriate person–

(i) if the constable is not in uniform, documentary evidence that he is a constable; and
(ii) whether he is in uniform or not, the matters specified in subsection (3) below;

and the constable shall not commence the search until he has performed that duty.'

Paragraphing is also helpful where there are several items and it is necessary to make it clear that certain words apply to all of them, and not just to the last item. In the following example from section 100(1) of the Representation of the People Act 1983, it is clear that 'wholly or partly within the police area' qualifies both 'constituency' and 'electoral area':

'No member of a police force shall by word, message, writing or in any other manner, endeavour to persuade any person to give, or dissuade any person from giving, his vote, whether as an elector or as a proxy–

(a) at any parliamentary election for a constituency, or
(b) at any local government election for any electoral area,

wholly or partly within the police area.'

Similarly, in section 3(1) of the Official Secrets Act 1989 the 'tailpiece' about information being in the person's possession by virtue of his position as a Crown servant or government contractor qualifies both the information described in paragraph (a) as well as the items described in paragraph (b).

'(1) A person who is or has been a Crown servant or government contractor is guilty of an offence if without lawful authority he makes a damaging disclosure of–

(a) any information, document or other article relating to international relations; or
(b) any confidential information, document or other article which was obtained from a State other than the United Kingdom or an international organisation,

being information or a document or article which is or has been in his possession by virtue of his position as a Crown servant or government contractor.'

Similarly the new section 45 of the Justices of the Peace Act 1979:

'**45** An action shall lie against any justice of the peace or justice's clerk in respect of any act or omission of his–

(a) in the purported execution of his duty–

(i) as such a justice; or

(ii) as such a clerk exercising, by virtue of any statutory provision, any of the functions of a single justice; but

(b) with respect to a matter which is not within his jurisdiction,

if, but only if, it is proved that he acted in bad faith.'

Paragraphing also prevents confusion where a provision contains two or more items and an adjectival phrase intended to apply only to the last item. For example–

This clause applies to–

(a) any director; and
(b) any employee who is resident in the United Kingdom.

Paragraphing can be used to effect even in a simple provision; the following is section 11(1) of the Insolvency Act 1986:

'On the making of an administration order–

(a) any petition for the winding up of the company shall be dismissed, and
(b) any administrative receiver of the company shall vacate office.'

From the examples given in this chapter it will be seen that a paragraph never has more than one sentence. Each paragraph ends with either a semi-colon or a comma. If there are only two paragraphs, an 'and' or an 'or' is usually inserted between them. Where there are more than two paragraphs in a series, the word 'and' or the word 'or' is inserted only between the penultimate paragraph and the last one, except where there is a need to emphasise that the paragraphs concerned are cumulative or alternatives; in that case, the word 'and' or the word 'or' is inserted after each paragraph except the last.

CHAPTER 8

RECITALS

Recitals are the preambles in a deed or agreement introduced by the word 'WHEREAS'. Modern English practice is to put 'WHEREAS' only before the first recital and, if there are several recitals, to number or letter them. A commercial agreement of any complexity usually recites the previous transactions and events which have led up to the agreement; and even a straightforward agreement often contains an introductory recital about the transaction. For example, an agreement for the sale of a private company may start:

> WHEREAS the Vendors have agreed to sell to the Purchaser, and the Purchaser has agreed to purchase, the entire issued share capital of Barchester Chemicals Limited ('the Company') on the terms set out in this Agreement.

A recital is often used to estop a party from denying, for example, that he is the absolute owner of a particular property, or that he is indebted to another party in a specified amount. However, to have this effect a recital must be 'a distinct statement of a particular fact'.[1] The statement must be 'clear and unambiguous'. A recital in a conveyance that the vendors were 'seised in unencumbered fee simple' did not estop them from setting up a lease because 'an incumbrance, normally, is something in the nature of a mortgage and not something in the nature of a lease'.[2] It is sometimes unclear whether a recital was intended to be a representation by one of the parties or a statement by all of them; in the latter case it might be more difficult to claim an estoppel. It also seems that a recital only estops if it is in a deed. A more effective way of creating an estoppel is to include in the operative clauses an acknowledgement of the fact concerned or a representation and warranty as to that fact.

1 Parke B in *Carpenter v Buller* (1841) 8 M & W 209 at 212.
2 *District Bank Ltd v Webb* [1958] 1 All ER 126, [1958] 1 WLR 148.

A recital can be used to state that an agreement is 'supplemental to' an earlier agreement. For example, an amending agreement may start:

> WHEREAS this Agreement is supplemental to an agreement dated 5 December 1989 and made between the parties to this Agreement ('the Principal Agreement') under which the Purchaser agreed to buy certain assets of the Vendor for an aggregate sum of £3 million.

Similarly, if a company has already executed a debenture charging certain property, a further charge covering additional property may be stated to be 'supplemental' to the debenture and incorporate, by reference, many of the debenture's provisions about the bank's power of sale, its right to appoint a receiver and so on.

Section 58 of the Law of Property Act 1925 provides that an instrument which is expressed to be supplemental to a previous instrument shall have effect as if it contained 'a full recital of the previous instrument'. In practice, section 58 is seldom relied on, and a general statement is made about the effect of the previous instrument.

There is a considerable body of case law about how a conflict between a recital and an operative clause is to be resolved. In *Re Moon, ex p Dawes*,[3] Lord Esher MR formulated three rules:

> 'If the recitals are clear and the operative part is ambiguous, the recitals govern the construction. If the recitals are ambiguous, and the operative part is clear, the operative part must prevail. If both the recitals and the operative part are clear, but they are inconsistent with each other, the operative part is to be preferred.'

However, general words in the operative part are not within the category of 'clear words' which cannot be controlled by a recital. In *Danby v Coutts & Co*[4] the operative part of a power of attorney appointed two partners in a firm of solicitors to be the attorneys without limiting in terms the duration of their powers; but there was a recital that the principal was going abroad and was desirous of appointing attorneys to act for him during his absence. It was held that the recital controlled the operative part and limited the powers to the duration of the principal's absence from England.

If a draft agreement has a recital describing the transaction, and the transaction is modified during negotiations, care should be taken to amend the recital to reflect the alterations in the operative clauses.

In two limited situations, a recital can operate as a covenant or undertaking. The first is where a deed (or, it is thought, an agreement under hand only) recites that a particular party to it has agreed to do something, but there is missing from the operative part any covenant (or undertaking) by that party relating to that subject

3 (1886) 17 QBD 275 at 286.
4 (1885) 29 Ch D 500.

matter.[5] The second is where a deed contains an unqualified recital that a certain sum is due and owing from one party to another; here a covenant to pay will be implied if the sole object of the recital is to obtain an acknowledgement of the debt, and there is no other purpose, for example, to have a statement of the debt on which to base the creation of a mortgage or charge.[6]

Although recitals have almost entirely disappeared from English legislation (except private Acts and subordinate legislation), they are used extensively in EC Directives and Regulations, and can have considerable significance. In *Litster v Forth Dry Dock and Engineering Co Limited*[7] both Lord Templeman and Lord Oliver of Aylmerton invoked a recital of purpose in Council Directive 77/187, which safeguards employees' rights on a transfer of business, in order to defeat a literal interpretation of the statutory instrument that gave effect to the Directive in the United Kingdom. Another example is Council Regulation 418/85, which exempts certain joint ventures for research and development from article 85(1) of the Treaty of Rome; Professor Korah describes[8] the second recital as 'the most important provision in the whole regulation'. This recital sets out the Commission's view that joint ventures applying only to r & d and terminating short of industrial application rarely infringe article 85(1). In Regulation 2137/85, which governs European Economic Interest Groupings, it is the fifth and sixth recitals, and not any of the operative articles, that make it possible for a member of a profession to join an EEIG. Commercial agreements may come to adopt the Brussels technique of using recitals to describe the broad policy background or to deal with sensitive issues. Careful drafting is, however, necessary to ensure that a provision in a recital is not overridden by the operative clauses.

5 See the statement of Sir George Jessel MR in *Dawes v Tredwell* (1881) 18 Ch D 354 at 359; *Buckland v Buckland* [1900] 2 Ch 534; and *Stephens v Junior Army and Navy Stores Ltd* [1914] 2 Ch 516.
6 *Jackson v North Eastern Rly Co* (1877) 7 Ch D 573 at 582–587.
7 [1990] 1 AC 546, [1989] 1 All ER 1134.
8 *EEC Competition Law and Practice* (ESC Publishing Limited) p 207.

CHAPTER 9

DEFINITIONS

There are four main types of definition.

Nicknames

The first is the 'nickname', for example:

> 'the Trustees' means the trustees for the time being of the settlement dated 1 September 1980 and made between John Smith of the one part and George White and Arthur Brown of the other part.
>
> 'the Finance Documents' means this Agreement, the mortgage to be delivered by the Borrower under clause 2 below and the guarantee to be delivered by the Guarantor under that clause.

Nicknames are used only for brevity; their purpose is seldom to achieve a specific legal result. By convention the first letters of 'nickname' definitions are in upper case.

'Means'

A similar type of definition sets out comprehensively the scope of a term, often by specifying all the items which it covers. For example,

> 'Security interest' means any mortgage, charge, pledge or lien.

A definition of this type is useful where there is a multi-word phrase which would otherwise have to be repeated throughout a clause or contract:

> 'non-resident employee' means an employee of the Company who is not at any time during the relevant calendar year resident in the United Kingdom for the purposes of income tax.

'Includes'

The third type of definition extends a term to an item which it would not normally cover. For example:

> '"term of years" includes a term for less than a year';[1]

> '"loss" includes a loss by not getting what one might get, as well as parting with what one has';[2]

> '"noise" includes vibration'.[3]

This type of definition is generally introduced by the word 'includes'. However, the court will sometimes limit the items which are listed after 'includes' to the phrase which precedes that word. *Customs and Excise Comrs v Savoy Hotel Ltd*[4] arose out of the following Purchase Tax Group in the Purchase Tax Act 1963:

> 'Manufactured beverages, including fruit juices and bottled waters, and syrups, concentrates, essences, powders, crystals or other products for the preparation of beverages.'

The issue was described by Sachs J:

> 'In this case the court is called on to decide the fascinating and no doubt important problem as to whether the guest who from his bedroom in Claridge's (or for that matter the Savoy or the Berkeley) calls at breakfast time for his orange juice and a few minutes later receives the juice of a single orange freshly pressed out for his benefit in its purest form - unsweetened at that - is provided with a manufactured beverage within the meaning of those words in Group 35 of Sch 1 to the Purchase Tax Act 1963. Any tendency to approach this question with undue levity was checked by the information that in the course of a single year there were served in those three hotels no less than one hundred thousand of what is convenient to call "portions" of orange juice, and that the Commissioners of Customs and Excise were industriously chasing a sum of the order of £1,500, having previously succeeded in bringing into the purchase tax net the ices consumed by diners at those institutions.'

Counsel for the Commissioners (Mr Nigel Bridge) argued that the word 'includes' extended the definition beyond the natural meaning of the term 'manufactured beverages'. Sachs J rejected this argument:

> 'To talk of natural juice extracted by hand from a single orange for the use of the particular person who wishes to have it fresh to drink,

1 Law of Property Act 1925, s 205(1)(xxvii).
2 Theft Act 1968, s 34(2).
3 Environmental Protection Act 1990, s 79(7).
4 [1966] 2 All ER 299, [1966] 1 WLR 948; see also *Beswick v Beswick* [1968] AC 58, [1967] 2 All ER 1197, and *Guinness plc v Saunders* [1990] 2 AC 663, [1990] 1 All ER 652 discussed in Chapter 11.

as a "manufactured beverage" does not, as I have already indicated, make sense; and there is nothing here in the use of the word "included" that compels the court to say that "fruit juices" must be construed without reference to the two words with which the sentence begins and which should, where practicable, be given some effect in relation to the words that follow.'

'Does not include'

The fourth type of definition narrows a term's meaning. For example:

> '"animal" does not include bird or fish.'[5]

The same definition can include some items and exclude others:

> '"milk" includes cream and separated milk, but does not include dried milk or condensed milk.'[6]

'In relation to'

Some defined terms make sense only in relation to a particular subject. For example:

> 'In this Part "author", in relation to a work, means the person who creates it';[7]

> 'In this section "chief executive", in relation to an institution, means a person who, either alone or jointly with one or more other persons, is responsible under the immediate authority of the directors for the conduct of the business of the institution';[8]

> '"address" means–
>
> (a) in relation to an individual, his usual residential or business address, and
>
> (b) in relation to a firm, its registered or principal office in Great Britain.'[9]

Narrative definitions

A definition does not always have to put the defined term in inverted commas and use a word such as 'means' or 'includes'. The following is section 2(1) of the Sale of Goods Act 1979:

> 'A contract of sale of goods is a contract by which the seller transfers

5 Food Act 1984.
6 Ibid.
7 Copyright, Designs and Patents Act 1988, s 9(1).
8 Banking Act 1987, s 105.
9 Companies Act 1989, s 53.

or agrees to transfer the property in goods to the buyer for a money consideration, called the price.'

And section 247(2) of the Insolvency Act 1986:

> 'For the purposes of any provision in this Group of Parts, a company goes into liquidation if it passes a resolution for voluntary winding up or an order for its winding up is made by the court at a time when it has not already gone into liquidation by passing such a resolution.'

Similarly, section 12(1) of the Unfair Contract Terms Act 1977:

> 'A party to a contract "deals as consumer" in relation to another party if–
>
> (a) he neither makes the contract in the course of a business nor holds himself out as doing so; and
> (b) the other party does make the contract in the course of a business; and
> (c) in the case of a contract governed by the law of sale of goods or hire purchase ... the goods passing under or in pursuance of the contract are of a type ordinarily supplied for private use or consumption.'

The 'a reference to' formula is common. For example:

> 'A reference to a class of shares is to shares to which the same rights are attached as to voting and as to participation, both as respects dividends and as respects capital, in a distribution.'[10]

> 'Any reference to the time of any sale shall be construed as a reference to the time of completion or the time when possession is given, whichever is the earlier.'[11]

> 'Subject to the following provisions of this section, references in this Act to supplying goods shall be construed as references to doing any of the following, whether as principal or agent, that is to say–
>
> (a) selling, hiring out or lending the goods;
> (b) entering into a hire purchase agreement to furnish the goods;
> (c) the performance of any contract for work and materials to furnish the goods;
> (d) providing the goods in exchange for any consideration (including trading stamps) other than money;
>
> ...'[12]

Definitions often appear as part of an operative provision. For example, section 402 of the Income and Corporation Taxes Act 1988:

> '(1) Subject to and in accordance with this Chapter and section 492(8), relief for trading losses and other amounts eligible for relief from corporation tax may, in the cases set out in subsections (2) and (3) below,

10 Companies Act 1985, s 94(6).
11 Capital Allowances Act 1990, s 161(8).
12 Consumer Protection ACt 1987, s 46(1).

be surrendered by a company ("the surrendering company") and, on the making of a claim by another company ("the claimant company") may be allowed to the claimant company by way of a relief from corporation tax called "group relief".

(2) Group relief shall be available in a case where the surrendering company and the claimant company are both members of the same group.'

Definitions within definitions

Sometimes elements of a definition need themselves to be defined; this can best be done if the definition is set out as a separate provision (rather than as one of the defined terms in the general definitions clause), and additional provisions are used for the supplemental definitions. In the following example, taken from section 17 of the Computer Misuse Act 1990, subsection (2) sets out the main definition and subsections (3) and (4) define terms used within the main definition:

'(2) A person secures access to any program or data held in a computer if by causing a computer to perform any function he–

(a) alters or erases the program or data;
(b) copies or moves it to any storage medium other than that in which it is held or to a different location in the storage medium in which it is held;
(c) uses it; or
(d) has it output from the computer in which it is held (whether by having it displayed or in any other manner);

and references to access to a program or data ... shall be read accordingly.

(3) For the purposes of subsection (2)(c) above a person uses a program if the function he causes the computer to perform–

(a) causes the program to be executed; or
(b) is itself a function of the program.

(4) For the purposes of subsection (2)(d) above–

(a) a program is output if the instructions of which it consists are output; and
(b) the form in which any such instructions or any other data is output ... is immaterial.'

Undefined terms

Sometimes it is inappropriate to attempt a precise definition, and a term should be left undefined or there should be a statement that its meaning is to be determined, for example, in accordance with accepted practice among leading firms in London engaged in the relevant type of business. Such a clause is useful where the defined term is 'dynamic', in the sense that its meaning or scope is to be determined by reference to practice at the date of the contract or practice at the date when the relevant transaction comes to be carried out. For example,

> 'derivative instrument' means any security or contract which, at the relevant time, is generally regarded as a derivative instrument by firms in London which regularly lead manage issues on the international capital markets of bonds having an aggregate principal amount of US$ 500 million or more (or the equivalent), regardless of whether transactions in securities or contracts of that type are regularly entered into at that time by such firms.

A notable statutory example of such a definition is section 262(3) of the Companies Act 1985, which provides:

> 'References in this Part to "realised profits" and "realised losses" ... are to such profits and losses of the company as fall to be treated as realised in accordance with principles generally accepted, at the time when the accounts are prepared, with respect to the determination for accounting purposes of realised profits or losses.
>
> This is without prejudice to ... the construction of any other expression (where appropriate) by reference to accepted accounting principles or practice.'

Relevant here is a well-known opinion given in 1984 by Mr Leonard Hoffmann and Miss Mary Arden (now Hoffmann J and Miss Arden QC) as to the meaning of the Companies Act requirements for accounts to 'give a true and fair view'. They considered that the question of whether accounts complied with this requirement was a legal issue to be decided by a judge; but that the courts would look for guidance on this question to 'the ordinary practices of professional accountants'.

A similar approach is taken by section 64 of the Courts and Legal Services Act 1990 (which amends the Sex Discrimination Act 1975 and the Race Relations Act 1976):

> '"Pupil", "pupillage", "tenancy" and "tenant" have the meanings commonly associated with their use in the context of a set of barristers' chambers.'

Occasionally, it is decided not to define a term used in legislation, but to leave its interpretation to the courts. Neither the Data Protection Act 1984 nor the Computer Misuse Act 1990 define 'computer'; section 349(3) of the Income and Corporation Taxes Act 1988 (which permits interest to be paid gross on an advance from a UK bank) does not define 'a bank carrying on a bona fide banking business in the United Kingdom'. Although, in the case of legislation, it may be a legitimate policy option to leave it to the courts to decide what a particular term means, that might increase the risk of litigation in the case of a contract. *Tandon v Trustees of Spurgeons Homes*[13] arose out of section 2(1) of the Leasehold Reform Act 1967 which defined 'house' to include 'any building designed or adapted for living in and reasonably so called'. The county court judge held that this covered a shop with living accommodation above. His decision was reversed by a majority of the Court of Appeal, but restored by a bare majority of the House of Lords. Delivering the leading speech for the majority, Lord Roskill said that as long as a building of mixed use could reasonably be called a house, it was within the definition, even though it might also reasonably be called something else; and that it was a question of law whether it was reasonable to call a building a 'house'.

Definitions not to contain operative substantive provisions

The better practice is that a definition should not incorporate a substantive provision. For example–

> 'Reference Banks' means A Bank, B Bank and C Bank or any other bank with a branch in London which the Majority Banks may, after consulting the Borrower and the Facility Agent, appoint to replace any of those banks or any bank previously appointed by them.

would be better as–

> 'Reference Banks' means A Bank, B Bank and C Bank or any other bank which the Majority Banks appoint under clause 23.

Clause 23 would give the Majority Banks the power to appoint a replacement bank; it would also set out the requirements for a London branch and consultation with the Borrower and the Facility Agent. Moreover, the House of Lords decisions in *Beswick v Beswick* and *Guinness plc v Saunders*[14] indicate that it is unsafe to use a general definition to bring about important modification in how a substantive provision operates.

Position of definitions

The definitions of terms used throughout an Act appear in an interpretation section at the end of the Act – for example, section 744 of the Companies Act 1985 which defines such terms as 'debenture' and 'officer'. By contrast, the normal practice for commercial agreements is to put the general definitions at the beginning. However, this requires the reader to go through a set of technical and legalistic provisions before arriving at the essential

13 [1982] AC 755, [1982] 1 All ER 1086.
14 See Chapter 11.

business terms; and the significance of some definitions can only be appreciated after seeing the clauses in which they operate. A tendency may therefore develop for commercial agreements to follow the statutory practice of putting general definitions at the end.

The statutory practice is that a term used only or primarily in a particular section or group of sections is defined in the section or sections concerned – so 'share premium account' is defined in section 130 of the 1985 Act, which is the first in a set of four sections dealing with the application of share premiums.

A term of fundamental importance to an Act is often defined at the start of the Act. In the Unfair Contract Terms Act 1977, section 1 defines 'negligence'; in the Banking Act 1987, sections 5 and 6 define 'deposit' and 'deposit-taking business'; and in Part I of the Environmental Protection Act 1990, section 1 defines the 'environment' and 'pollution of the environment'.

Placing definitions in the place most appropriate to the term defined can result their being widely scattered. Accordingly, it is increasingly common for a long Act to contain an index of defined expressions: examples are section 155(4) of the Capital Gains Tax Act 1979 and section 744A of the Companies Act 1985.

Common definitions

By way of illustration, the following are some definitions which might typically appear in a commercial agreement.

> 'agreement' includes any commitment, scheme or arrangement, whether legally binding or not, and references to being party to an agreement shall be construed accordingly;
>
> 'business day' means a day on which banks and foreign exchange markets are open for business in London and New York;
>
> 'document' includes information recorded in any form;
>
> 'expenses' includes costs, charges and expenses of every description;
>
> 'intellectual property right' means the following in any part of the world:
>
> (a) a patent, trade mark, service mark, registered design, copyright or design right or any right which is similar or analogous to any of the foregoing;
> (b) any moral right;
> (c) any know-how, as defined in section 533(7) of the Income and Corporation Taxes Act 1988;
> (d) any licence, right or interest of any kind arising out of or granted or created in respect of any of the foregoing;
> (e) any right to bring an action for passing off or any similar or analogous proceeding;
>
> 'legislation' means any enactment, subordinate legislation or Order in Council not made under an enactment and any analogous law, regulation

or decree in force in a country or territory outside the United Kingdom; also any of the Treaties and a Community instrument, as defined in the European Communities Act 1972;

'notice' includes a demand, consent or waiver;

'proceedings' means any proceedings before a court or tribunal (including an arbitration), whether in England or elsewhere;

'property' means property, assets, interests and rights of every description, wherever situated;

'tax' includes every description of tax, duty or levy, whether or not similar to any tax payable in the United Kingdom or in force at the date of this Agreement, and any related interest, penalty, fine or other amount;

'written', in relation to a notice under this Agreement, includes sent by telex or fax.

There might well be additional definitions based on various statutory provisions:

'control', in relation to a company or partnership, has the meaning given in section 840 of the Income and Corporation Taxes Act 1988;

'group company' means any company or other undertaking which at the relevant time is a group undertaking (as defined in section 259(5) of the Companies Act 1985) in relation to the Purchaser;

'land' has the meaning given in Schedule 1 to the Interpretation Act 1978;

'liability' means every description of debt or liability, including any which falls within section 382(3) or (4) of the Insolvency Act 1986 (or any corresponding provision relating to companies) or to which a person becomes subject after, or would become subject but for, his bankruptcy or its winding up;

'parent undertaking' has the meaning given in section 258 of the Companies Act 1985;

'personal representative' has the meaning given in section 272 of the Inheritance Tax Act 1984;

'securities' has the meaning given in section 228(6) of the Companies Act 1985;

'subsidiary undertaking' has the meaning given in section 258 of the Companies Act 1985;

'trust' has the meaning given in article 2 of the Convention referred to in the Recognition of Trusts Act 1987;

'undertaking' has the meaning given in section 259 of the Companies Act 1985.

'Subsidiary' and 'subsidiary undertaking'

The concepts of 'group' and 'subsidiary' are important for many contracts. The Companies Act 1989, which amended the 1985 Act, introduced two concepts of subsidiary. The first is 'subsidiary undertaking', which is defined in the new sections 258 to 260 and the new Schedule 10A. These provisions implement the EC Seventh Directive on consolidated accounts and form the basis of the rules about which companies have to be included in group accounts under the Companies Act.

Side by side with the 'subsidiary undertaking' concept is the definition of 'subsidiary' in the new section 736 of the Companies Act 1985. This definition applies for the purposes of the companies legislation and certain related legislation, such as the Financial Services Act 1986. For example, section 736 (and not the definition of 'subsidiary undertaking') applies to the prohibition in section 151 of the Companies Act 1985 on a company giving financial assistance for the purpose of an acquisition of shares in itself or its holding company.

Essentially, S is a 'subsidiary undertaking' of P if any of the following six tests is met.

(1) P has a '*participating interest*' in S and '*actually exercises a dominant influence*' over S; whether or not P actually exercises a dominant influence is a pure question of fact and the position could change from one year to another.

(2) P has a '*participating interest*' in S, and P and S '*are managed on a unified basis*': this is another factual issue.

(3) P holds a majority of the voting rights in S.

(4) P is a member of S and has the right to appoint or remove a majority of S's board of directors; this is defined to mean 'directors holding a majority of the voting rights at meetings of the board on all, or substantially all, matters'. P therefore cannot keep S off the balance sheet by having the power to appoint directors, who, although a minority in number, possess loaded rights giving a majority of the votes.

(5) P is a member of S and, under an agreement with other members of S, P controls *alone* a majority of the voting rights in S.

(6) P has *the right* to exercise a dominant influence over S by virtue of S's memorandum or articles or 'a control contract' (defined in Sch 10A, para 4(2)); unlike test (1) this test does not depend on the influence actually being exercised.

'Participating interest' is defined as an interest in shares which an undertaking–

> 'holds on a long-term basis for the purpose of securing a contribution to its activities by the exercise of control or influence arising from or related to that interest.'

There is a prima facie presumption that a shareholding of 20 per cent or more is a participating interest.

For the definition of 'subsidiary' in section 736, the only applicable tests are (3), (4) and (5) above. Since the concepts of 'actually exercising a dominant influence' and being 'managed on a unified basis' do not apply to section 736, the definition of 'subsidiary' is much narrower than that of 'subsidiary undertaking'.

Which definition is more appropriate depends on the type of contract and provision concerned. However, it is thought that prima facie the 'subsidiary undertaking' definition should be more suitable to most provisions of a commercial contract since, essentially, it governs what is an economic group for accounting purposes. Also, being based on the EC Seventh Directive, it is similar to corresponding accounting definitions in other EC countries. It should be kept in mind, however, that in certain circumstances the Companies Act 1985 requires or permits a subsidiary undertaking to be excluded from group accounts and requires a company which is not a subsidiary undertaking to be included.

'As amended'

If an agreement contains references to statutory provisions, the definitions clause should include a subclause to the following effect:

> In this Agreement any reference to an enactment includes a reference to it as amended (whether before or after the date of this Agreement) and to any other enactment which may, after the date of this Agreement, directly or indirectly replace it, with or without amendment.[15]

This is wider than section 17(2)(a) of the Interpretation Act 1978 (the only provision of that Act which applies to deeds and agreements). Under section 17(2)(a) a reference to enactment 1 only includes a reference to enactment 2 if enactment 2 repeals, as well as re-enacts, enactment 1.

The need for such a provision is illustrated by *Brett v Brett Essex Golf Club*[16] in which the Court of Appeal had to decide whether in a lease granted in 1978 a reference to section 34 of the Landlord and Tenant Act 1954 was a reference to that section as amended by the Law of Property Act 1969 or in the form in which it was originally enacted. Slade LJ, who delivered the main judgment, said:

15 If an agreement refers to any statutory instrument, this clause should be extended to subordinate legislation.
16 (1986) 52 P & CR 330.

> '...in many, perhaps the majority of, cases where parties to a written contract have incorporated in it a reference to a statute, it may be reasonable to impute to them an intention to refer to the statute in its amended form. However, no authority has been cited to us which suggests that under the ordinary law there is any presumption of construction to this effect.'

It was held that the 1978 lease referred to section 34 in the form in which it had stood before the 1969 amendment.

A fortiori, it is thought that in the absence of express words, a reference in an agreement to an enactment will not normally cover amendments to the enactment which are made *after* the date of the agreement unless the context clearly indicates that post-agreement amendments were intended to be covered.

A definitions clause often contains a similar 'as amended' provision applicable to itself and other agreements:

> References to (or to any provision of) this Agreement or any other agreement, instrument or document include references to it as altered, supplemented or replaced in any manner.

It should be noted that a provision of this kind has the effect of altering the contract's terms automatically, and without the parties' consent being required, if there is an amendment to any of the statutory provisions referred to. For example, if a contract signed in 1987 had defined 'subsidiary' by reference to the definition in section 736 of the Companies Act 1985, that definition would have changed automatically when section 144 of the 1989 Act brought in a new version of section 736.

'From time to time' and 'for the time being'

The question sometimes arises whether a particular power or right conferred by an agreement can be exercised more than once; for example, if a clause requires A to execute any documents which B may request for a particular purpose, can B make a second request if he finds that the documents which A executed pursuant to the first request are insufficient? Or if A is required to indemnify B against certain expenses or claims 'on demand', can B make a second demand if he incurs further expenses after serving the first? The traditional way of dealing with such questions is to insert the phrase 'from time to time' in the appropriate place in the clause concerned; for example–

> A shall execute any deeds or documents which B may from time to time request.

However, this can be rather cumbersome. Also, if only some clauses in an agreement include this phrase, there can be an implication that the rights given by the other clauses can be exercised only once. It is therefore preferable for an agreement's general definitions clause to contain the following subclause:

Unless the contrary intention appears–

(a) any right or power conferred by this Agreement may be exercised; and
(b) any duty or obligation imposed by this Agreement is to be performed;

from time to time as occasion requires.

This is in similar terms to section 12(1) of the Interpretation Act 1978. The operation of such a provision is illustrated by the Court of Appeal's decision in *R v Ealing Borough Council, ex p McBain*.[17] Section 12 converted a housing authority's duty under the Housing (Homeless Persons) Act 1977 into a duty to be performed from time to time as occasion required. It followed that, where a homeless person had unreasonably refused a previous offer of accommodation, and later a change in her circumstances occurred which rendered the accommodation previously offered clearly unsuitable, the housing authority came under a fresh duty to offer her accommodation.

'From time to time' is adverbial, whereas 'for the time being' is adjectival. For example, if it is necessary to refer to the persons who are the trustees of a settlement at some future date when a particular clause may come to apply, the reference would be to the trustees 'for the time being' of the settlement. A modern equivalent is 'at the relevant time'.

Law of Property Act 1925, section 61

There are several definitions which a contract does not need to contain because, unless the context otherwise requires, they apply automatically under section 61 of the Law of Property Act in any deed, contract or other instrument which is governed by English law:

Month includes calendar month;[18]

The singular includes the plural and vice versa;

The masculine includes the feminine and vice versa.

'Person'

It is sometimes thought necessary to define 'person'. The main problem is that the term might not cover a joint venture, an unincorporated body (such as the Panel or Take-overs and Mergers)

17 [1986] 1 All ER 13, [1985] 1 WLR 1351.
18 See Chapter 14.

or an international organisation on the grounds that some of these do not have legal personality.[19]

The following is a suggested definition:

'person' means–

(a) a natural person and any corporation or other entity which is given, or is recognised as having, legal personality by the law of any country or territory;

(b) any unincorporated association or unincorporated body of persons, whether formed in the United Kingdom or elsewhere, including a partnership, joint venture or consortium;

(c) the government of a country or territory, any public, local or municipal authority in the United Kingdom or elsewhere and any international organisation or body, whether or not its members include the United Kingdom and whether or not having legal personality;

and any persons who, under the law of any country or territory, together hold a fiduciary, representative or official position (for example, the trustees of a settlement, an individual's personal representatives or joint receivers, administrators or liquidators) shall be treated as a single person.

A European Economic Interest Grouping registered in Great Britain is covered by paragraph (a) of the above definition, since such an EEIG is a body corporate: see regulation 3 of the European Economic Interest Grouping Regulations 1989, 1989 No 638. Paragraph (b) of that definition would apply to an EEIG registered in a Member State which does not accord legal personality to EEIGs. The European Economic Community itself is covered by paragraph (a) of the above definition. Articles 210 and 211 of the Treaty of Rome provide for the EEC to have legal personality and 'the most extensive legal capacity accorded to legal persons' and these articles are incorporated into United Kingdom law by section 2 of the European Communities Act 1972.[20]

Section 61 of the Law of Property Act 1925 also defines 'person' to include a corporation; this is narrower than the definition in the Interpretation Act:

'"Person" includes a body of persons corporate or unincorporate.'

Unlike the section 61 definition, this covers a partnership or a joint venture, and also a fluctuating body of persons such as a committee: *R v Minister of Agriculture and Fisheries, ex p Graham*.[1] However, the wider Interpretation Act definition applies only in legislation and not contracts.

Where it is intended to make a provision apply only to natural

19 See, for example, *R v Panel on Take-overs and Mergers, ex p Datafin plc* [1987] QB 815 at 824H) and *Arab Monetary Fund v Hashim (No 3)* [1991] 1 All ER 871, [1991] 2 WLR 729, HL; also article by G Marston (1991) 40 ICLQ 403.

20 See *J H Rayner Ltd v Department of Trade and Industry* [1989] Ch 72 at 198B and 200E to 201D, 223C and 252H.

1 [1955] 2 QB 140, [1955] 2 All ER 129.

persons, the term 'individual' should be used instead of 'person'. Statutory examples are the Company Securities (Insider Dealing) Act 1985, section 264 of the Insolvency Act 1986 (bankruptcy petitions) and section 256 of the Income and Corporation Taxes Act 1988 (personal reliefs). Exceptionally, however, 'individual' can be construed as including a company if there is a strong contextual implication to that effect.[2]

Singular includes the plural

The statement in section 61 that the singular includes the plural and vice versa cannot be invoked to alter the nature of a clause. In *Blue Metal Industries Ltd v Dilley*,[3] the Privy Council held that a similar statement in the Interpretation Act of New South Wales was a drafting convenience which could not be used to change 'the character' of legislation, that is, to rewrite a section in terms that would presuppose a different legislative policy. However, in *Dawson v IRC*,[4] the House of Lords had no hesitation in applying the Interpretation Act to pluralise a reference to 'a person' in paragraph (a)(i) of Schedule D (now in section 18, Income and Corporation Taxes Act 1988). In *Floor v Davis*,[5] the House of Lords had to consider whether the Interpretation Act could be invoked to pluralise the expression 'a person having control' in what is now section 25(2) of the Capital Gains Tax Act 1978. By a bare majority, the House rejected the taxpayer's argument that applying the Interpretation Act would change the character of the provision. The speeches of the dissenters, Lord Wilberforce and Lord Keith of Kinkel, indicate that it is unsafe to rely on section 61 where pluralisation (or singularisation) might possibly be regarded as altering the character of a provision; in such a case, express pluralised (or singularised) wording should be included and any points arising from the provision applying to two or more persons or items should be expressly dealt with.[6]

Significance of definitions

The definitions are often a contract's most difficult provisions to draft. A flawed definition can produce an incorrect result each time

2 *Societe United Docks v Government of Mauritius* [1985] AC 585 at 601C.
3 [1970] AC 827, [1969] 3 All ER 437.
4 [1990] 1 AC 1 at 11.
5 [1980] AC 695, [1979] 2 All ER 677.
6 *Featherstone v Staples* [1986] 2 All ER 461 illustrates the problems which can arise if this is not done. *Prior v Sovereign Chicken Ltd* [1984] 2 All ER 289, [1984] 1 WLR 921, CA shows how the context can negative the Interpretation Act provision that the plural includes the singular.

the defined term is used. The more usual problem, however, is that a definition fits most clauses correctly, but is too wide or too narrow for others. It is a difficult but necessary task to check that a definition does not produce an anomaly in any of the provisions in which the defined term appears.

There is a tendency for agreements to contain unnecessary definitions; for example, 'sterling' means the lawful currency of the United Kingdom. The observations of Lord Thring, the distinguished nineteenth-century Parliamentary counsel, are salutary:

> 'The proper use of definitions is to include or exclude something with respect to the inclusion or exclusion of which there is a doubt without such a definition, and no attempt should be made to make a pretence of scientific precision by defining words of which the ordinary meaning is sufficiently clear and exact.'[7]

Excluding reference to headings

In *DPP v Schildkamp*,[8] Lord Reid and Lord Upjohn indicated that, in construing an Act, reference can be made to a cross-heading or to a marginal note. A cross-heading is the heading given to a Part or a group of sections, for example, in Part VII of the Companies Act 1989:

'FINANCIAL MARKETS AND INSOLVENCY

Introduction

Recognised investment exchanges and clearing houses.'

Marginal notes are the titles of sections; for example, 'Market contracts' in the case of section 155 of that Act. However, in *Schildkamp* Lord Reid said that a marginal note is a poor guide to the scope of a section because it can do no more than indicate the main subject with which the section deals.

In a statutory context, the main constraint against referring to headings and marginal notes is that these are not considered or debated by Parliament: see 44 Halsbury's Laws 818 and 819. This constraint does not apply to clause headings in contracts and on this account a court may be readier to refer to them. On the other hand, Lord Reid's point about a marginal note being no more than an indication of the main subject matter of a section is equally applicable to clause and Schedule headings in contracts. For this reason, it is thought that a court would not usually attach significance to a clause heading, and that only exceptionally would such a heading be the decisive factor in a court's interpreting a clause in one way rather than another.

7 *Practical Legislation* (1902) p96.
8 [1971] AC 1, [1969] 3 All ER 1640, HL.

Nevertheless, it is normal for agreements to provide that–

> No regard shall be had to the heading or title of any Part, clause or Schedule of this Agreement in construing any of its provisions.

Whether this is desirable is finely-balanced. It is thought that the better view is that the court's discretion should not be excluded and that, in practice, a court would only invoke a clause heading to support a more reasonable interpretation than would result from a literal reading. It is considered unlikely that a court would invoke a clause heading to reinforce an interpretation which produces a result that is unreasonable in business terms.

CHAPTER 10

NON-LITERAL INTERPRETATION

Parties are often anxious that a court might give their contract a strict literal interpretation which will defeat their intentions. This Chapter considers whether any purpose is served by a contract including a stipulation against literal interpretation, and whether such a stipulation is valid. It should be emphasised that this is quite different from the type of clause which purports to permit or oblige a court or an arbitrator to apply 'principles of equity' instead of legal rules: as to these, see the discussion of 'equity clauses' in *Commercial Arbitration* by Mustill and Boyd at pp 74–86.

To some extent the risk of literal interpretation is more perceived than real. In *Prenn v Simmonds*,[1] the House of Lords rejected what Lord Wilberforce referred to as 'the idea that English law is left behind in some island of literal interpretation'. Lord Wilberforce (with whom all the other Law Lords agreed) stated–

> 'We must . . . enquire beyond the language and see what the circumstances were with reference to which the words were used, and the object, appearing from those circumstances, which the person using them had in view.'

The decision establishes that 'the commercial, or business object of the transaction, objectively ascertained, may be a surrounding fact' to which the court should have regard. On the other hand, the decision makes it clear that evidence of pre-contractual negotiations or of the parties' subjective intentions cannot be received. In *Prenn v Simmonds* the House of Lords held that a clause which provided that a party would have a right to purchase shares in a particular company if the aggregate profits of that company available for dividend on its ordinary stock reached a particular figure referred to the consolidated profits of the group consisting of that company and its subsidiaries, and not to the profits of the company alone.

1 [1971] 3 All ER 237, [1971] 1 WLR 1381.

In *Reardon Smith Line Ltd v Yngvar Hansen-Tangen and Sanko SS Co Ltd*,[2] the House of Lords again asserted that, in interpreting a contract, a court should have regard to the factual background against which the contract was made, including the commercial purpose of the transaction. As Lord Wilberforce put it–

> 'What the court must do must be to place itself in thought in the same factual matrix as that in which the parties were'.

Lord Wilberforce also said:–

> 'When one speaks of the intention of the parties to the contract, one is speaking objectively – the parties cannot themselves give direct evidence of what their intention was – and what must be ascertained is what is to be taken as the intention which reasonable people would have had if placed in the situation of the parties. Similarly, when one is speaking of aim, or object, or commercial purpose, one is speaking objectively of what reasonable persons would have in mind in the situation of the parties.'

In *Prenn v Simmonds* Lord Wilberforce referred to the judgment of Cardozo J in the *Utica City National Bank v Gunn*[3] in order 'to dispel the idea that English law is left behind in some island of literal interpretation'. The judgment of this celebrated New York judge is reproduced in Appendix 2. 'The whole judgment', Lord Wilberforce observed, 'combines classicism with intelligent realism.'

In *Black-Clawson International Ltd v Papierwerke Waldhof-Aschaffenburg AG*,[4] Lord Reid stated:

> 'The general rule in construing any document is that one should put oneself "in the shoes" of the maker or makers and take into account relevant facts known to them when the document was made.'

In *Schuler AG v Wickman Machine Tool Sales Ltd*[5] the House of Lords searched for, and found, a possible alternative meaning of a contract in order to avoid a clearly unreasonable result. A contract by which the manufacturers of panel presses granted a company the sole selling rights for four-and-a-half years stated that 'it shall be [a] condition of this agreement' that the company granted the selling rights should send its representatives to visit the six largest United Kingdom motor manufacturers at least once in every week to solicit orders for the panel presses. The manufacturers sought to terminate the contract on the ground of immaterial breaches of this obligation. The House of Lords held that the clause was not

2 [1976] 3 All ER 570, [1976] 1 WLR 989.
3 222 NY 204, 118 NE 607 (1918).
4 [1975] AC 591, [1975] 1 All ER 810.
5 [1974] AC 235, [1973] 2 All ER 39.

a 'condition' in the primary sense such that a single breach of it, however trivial, would entitle the innocent party to terminate the contract. Lord Reid said:

> 'The fact that a particular construction leads to a very unreasonable result must be a relevant consideration. The more unreasonable the result the more unlikely it is that the parties can have intended it, and if they do intend it the more necessary it is that they shall make that intention abundantly clear.'

The House of Lords adopted the same approach in *Antaios Cia Naviera SA v Salen AB*.[6] Against a background of rising rates of charterhire, the owners of a vessel had withdrawn it from a charter party on the grounds that inaccurate bills of lading had been issued. The relevant clause in the charter entitled the owners to withdraw the vessel 'failing the punctual and regular payment of the hire or on any breach of this charter party'. The arbitrators, however, decided that 'any other breach of this charter party' meant only a repudiatory breach, a category into which they considered that the breach complained of did not fall. The arbitrators based their opinion on what Lord Diplock described as a 'semantic analysis, buttressed by generous citation of judicial authority'. The arbitrators added, as Lord Diplock put it, 'an uncomplicated reason based simply upon business commonsense':

> 'We always return to the point that the owners' construction is wholly unreasonable, totally uncommercial and in total contradiction to the whole purpose of the NYPE time charter form. The owners relied on what they said was "the literal meaning of the words in the clause". We would say that if necessary, in a situation such as this, a purposive construction should be given to the clause so as not to defeat the commercial purpose of the contract.'

Lord Diplock agreed with this reason (although he deprecated the extension of the use of the expression 'purposive construction' from the interpretation of statutes to the interpretation of private contracts). He said that the arbitrators were anticipating the commonsense approach to the construction of commercial documents which, with the concurrence of his fellow Law Lords, he had described in *Miramar Maritime Corpn v Holborn Oil Trading Ltd*.[7] Lord Diplock, whose speech was concurred in by all the other Law Lords, added this:

> 'I take this opportunity of re-stating that if detailed semantic and syntactical analysis of words in a commercial contract is going to lead to a conclusion that flouts business commonsense, it must be made to yield to business commonsense.'

6 [1985] AC 191, [1984] 3 All ER 229.
7 [1984] AC 676, [1984] 2 All ER 326.

However, it is not necessary for an interpretation to 'flout common sense' in order for the court to reject it for business reasons. In *Harvela Investments Ltd v Royal Trust Co of Canada (CI) Ltd*[8] the House of Lords had to consider whether telexes which a shareholder in a family company sent to two of the shareholders inviting them to make offers to purchase the first shareholder's shares and undertaking to accept 'the highest offer' permitted an offer of C$2.1m 'or C$101,000 in excess of any other offer which you may receive ..., whichever is the higher'. The Court of Appeal had held that such a referential bid was permitted and valid. The unsuccessful tenderer appealed from this decision; its main argument was that the Court of Appeal had lost sight of the essential purpose of sealed bidding. The House of Lords accepted that argument and reversed the Court of Appeal. Lord Diplock said that 'the whole business purpose' of inviting two or more persons to submit sealed tenders which are not to be disclosed to any competing bidder, where the invitation to tender contains a binding obligation to transfer the property to the bidder whose tender specifies the highest price, is that each bidder should make up his mind as to the maximum sum which he estimates the property is worth to him. Lord Diplock stated that that business purpose would be defeated by a referential tender. Business considerations were also emphasised by Lord Templeman who delivered the main speech:

> 'The argument put forward by Mr Price on behalf of Sir Leonard was that the referential bid is an "offer" and therefore Sir Leonard was entitled to submit a referential bid. In acceding to this argument, the Court of Appeal recognised that the consequences could be unfortunate and would be unforeseeable; the Court of Appeal were inclined to blame such unfortunate and unforeseeable consequences on the vendors for binding themselves to accept the highest bid or for not expressly forbidding the submission of a referential bid. My Lords, in my opinion the argument based on the possible meaning of the word "offer" confuses definition with construction .... The court is not concerned to define the word "offer" in isolation, without regard to its context and by reference to the widest possible meaning which can be culled from the weightiest available dictionary.'

There is therefore ample House of Lords authority to show that a court will not adopt a literal, but uncommercial, interpretation unless the words used leave no room for a reasonable interpretation.[9]

8 [1986] AC 207, [1985] 2 All ER 966.

9 A similar approach was taken by the House of Lords in *McMonagle v Westminster City Council* [1990] 2 AC 716, [1990] 1 All ER 993 in the context of statutory interpretation. That case establishes that express words in a statutory provision will be disregarded where they would cause the substantial frustration of the provision's main object and the court is satisfied that the words are surplusage and have been introduced by incompetent draftsmanship.

Moreover, the judgment of Bingham LJ in *Pagnan SpA v Tradax Ocean Transportation SA*[10] indicates that interpreting commercial contacts is a two-stage process; a meaning arrived at by legal analysis must then be tested 'against the touchstone of commercial common sense: is this an apportionment of risk which the parties could reasonably be supposed to have intended?'

However, there are limits to a court's power to depart from the literal meaning. Where a contract fails to cover a particular situation expressly, the court cannot imply a clause that will cover the situation unless, on considering the terms of the contract in a reasonable and business manner, an implication *necessarily* arises that the parties must have intended that the suggested clause should exist.[11] It is not enough to say that it would be reasonable to make such an implication. This is a strict test under which the criterion is always necessity and not merely reasonableness.[12] However, it seems that a term will be more readily implied if it reduces, rather than adds to, a party's obligations. In *Associated Japanese Bank (International) Ltd v Crédit du Nord SA*[13] Steyn J said that a term could be implied if either (a) it was necessary to render a contract workable or (b) reasonable men, faced with the suggested term, would without hesitation say 'yes, of course, that is so obvious that it goes without saying'. Applying the second test, he held that a bank's guarantee of a lessee's payment obligations under an equipment lease was subject to an implied condition precedent that the equipment concerned actually existed. In *Davis v Richards & Wallington Industries Ltd*[14] Scott J had no hesitation in implying into an interim trust deed for a company pension scheme a term that execution of a definitive deed and approval of the rules would not be required of any associated company which was not for the time being a contributing employer.

The other main restriction on a court's power to depart from the language used in a contract is the rule, noted above, against admitting evidence of pre-contractual documents. In *Rabin v Gerson Berger Association Ltd*[15] a dispute arose about the meaning of certain trust deeds. The Court of Appeal refused to admit opinions regarding the trust deeds, which, some months before the trust deeds were

10 [1987] 3 All ER 565 at 575.
11 This is apart from the implied terms or obligations which the law imposes as a legal incident of certain kinds of contractual relationship: see 9 Halsbury's Laws 354 and Treitel, *The Law of Contract* at 162 to 164.
12 *Liverpool City Council v Irwin* [1977] AC 239, [1976] 2 All ER 39, HL.
13 [1988] 3 All ER 902, [1989] 1 WLR 255.
14 [1990] 1 WLR 1511.
15 [1986] 1 All ER 374, [1986] 1 WLR 526.

executed, had been written by the tax counsel who in fact had drafted the deeds in issue.[16]

It should be clear from this discussion that where a contract's applicable law is English law, it is not necessary to include a provision against literal interpretation. Nevertheless, it is thought that such a provision can be useful because there is a tendency, not least among English lawyers, to rely exclusively on purely semantic analysis in interpreting contracts. Moreover, an observation which Lord Bridge made when delivering the advice of the Privy Council in *Mitsui Construction Co Ltd v A-G of Hong Kong*[17] suggests that the more precisely drafted a contract the more difficult it may be for a court to depart from a literal interpretation.[18]

A provision against literal interpretation was upheld by the Court of Appeal in *Home and Overseas Insurance Co Ltd v Mentor Insurance Co (UK) Ltd.*[19] An arbitration clause in a reinsurance contract included the following:

> 'The Arbitrators and the Umpire shall interpret this Reinsurance as an honourable engagement and they shall make their award with a view to effecting the general purpose of this Reinsurance in a reasonable manner rather than in accordance with a literal interpretation of the language.'

16 However, in *Kleinwort Benson Ltd v Malaysia Mining Corpn Bhd* [1989] 1 All ER 785, [1989] 1 WLR 379 the Court of Appeal did admit evidence about pre-contractual negotiations. In making a facility available to the defendant's wholly-owned subsidiary, Kleinwort Benson had originally requested that the defendants give a guarantee; but they would only agree to give a comfort letter. The Court of Appeal admitted evidence about these pre-contractual negotiations. Delivering the judgment of the court, Ralph Gibson LJ said:

> 'The context in which the comfort letter was requested and given is before the court without dispute as to the relevance or admissibility of that context. That concession was, in my view, rightly made.... Those facts are not available to show merely that the defendants did not themselves subjectively intend to assume legal liability and that, therefore, the words eventually included in the comfort letter provided by the defendants should be construed so as to exclude such liability. That, as I understand it, would be misapplying the principles stated in *Prenn v Simmonds*, by which evidence of the factual background is admitted. But the evidence of the refusal by the defendants to assume legal responsibility for the liabilities of Metals to the plaintiffs in the normal form of joint and several liability or of a guarantee, and the consequent resort by the parties to what they described as a comfort letter substantially in the terms submitted by the plaintiffs to the defendants, is, in my judgment, admissible on the question whether ... the defendants' affirmation in para 3 appears on the evidence to have been intended as a warranty or contractual promise.'

17 (1986) 10 Con LR 1.

18 That advice is also notable for indicating that, in interpreting a contract, it is seldom useful to consider previous decisions on analogous but differently worded terms in other forms of contract commonly in use.

19 [1989] 3 All ER 74, [1990] 1 WLR 153, CA.

Parker LJ considered that the clause did no more than give the arbitrators liberty to do that which was approved by the House of Lords in *Antaios Cia SA v Salen AB*;[20] that is, making detailed semantic and syntactical analysis of the words used yield to 'business common sense' where such analysis would otherwise lead to a conclusion which flouts business common sense. Parker LJ very much doubted whether the clause conferred any further latitude. However, he said that a clause would not be valid if it purported to authorise the arbitrators 'to decide without regard to the law and according, for example, to their own notions of what would be fair'.

Lloyd LJ quoted the following passage from the judgment of May LJ in the *Ashville Investments* case:[1]

> 'It can happen that ... one is driven to the conclusion that [a] clause is ambiguous, that it has two possible meanings. In those circumstances the court has to prefer one above the other in accordance with settled principles. If one meaning is more in accord with what the court considers to be the underlying purpose and intent of the contract, or part of it, than the other, then the court will choose the former rather than the latter.'

Lloyd LJ then continued:

> 'Just as a clause may be ambiguous in the strict sense, so also a contract may be "ambiguous" in the sense that it is not clear whether a particular provision, or series of provisions, is to apply in a particular set of circumstances which may not have been foreseen, or for which no express provision has been made. If it is open to the court to prefer a meaning which is more in accordance with the "underlying purpose and intent of the contract" in the case of a true ambiguity, I do not see why it should not be open to arbitrators, when so required, to determine the rights of the parties in accordance with the "general purpose" of the reinsurance, in order to resolve a contractual "ambiguity" in the wider sense.'

Balcombe LJ agreed with the judgments of Parker and Lloyd LJJ. The clause in issue had also been upheld by Hirst J sitting in the Commercial Court in chambers.

Similar clauses requiring arbitrators to decide 'according to an equitable rather than a strictly legal interpretation' were approved by the Court of Appeal (Lord Denning MR and Goff and Shaw LJJ) in *Eagle Star Insurance Co Ltd v Yuval Insurance Co Ltd*[2] and by Parker J (as he then was) in *Home Insurance Co v Administratia Asigurarilor de Stat*.[3]

In the light of these cases, a clause in the following terms is considered to fall well within the limits laid down by English law:

20 [1985] AC 191, [1984] 3 All ER 229.
1 [1989] QB 488, [1988] 2 All ER 577.
2 [1978] 1 Lloyd's Rep 357.
3 [1983] 2 Lloyd's Rep 674.

> 'To the fullest extent permitted by law, this Agreement shall be interpreted in a reasonable and commercial manner rather than in strict accordance with the literal meaning of the language used; and, in particular, due weight shall be given to the underlying business purposes of this Agreement and of the provision in issue.'

The words 'To the fullest extent permitted by law' make it clear that the clause does not attempt to give more latitude than the law allows. The first half of the clause is similar to the provision upheld in *Home and Overseas Insurance Co v Mentor Insurance* and reflects the approach sanctioned by the House of Lords in *Antaios Compania SA v Salen AB.* The second half of the clause owes more to the decision of the House of Lords in *Prenn v Simmonds.*

However, it is not thought that this clause enables a term to be implied into an agreement where that would be reasonable but would not satisfy the test of necessity imposed by the case law on implied terms. There must be a considerable risk that a clause which purports to permit a term to be implied where the test of necessity is not satisfied would be invalid or make the entire agreement void for uncertainty.

Nor does the above clause authorise the admission of evidence about pre-contractual documents, such as drafts of the agreement, correspondence between the parties' lawyers and counsels' opinions. On balance, it is thought that a clause can validly provide that a specified document, for example heads of agreement, shall be considered in ascertaining the meaning or effect of any provision in the agreement. Such a clause would be similar to the provisions in the Civil Jurisdiction and Judgments Act 1982 and the Contracts (Applicable Law) Act 1990 which allow reference to be made to the official reports on the Brussels and Rome Conventions respectively in interpreting those Conventions. A clause of this type has a higher prospect of validity if the document to which reference is permitted (for example, a counsel's opinion) is reproduced within the contract as a Schedule; this makes it possible to argue that evidence about the document is not excluded by the rule against 'extrinsic' evidence.

It is thought that, in a standard form contract which has been the subject of judicial decisions, the above clause would provide only limited scope for a court to depart from the previous decisions: see Lord Diplock's speech in *Pioneer Shipping Ltd v BTP Tioxide Ltd.*[4]

4 [1982] AC 724, [1981] 2 All ER 1030, HL.

CHAPTER 11

GENERAL PROVISIONS

Particular problems arise in drafting general provisions. This is owing to four rules of interpretation which can be used to give a general provision a more restricted scope than its literal meaning. There are also the principles which require exclusion and limitation clauses to be construed narrowly.

The ejusdem generis rule

The first rule is the ejusdem generis rule; under this general rule words which follow two[1] or more specific words are restricted to the same genus or category as the specific words. For example–

> 'disposal' means any conveyance, transfer, assignment or other disposal

would not cover a surrender of a lease. 'Disposal' would be read as covering only transactions in which property passes from A to B, and not a transaction in which A extinguishes an interest in property.[2]

In *Quazi v Quazi*[3] Lord Scarman described the ejusdem generis rule as 'at best, a very secondary guide to the meaning of a statute. The all-important matter is to consider the purpose of the statute.'

1 This is the opinion expressed by Lord Diplock in *Quazi v Quazi* [1980] AC 744 at 807G to 808D. However, he stated that, even where the eiusdem generis rule is inapplicable, because there is only one specific term, the general expression can be cut down 'if to give it its wide prima facie meaning would lead to results that would be contrary to the manifest policy of the Act looked at as a whole, or would conflict with the evident purpose for which it was enacted'.

2 For an example of the rule in operation, see the decision of the Divisional Court in *Wood v Metropolitan Police Comr* [1986] 2 All ER 570, [1986] 1 WLR 796.

3 [1980] AC 744, 823H to 824A.

He continued:

> 'If the legislative purpose of a statute is such that a statutory series should be read ejusdem generis, so be it: the rule is helpful. But, if it is not, the rule is more likely to defeat than to fulfil the purpose of the statute. The rule, like many other rules of statutory interpretation, is a useful servant but a bad master.'

The noscitur a sociis rule

The second rule of restricted interpretation is the noscitur a sociis rule. Under this rule general words may be limited by reference to the subject matter in the context of which they are used. For example, if the word 'property' appears in an agreement concerned with a transaction in land, it is doubtful whether it would be read as including intellectual property rights, unless the context in which it appears makes it clear that intellectual property rights are intended to be covered. The basic principle was described by Viscount Simonds in *A-G v Prince Ernest Augustus of Hanover*:[4]

> '... words, and particularly general words, cannot be read in isolation: their colour and content are derived from their context. So it is that I conceive it to be my right and duty to examine every word of a statute in its context, and I use "context" in its widest sense, which I have already indicated as including not only other enacting provisions of the same statute, but its preamble, the existing state of the law, other statutes in pari materia, and the mischief which I can, by those and other legitimate means, discern the statute was intended to remedy.'

A striking illustration of this approach is the speech of Lord Halsbury LC in *Cox v Hakes*[5] in which the House of Lords held that the Court of Appeal had no jurisdiction to hear an appeal from a High Court habeas corpus order discharging a person from custody. (This was changed by the Administration of Justice Act 1960.) The relevant section of the Judicature Act provided that the Court of Appeal had jurisdiction 'to hear and determine appeals from any judgment or order ... of Her Majesty's High Court of Justice.' Literally this covered an order of discharge made on a writ of habeas corpus. Lord Halsbury cited the celebrated judgment in the Elizabethan case of *Stradling v Morgan*:

> 'From which case it appears that the sages of the law heretofore have construed statutes quite contrary to the letter in some appearance, and those statutes which comprehend all things in the letter, they have expounded to extend but to some things, and those which generally prohibit all people from doing such an act, they have interpreted to permit some people to do it, and those which include every person in

4 [1957] AC 436 at 461.
5 (1890) 15 App Cas 506.

> the letter they have adjudged to reach to some persons only, which expositions have always been founded on the intent of the Legislature, which they have collected sometimes by considering the cause and necessity of making the Act, sometimes by comparing one part of the Act with another, and sometimes by foreign circumstances. So that they have ever been guided by the intent of the Legislature, which they have always taken according to the necessity of the matter and according to that which is consonant to reason and good discretion.'

Lord Halsbury continued that, if the Judicature Acts were looked at by the light of these principles, 'I cannot conceive it to be possible that the framers of those Acts had in their minds the dealing with such an important branch of the law by the use of one word.'

'Unless the context otherwise requires'

The third rule arises from the almost invariable practice of providing that the general definitions in an agreement apply 'unless the context otherwise requires' or 'unless a contrary intention appears'. There is high authority that such a qualification is to be implied if not stated: see the observations of Lord Selborne in *Meux v Jacobs*.[6] Two House of Lords cases illustrate the restrictive effect of the 'unless the context otherwise requires' qualification.

Beswick v Beswick[7] arose out of an agreement for the sale of a business which provided that the purchaser would make certain payments to the vendor for the rest of the vendor's life, and, after the vendor's death, would pay an annuity to the vendor's widow. She, however, was not party to the agreement and her attempt to enforce it was met with the defence of privity of contract (see Chapter 2 above). The vendor's widow invoked section 56(1) of the Law of Property Act 1925:

> 'A person may take an ... interest in land *or other property*, or the benefit of any condition, right of entry, covenant or agreement over or respecting land *or other property*, although he may not be named as a party to the conveyance or other instrument....'

She also relied on section 205(1) of the Act which provides that, 'unless the context otherwise requires'–

> '"Property" includes any thing in action, and any interest in real or personal property.'

Lord Reid (at page 77) said this:

> 'By express provision in the definition section [ie section 205(1)] a definition contained in it is not to be applied to the word defined if

6 (1875) LR 7, HL 481 at 493.
7 [1968] AC 58, [1967] 2 All ER 1197, HL.

in the particular case the context otherwise requires. If application of that definition would result in giving to section 56 a meaning going beyond that of the old section, then, in my opinion, the context does require that the definition of "property" shall not be applied to that word in section 56. The context in which this section occurs is a consolidation Act. If the definition is not applied the section is a proper one to appear in such an Act because it can properly be regarded as not substantially altering the pre-existing law. But if the definition is applied the result is to make section 56 go far beyond the pre-existing law. Holding that the section has such an effect would involve holding that the invariable practice of Parliament has been departed from per incuriam so that something has got into this consolidation Act which neither the draftsman nor Parliament can have intended to be there. I am reinforced in this view by two facts. The language of section 56 is not at all what one would have expected if the intention had been to bring in all that the application of the definition would bring in. And, secondly, section 56 is one of 25 sections which appear in the Act under the cross-heading "Conveyances and other Instruments". The other twenty-four sections come appropriately under that heading and so does section 56 if it has a limited meaning: but, if its scope is extended by the definition of property, it would be quite inappropriately placed in this part of the Act. For these reasons I am of opinion that section 56 has no application to the present case.'

The second House of Lords decision relevant to 'unless the context otherwise requires' is *Guinness Plc v Saunders*.[8] This was a claim by Guinness for the recovery of £5.2 million which it had paid to Mr Thomas Ward, a former director, for his services in connection with a takeover bid which Guinness had made for The Distillers Company plc. Mr Ward argued that the payment had been sanctioned by the committee of Guinness's board under an article in Guinness's articles of association which was in the following terms:

'The board may ... grant special remuneration to any director who devotes special attention to the business of the company or who otherwise performs services which in the opinion of the board are outside the scope of the ordinary duties of a director.'

Although the terms of this article required any special remuneration to be sanctioned by the board, Mr Ward claimed that a committee had power to do this by virtue of the general definition of 'the board' in Guinness's articles:

'The directors of the company for the time being ... or any committee authorised by the board to act on its behalf.'

Lord Templeman (at page 687) pointed out that the general definitions in the articles were stated to apply 'if not inconsistent with the subject or context'. He said that the subject and context

8 [1990] 2 AC 663, [1990] 1 All ER 652.

of the relevant article were inconsistent with the expression 'the board' in that article meaning anything except the board.

However, a clause can state that nothing in it shall be taken to exclude the application of a particular definition.[9]

The good commercial sense principle

What may be described as 'the good commercial sense principle' was formulated by Lord Diplock in *Miramar Maritime Corpn v Holborn Oil Trading Ltd.*[10] The Exxonvoy bill of lading contained a clause providing that 'all the terms whatsoever' of the charter under which the shipment was carried 'except the rate and payment of freight specified therein apply to and govern the rights of the parties concerned in this shipment'. One of the terms of the charter required the charterer to pay demurrage. The owners of the vessel tried to recover the demurrage from the consignees of the cargo, as holders of the bill of lading, on the basis that the demurrage clause in the charter had been incorporated into the bill of lading, but with the implied substitution of references to a consignee under a bill of lading in respect of the cargo for references to the charterer. Lord Diplock pointed out that the bill of lading could be issued in a variety of different situations and drew attention to the extent of the liability which a consignee might incur if it were held that the demurrage clause in the charter had been incorporated into the bill of lading. Lord Diplock said:

> 'There must be ascribed to the words a meaning that would make good commercial sense if the Exxonvoy bill of lading were issued in *any* of these situations, and not some meaning that imposed upon a transferree to whom the bill of lading for goods afloat was negotiated, a financial liability of unknown extent that no business man in his senses would be willing to incur .... My Lords, I venture to assert that no businessman who had not taken leave of his senses would intentionally enter into a contract which exposed him to a potential liability of this kind; and this, in itself, I find to be an overwhelming reason for not indulging in verbal manipulation of the actual contractual words used in the charterparty so as to give to them this effect when they are treated as incorporated in the bill of lading.'

All the other Law Lords concurred in Lord Diplock's speech.

In *Antaios Cia Naviera SA v Salen AB*,[11] the House of Lords applied what Lord Diplock termed 'business common sense' to restrict a clause in a charterparty which entitled the owner to terminate on 'any breach' of the charterparty so that it would apply only if there were a repudiatory breach. Lord Diplock declared:

9 See, for example, Town and Country Planning Act 1990, s 164(4).
10 [1984] AC 676, [1984] 2 All ER 326, HL.
11 [1985] AC 191, [1984] 3 All ER 229.

'... if detailed semantic and syntactical analysis of words in a commercial contract is going to lead to a conclusion that flouts business commonsense, it must be made to yield to business commonsense.'

A similar approach was adopted in *Re Melbourne Brewery and Distillery*,[12] a case of some significance for capital markets and banking transactions. A trust deed securing debenture stock provided that one of the events in which the security would become enforceable was if the company should commit a breach of 'any covenant herein contained'. Wright J said this:

'In my judgment it would be hardly possible to so construe this deed as to hold that the security should become enforceable by a particular stockholder upon a breach of any one of these most trifling obligations which the company has brought itself under by this deed. It has undertaken a great variety of obligations of various degrees of importance, and I do not think it could possibly be supposed that the security was to become enforceable by any stockholder whenever any of the provisions of the deed could be shown to have been disregarded.'

This approach[13] was also followed by the House of Lords in *Schuler AG v Wickman Machine Tool Sales Ltd*[14] (considered in the Chapter 10).

Exclusion and limitation clauses

Exclusion and limitation clauses are narrowly construed. An exclusion clause is a clause which purports to exclude liability altogether, a limitation clause being a clause which limits liability to a maximum amount (for instance, the price payable to the party concerned under the contract), or to claims notified before a specified date. Broadly similar principles of interpretation apply to clauses which purport to disapply a duty or restriction which the law would otherwise impose; an example is a clause in a contract between an investor and a securities firm which will manage his portfolio on a discretionary basis under which the securities firm is permitted to buy for its own account securities from the investor and sell its own securities to him. Such a clause disapplies the restrictions on a fiduciary entering into transactions with a beneficiary.

In *The 'Pera'*[15] Staughton J identified two separate principles:

'The first is that a party relying on an exemption clause must show that the case comes within it and that there is no ambiguity or equivocation. The second principle is that a party relying on a clause

12 [1901] 1 Ch 453.
13 Different considerations may apply to legislation; see *R v Broadcasting Complaints Commission, ex p Owen* [1985] QB 1153 at 1174C, but also *Cox v Hakes* (1890) 15 App Cas 506.
14 [1974] AC 235, [1973] 2 All ER 39.
15 [1984] 2 Lloyd's Rep 363 at 365.

which he himself has put forward as part of the contract must bring himself within it clearly and without ambiguity or equivocation.'

Limitation clauses are not subjected to the first principle in its 'full rigour', although it is applied to them: see the statement of Lord Fraser of Tullybelton in *Ailsa Craig Fishing Co Ltd v Malvern Fishing Co Ltd*[16] cited by Lord Bridge of Harwich in *George Mitchell (Chesterhall) Ltd v Finney Lock Seeds Ltd.*[17]

In *Photo Production Ltd v Securicor Transport Ltd*[18] Lord Diplock described the basis of the first principle:

'... an exclusion clause is one which excludes or modifies an obligation ... that would otherwise arise under the contract by implication of law. ... Since the presumption is that the parties by entering into the contract intended to accept the implied obligations exclusion clauses are to be construed strictly and the degree of strictness appropriate to be applied to their construction may properly depend upon the extent to which they involve departure from the implied obligations. Since the obligations implied by law in a commercial contract are those which, by judicial consensus over the years or by Parliament in passing a statute, have been regarded as obligations which a reasonable businessman would realise that he was accepting when he entered into a contract of a particular kind, the court's view of the reasonableness of any departure from the implied obligations which would be involved in construing the express words of an exclusion clause in one sense that they are capable of bearing rather than another, is a relevant consideration in deciding what meaning the words were intended by the parties to bear. But this does not entitle the court to reject the exclusion clause, however unreasonable the court itself may think it is, if the words are clear and fairly susceptible of one meaning only.'

Lord Diplock's statement was applied by the Court of Appeal in *Bishop v Bonham*[19] in which it was held that a mortgagee of shares was not protected from liability for having negligently exercised his power of sale by a clause in the mortgage which stated that the mortgagee 'shall have no liability for any loss howsoever arising in connection with any such sale'. The clause only covered a proper exercise of the power of sale, that is to say, with the exercise of reasonable care to obtain a proper price.

Bishop v Bonham is also important for showing that a clause giving a person a power exercisable at his 'absolute discretion' can be read subject to the implicit restriction that it should be exercised properly and not in any way which is unreasonable.

Additional interpretative guidelines apply to a clause which excludes or restricts negligence liability. These have to be applied before

16 [1983] 1 WLR 964 at 970.
17 [1983] 2 AC 803 at 813.
18 [1980] AC 827 at 850.
19 [1988] 1 WLR 742, [1988] BCLC 656.

considering whether the clause is valid under the Unfair Contract Terms Act 1977 because, if, on its true construction, the clause does not cover the circumstances which have arisen, the question of whether it is valid under the 1977 Act never arises. Moreover, Schedule 1 to the 1977 Act places several important categories of contract outside the Act's scope; in particular, the Schedule excludes any contract so far as it relates to the creation or transfer of an interest in land, of any patent or other intellectual property or of securities.

These guidelines were summarised by Lord Morton of Henryton in the Privy Council in *Canada SS Lines Ltd v R*,[20] and explained by the Court of Appeal in *The 'Raphael'*:[1]

> '(i) If the clause contains language which expressly exempts the person in whose favour it is made (hereafter called "the proferens") from the consequence of the negligence ..., effect must be given to that provision ... (ii) If there is no express reference to negligence, the court must consider whether the words used are wide enough, in their ordinary meaning, to cover negligence .... If a doubt arises at this point, it must be resolved against the proferens .... (iii) If the words used are wide enough for the above purpose, the court must then consider whether "the head of damage may be based on some ground other than that of negligence" .... The "other ground" must not be so fanciful or remote that the proferens cannot be supposed to have desired protection against it, but subject to this qualification, ... the existence of a possible head of damage other than that of negligence is fatal to the proferens even if the words used are, prima facie, wide enough to cover negligence ...'

Moreover, in *Interfoto Picture Library Ltd v Stiletto Visual Programmes Ltd*[2] Dillon and Bingham LJJ held that, if a condition in a set of printed conditions in a standard form contract is particularly onerous or unusual, the party seeking to enforce it must show that that particular condition was fairly brought to the attention of the other party. It is thought that this requirement is normally inapplicable to a negotiated contract. However, it might apply in an exceptional case, for example, to a lengthy loan agreement which is sent out to a large number of banks for syndication and which has embedded within it a clause which subjects the banks to highly unusual obligations or restrictions.

Methods of excluding the restrictive rules

The following are some techniques for protecting a general provision against the risk of a restrictive interpretation.

The ejusdem generis rule can be negatived by adding to the general

20 [1952] AC 192, [1952] 1 All ER 305.
1 [1982] 1 Lloyd's Rep 42.
2 [1989] QB 433, [1988] 1 All ER 348, CA.

term the phrase 'whether or not similar to any of the foregoing'. For example,

> 'securities' includes debentures, loan stock, bonds and any other securities of any kind, whether or not in any respect similar to any of the foregoing,

would cover shares. If the definition merely read 'or any other securities whatsoever', this would probably be insufficient to prevent 'securities' being restricted to the genus or category of debt securities.

A second way of excluding the eiusdem generis rule is to put the general wording first and to follow it with certain specific items which it is wished to mention expressly. In the following example, taken from section 785 of the Income and Corporation Taxes Act 1988, the draftsman wanted to make sure that finance leases were caught:

> '"lease", in relation to an asset, means any kind of agreement or arrangement under which payments are made for the use of, or otherwise in respect of, an asset, and includes, in particular, any agreement or arrangement all or any of the payments under which represent instalments of, or payments towards, a purchase price.'

By adding the words 'in particular' after the word 'includes' the draftsman wanted to ensure that the specific mention of finance leases would not result in the general language in the first half of the definition being restricted. Another formula which can be used for this purpose is 'without prejudice to the generality of the foregoing', as in this example in section 670 of the Taxes Act:

> '"settlor", in relation to a settlement includes any person by whom the settlement was made or entered into directly or indirectly, and in particular (but without prejudice to the generality of the preceding words of this definition) includes any person who has provided ... funds directly or indirectly for the purpose of the settlement....'

The 'without prejudice to the generality' formula is often used to ensure that a general power is not restricted as a result of specific items being mentioned. Section 144 of the Financial Services Act 1986 authorises the competent authority, that is, the London Stock Exchange, to require, as a condition of the admission of any securities to the Official List, that listing particulars are submitted to, and approved by, it, and that the particulars are published. This specific power is, however, prefaced by the words–

> 'Without prejudice to the generality of the power of listing authority to make listing rules for the purposes of this section.'

Similarly, in section 413 of the Companies Act 1985 (as inserted by section 102 of the 1989 Act), subsection (1) gives the Secretary of State a general power by regulations to make further provision in relation to the registration of charges, and subsections (2) to (6) specify particular matters which the regulations can address. To prevent the specific matters described in the later subsections restricting the scope of the general power in subsection (1), the general power is followed by the following statement in subsection (1):

> 'Nothing in the following provisions shall be construed as restricting the generality of that power.'

The third method of safeguarding generality is to state that the specific items mentioned are only 'examples' of the matters covered by the general provision. Subsection (1) of section 20 of the Race Relations Act 1976 prohibits a person concerned with the provision of facilities or services to the public from discriminating against a person by refusing to provide him with those facilities or services; subsection (2) is as follows:

> '(2) The following are examples of the facilities and services mentioned in subsection (1)–
>
> (a) access to and use of any place which members of the public are permitted to enter;
> (b) accommodation in a hotel, boarding house or other similar establishment;
> (c) facilities by way of banking or insurance or for grants, loans, credit or finance;
> (d) facilities for education;
> (e) facilities for entertainment, recreation or refreshment;
> (f) facilities for transport or travel;
> (g) the services of any profession or trade, or any local or other public authority.'

Describing the specific items mentioned in subsection (2) as 'examples' serves two purposes. First, it indicates that significance must be given to these items as illustrations of wider principles underlying subsection (1). For instance, the banking example shows that financial facilities, as well as commercial goods and services, are covered; and the examples of education and local or public authority services show that the subsection extends beyond business services and the private sector. Second, describing the specific items as 'examples' emphasises that the list is far from comprehensive.

Wide interpretation clause

Sometimes it is possible to include an express provision for wide interpretation. The objects clause of English company often concludes with a declaration that the subclauses setting out the company's powers shall be given 'the widest and most general interpretation'. Such a declaration may also be appropriate to other types of powers, for example, those of the trustees of a settlement or of a loan stock trust deed.

Anti-avoidance clauses

Another technique is an anti-avoidance clause. Such a clause recognises that a provision which applies to certain transactions that are classified according to their legal character can be avoided by a transaction which is not in any of the specified legal categories but which produces a similar financial or business result. For example, a clause which applies if a party sells an asset can be circumvented by the grant of a long lease or licence for a capital sum and a nominal rental.[3] The following is an anti-avoidance clause designed to deal with this type of problem:

> The previous subclauses also apply if the Company enters into a transaction which, although not of the same or a similar legal type as any mentioned in those subclauses, produces an economic or financial effect similar to that which would be produced by such a transaction.

A different kind of anti-avoidance clause concentrates on the purpose of a transaction, rather than its effect. This is similar to the approach taken by section 703 of the Income and Corporation Taxes Act 1988 which gives the Inland Revenue power to counteract a tax advantage produced by a transaction which had as its main object to enable a tax advantage to be obtained.

> 'The previous subclauses extend to any transaction which is carried out in a way which is designed to place it outside the scope of any of those subclauses or which has one or more elements designed for that purpose.'

Excluding negligence liability

It should be possible to draft an effective clause which excludes a restriction implied by law (for example, those to which fiduciaries are subject) or which limits negligence liability to a particular sum.[4] By contrast, it is seldom practicable to draft a provision which (as a matter of interpretation irrespective of the Unfair Contract Terms Act) will completely exclude negligence liability. *Bishop v Bonham* demonstrates that a clause which does not expressly exclude liability for 'negligence' may be ineffective, even though it has wide language, such as 'any loss howsoever arising'. In practice, a party is usually

3 See also the scheme which the House of Lords rejected in *Lyle and Scott Ltd v British Investment Trust Ltd* [1959] AC 763, [1959] 2 All ER 661.

4 See *George Mitchell (Chesterhall) Ltd v Finney Lock Seeds Ltd [1983]* 2 AC 803, [1983] 2 All ER 737, HL.

reluctant to insert in an exclusion clause which is to protect him an express reference to his 'negligence' since this is viewed as provocative.

It may be, however, that a common form of clause provides the basis for an effective exclusion provision. Clauses frequently exclude liability except in so far as it is caused by 'gross negligence or wilful default'. The term 'gross negligence' is notoriously obscure and it has been said that it means nothing more than negligence.[5] On the other hand, in the context of shortcomings by company directors, it has been said to mean 'gross and culpable negligence' by Sir Nathaniel Lindley MR (as he then was) in *Re National Bank of Wales Ltd*;[6] see also the observations of Dillon LJ in *Multinational*.[7] It is thought that, by necessary implication, liability for what may be termed 'ordinary' negligence would be excluded by the following:

> The Contractor shall have no liability for any losses of any kind, however they are caused, except those which are directly and wholly or mainly caused by–
>
> (a) dishonesty; or
> (b) serious and culpable negligence;
>
> by a director or an employee of the Contractor when acting within the scope of his office or employment.

5 *Pentecost v London District Auditor* [1951] 2 KB 759 at 766.
6 [1899] 2 Ch 629 at 672.
7 [1983] Ch 258 at 291.

CHAPTER 12

TECHNICAL ISSUES

'Subject to', 'notwithstanding' and 'without prejudice to'

These terms define how different provisions or agreements relate to one another.

If clause 5 begins 'Subject to clause 6', that means that clause 6 overrides it. In *C & J Clark Ltd v IRC*,[1] counsel for the Crown put forward an argument that, if a provision is stated to be 'subject to' another provision, that necessarily means that the two provisions are in conflict. Megarry J said this:

> 'The highest compliment that I can pay this argument is that it is ingenious; but it seems to me to be fallacious and unreal. It drove counsel for the Crown into strange contentions. It requires the innocent and much-used phrase "Subject to" to be treated as implying that the master provisions [ie those referred to after "Subject to"] are contrary to each and every part of the subject provisions, and so require protecting from every part of the subject provisions by the words "Subject to". I have never met such a contention before, and if it were right I think that it would strike terror into the hearts of Parliamentary counsel when contemplating their output over the last two decades. Counsel for the Crown did not shrink from the contention that the phrase "Subject to" in effect warranted that without it each and every part of the two sets of provisions would be locked in conflict: he did not shrink, but I recoil. ... In my judgment, the phrase "subject to" is a simple provision which merely subjects the provisions of the subject subsections to the provisions of the master subsections. Where there is no clash the phrase does nothing: if there is collision, the phrase shows what is to prevail. The phrase provides no warranty of universal collision.'

If clause 5 begins 'Notwithstanding clause 6', it overrides clause 6. If it begins 'Notwithstanding any other provision of this Agreement',

1 [1973] 2 All ER 513, [1973] 1 WLR 905.

it overrides all the other clauses in that agreement. If two clauses in the same agreement begin that way, there is a mistake.

The word 'notwithstanding' does not have to be used. A clause can simply be stated to 'override' another clause or all other clauses in an agreement.

If clause 5 is expressed to be 'without prejudice' to clause 6, this merely means that nothing in clause 5 is to be taken to impair the effectiveness of clause 6. Sometimes a clause dealing with a specific matter is expressed to be 'without prejudice to the generality of' another clause setting out a general provision. This means that the fact that it was thought advisable to include an express reference to the specific matter is not to be used as an argument for reducing the scope of the general clause to the specific matter and matters closely connected with it.

Co-obligors

There are three different types of co-obligation.

If A, B and C *jointly* undertake with X to pay him £1000, that creates a single obligation binding all three. X cannot recover more than £1000 and a release of B discharges A and C (unless X only covenants not to sue B without actually releasing him). The common law rule that a judgment against B would bar an action against A or C was abolished by the Civil Liability (Contribution) Act 1978.

If A, B and C *severally* undertake with X to pay him £1000, there are three separate undertakings. A can recover £3000 in total and a release of B does not generally discharge C, although it may do so if A, B and C are co-sureties.

If A, B and C *jointly and severally* undertake with X to pay him £1000, there are four undertakings: one joint and three several. But there are two differences from purely several undertakings. Joint and several obligations are not cumulative, so X can recover only £1000.[2] Moreover, 'a release of one joint and several covenantor discharges the others, in precisely the same way as with purely joint covenants'.[3] Although there appears to be no authority on the point, it is thought that a court would uphold a clause providing that a release of one joint and several obligor will not discharge the several liabilities of the others.

A traditional formula creating several liability is that in Lloyd's policies–

2 See *Joint Obligations* by Glanville Williams (Butterworths, 1949) at pp 24, 34 and 42; and also *Set-off* by R Derham (Oxford, 1987) at pp 152–153.

3 Glanville Williams at p 135.

> 'We the underwriters ... hereby bind ourselves each for his own part and not one for another'

see the Court of Appeal's decision in *Touche Ross & Co v Baker*.[4]

There may be a difference between–

> A and B severally undertake that they will not compete with the Purchaser for 3 years,

and

> A and B each undertakes with respect to himself (but not with respect to the other) that he will not compete with the Purchaser for 3 years.

In the first example it seems that A might be liable if B competes although A does not.

Co-obligor clauses raise three potential problems.

(1) If the obligations of one co-obligor prove to have been invalid, the other co-obligor can often argue that his obligations are also ineffective, since they were conditional on the other co-obligor being bound. Similar arguments can be raised if one of the intended co-obligors fails to sign the agreement.[5]

(2) If all co-obligors are originally bound, but the obligee later releases one of them, that also releases the others where the obligation was either joint or joint and several.

(3) If two or more persons who originally contracted as principal co-debtors arrange between themselves, either when the debt is contracted or subsequently, that one of them shall be liable only secondarily as a surety, their arrangement binds the creditor after he is given notice of it; and, if the creditor agrees to give time to the primary debtors without the consent of the surety, the latter is discharged.[6]

4 (1991) Financial Times, 6 March.

5 *James Graham & Co (Timber) Ltd v Southgate-Sands* [1986] QB 80, [1985] 2 All ER 344, CA.

6 *Rouse v Bradford Banking Co* [1894] AC 586, HL. In *The Nature of the Judicial Process* (Yale University Press, 1921) Cardozo comments: 'It is a rule of the common law that a surety is discharged from liability if the time of payment is extended by contract between the principal debtor and the creditor without the surety's consent. Even an extension for a single day will be sufficient to bring about that result. Without such an extension, the surety would have the privilege upon the maturity of the debt of making payment to the creditor, and demanding immediate subrogation to the latter's remedies against the principal. He must, therefore, it is said, be deemed to have suffered prejudice if, by extension of the due date, the right has been postponed. ... The law has shaped its judgments upon the fictitious assumption that a surety, who has probably lain awake at nights for fear that payment may some day be demanded, has in truth been smarting under the repressed desire to force an unwelcome payment on a reluctant or capricious creditor.'

Accordingly, wording to the following effect should be included:

(1) The liabilities of the Companies under this Agreement are several and, if compatible with subclause (4) below, joint.

(2) However, if the Companies are liable to pay an amount, no more than that amount in aggregate is recoverable from them.

(3) Each of the Companies shall remain liable under this Agreement as a direct and principal debtor despite any notice received by the Bank (whether after the date of this Agreement or otherwise) to the effect that one or some of the Companies are only sureties.

(4) Notwithstanding subclause (1) above–

(a) if the liabilities of one or some of the Companies under this Agreement are, or become, void, unenforceable, invalid or illegal, or are discharged or avoided by or under any law, that shall not impair the liabilities of the other Companies or Company; and
(b) the Bank may release (wholly or partially) one or more of the Companies from their liabilities under this Agreement or enter into a rescheduling or other arrangement with or involving, or grant any concession to, any one or more of the Companies, and that shall not impair the liabilities under this Agreement of the other Companies or Company, even if their or its consent has not been obtained.

(5) Subclauses (3) and (4) above extend, with any necessary adaptations, to any security interest which a Company creates in or in pursuance of this Agreement as they apply to that Company's liabilities under this Agreement.

(6) In this clause 'liabilities' includes obligations, and 'liable' has a corresponding meaning.

Co-obligees

Problems can also arise where a person incurs an obligation in favour of two or more other persons. The agreement should make it clear–

(a) whether the obligation can be enforced or assigned only by all the obligees acting together, or whether any one of them can enforce or assign the obligation independently of the others; it is thought that the latter alternative applies under section 81 of the Law of Property Act 1925 to an obligation imposed by deed;[7] and

7 See the judgment of Greer LJ in *Josselson v Borst* [1938] 1 KB 723.

(b) whether, if obligee A breaches his obligations to the obligor, that will affect the obligations of the obligor towards obligees B and C.

An undertaking given to two or more persons jointly is enforceable, although only one of them provides consideration. It seems likely that an undertaking given to two or more persons severally can only be enforced by those of them who provide consideration. The position regarding an undertaking given to two or more persons jointly and severally is a matter of controversy.[8]

An undertaking by A in favour of himself and B takes effect as an undertaking in favour of B.[9]

'Beneficial owner'

In a conveyance of land the purpose of stating that the vendor conveys as 'beneficial owner' is to obtain the covenants for title implied under section 76 of the Law of Property Act 1925. It seems that the covenants implied under section 76(1)(A) only apply where a person, as well as being stated to convey as beneficial owner, in fact conveys in that capacity; but the point is not entirely clear.[10] It should be kept in mind, however, that section 76 extends to–

(a) mortgages and charges – see subsection (1)(c) and Part III of the Second Schedule; and

(b) personal property generally, including debts – see the definitions in section 205(1) of 'Conveyance', 'Mortgage' and 'Property'.

So 'beneficial owner' wording should be included, for example, in agreements for the purchase of shares or charges over shares.

Consideration

Some contracts expressly state the consideration, but, if consideration exists, failing to describe it will not invalidate the contract. In the case of guarantees, section 3 of the Mercantile Law Amendment Act 1856 specifically provides that the consideration does not need to be stated. However, where an agreement is chargeable with United Kingdom stamp duty, section 5 of the Stamp Act 1891 requires it to set forth 'fully and truly' all the facts affecting the amount of duty payable.

8 See *Chitty on Contracts* at 185 and *Essays on Contract* by Professor P S Attiyah at 221–2.
9 Law of Property Act 1925, s 82; see also s 72.
10 See Law Com No 199, paras 2.13 to 2.15. The concept of beneficial ownership has been considered in *J Sainsbury plc v O'Connor* (1991) Times, 29 May.

A statement of the consideration can operate as a condition precedent to a party's obligations. In *Burton v Gray*[11] an equitable mortgage to a bank was expressed to be 'in consideration of your lending Mr Frederick Burton £1000 for seven days'. The bank did not place £1000 to the credit of Mr Burton's account but allowed him by cheques to overdraw his account to £810. The Court of Appeal in Chancery held that the bank had no security.

A similar problem confronted the New York Court of Appeals in *The Utica City National Bank v Gunn.*[12] A guarantee stated that it was given 'on the consideration of the said party of the first part [the bank] shall and does make such loans and discounts in consideration of the execution and delivery of this agreement by us and each of us'. No new loans were made, but previous loans were renewed. The guarantee would fail unless 'loans and discounts' could be read to include post-guarantee renewals of pre-guarantee loans. Four of the Justices held that, having regard to the circumstances surrounding the issue of the guarantee, it could be read in this way; three of the Justices held that it could not. The judgment of Cardozo J, who spoke for the majority, is set out in Appendix 2. Lord Wilberforce cited this judgment with approval in *Prenn v Simmonds.*[13]

If token consideration, for example, the sum of £1 is stated, that does not prevent a party from showing that there was additional consideration provided to him, namely, a collateral undertaking or promise by another party. The only limitation is that the additional consideration has to be consistent with that stated in the agreement.[14] In *Pao On v Lau Yiu Long*[15] Lord Scarman, delivering the advice of the Privy Council, stated:

> 'There is no doubt ... that extrinsic evidence is admissible to prove the real consideration where (a) no consideration, or a nominal consideration, is expressed in the instrument, or (b) the expressed consideration is in general terms or ambiguously stated, or (c) a substantial consideration is stated, but an additional consideration exists. The additional consideration must not, however, be inconsistent with the terms of the written instrument. Extrinsic evidence is also admissible to prove the illegality of the consideration.'

It seems likely that the sum of £1, if actually paid, will normally be sufficient consideration to support a contract at common law.[16] However, in *Turner v Forwood* Lord Goddard CJ said that an acceptor of a bill not in the hands of a holder in due course can bring evidence

11 (1873) 8 Ch App 932.
12 222 NY 204, 118 NE 607 (1918).
13 [1971] 3 All ER 237 at 240.
14 *Turner v Forwood* [1951] 1 All ER 746, CA.
15 [1980] AC 614 at 631.
16 *Mountford v Scott* [1975] Ch 258.

to contradict a 'for value received' statement in the bill, and it seems that the same would apply to a statement in an agreement that it is made 'in consideration of the sum of £1 now paid by A to B, the receipt of which B acknowledges'. Even if actually paid, it is not clear that token consideration places the payer outside the rule that equity does not assist volunteers so that he can obtain specific performance or enforce an equitable assignment where a further step still has to be taken by the assignor to perfect the assignee's title.[17]

Section 205(i)(xxi) of the Law of Property Act 1925 defines 'purchaser' as 'a purchaser in good faith for valuable consideration' and continues that '"valuable consideration" does not include a nominal consideration in money'. In *Midland Bank Trust Co v Green*[18] Lord Wilberforce said that he would have great difficulty in holding that £500, which was the consideration for the conveyance in that case, was a nominal sum. Lord Wilberforce continued:

> '"Nominal consideration" and a "nominal sum" in the law appear to me, as terms of art, to refer to a sum or consideration which can be mentioned as consideration but is not necessarily paid.'

If this is correct, it seems unlikely that a conveyance or assignment made solely in consideration of £1 would attract the covenants for title implied under section 76(1)(A) of the Law of Property Act 1925. However, these covenants are implied where, as well as paying £1, the assignee assumes the obligations of the assignor.[19]

'Best endeavours'

Not all obligations can be undertaken in absolute and unqualified terms, particularly if the subject matter of the obligation is outside the control of the person undertaking it – for example, that a third party gives a necessary authorisation or consent. There is a variety of possible language descending, it is thought, from–

A shall do his utmost

A shall use his best endeavours

A shall use due diligence

A shall take all reasonable steps

17 The judgments in *Mountford v Scott* raise the point without resolving it. See also *Re McArdle* [1951] Ch 669, [1951] 1 All ER 905. In equity, the mere fact that a covenant is executed as a deed does not mean that the covenantee is not a volunteer.

18 [1981] AC 513, [1981] 1 All ER 153.

19 See the Court of Appeal's decision in *Johnsey Estates Ltd v Lewis and Manley Engineering Ltd* [1987] 54 P & CR 296.

to

> A shall use reasonable endeavours.

In *Terrell v Mabie Todd & Co*,[20] Sellers J (as he then was) held that an obligation to use 'best endeavours' to promote the sales of a product meant a duty to do what could reasonably be done in the circumstances; the standard of reasonableness was that of 'a reasonable and prudent board of directors acting properly in the interests of their company and applying their minds to their contractual obligations to exploit the inventions'.

However, the obligation was set higher by the Court of Appeal in *IBM United Kingdom Ltd v Rockware Glass Ltd*.[1] Rockware Glass had agreed to sell 37 acres of land at Greenford to IBM UK for £6 million. The agreement provided that 'the purchaser will make an application for planning permission and use its best endeavours to obtain the same'. Planning permission was sought and refused. However, IBM UK did not appeal to the Secretary of State against the refusal. The court (Buckley, Geoffrey Lane and Goff LJJ) granted the following declaration:

> '...that the plaintiffs as covenantors are bound to take all those steps in their power which are capable of producing the desired result, namely, the obtaining of planning permission, being steps which a prudent, determined and reasonable owner, acting in his own interests and desiring to achieve that result, would take.'

Buckley LJ said that the obligation was not to be measured by reference to somebody who is under a contractual obligation, but someone who is acting in his own interests. Geoffrey Lane LJ (as he then was) said this about the obligation to use 'best endeavours':

> 'Those words, as I see it, oblige the purchaser to take all those reasonable steps which a prudent and determined man, acting in his own interests and anxious to obtain planning permission, would have taken.'

All members of the court agreed that, if an appeal to the Secretary of State offered a reasonable chance of success, as to which there was no evidence before the court, the purchaser was obliged to appeal.[2]

In *Carreras Rothmans Distribution Services Ltd v Container Wear and Roadferry Ltd*,[3] Tudor Evans J rejected an argument that an

20 [1952] 2 TLR 574.

1 [1980] FSR 335. However, in *Oversea Buyers Ltd v Granadex* [1980] 2 Lloyd's Rep 608, 613 Mustill J (as he then was) seems to have doubted whether the test established by *IBM UK v Rockware* was different from 'doing all that can reasonably be expected'.

2 Goff LJ distinguished his judgment in *Bower v Bantam Investments Ltd* [1972] 3 All ER 349, [1972] 1 WLR 1120 on the ground that 'the object which the best endeavours were to be used to promote was left wholly uncertain'.

3 (1986) unreported.

obligation to use 'every endeavour' is stricter than an obligation to use 'best endeavours'. He said that he could see no real difference between the two expressions.

On the other hand, in *UBH (Mechanical Services) Ltd v Standard Life Assurance Co*,[4] Rougier J held that a covenant to use 'reasonable endeavours' was less onerous than one to use 'best endeavours'. A lessee required to use reasonable endeavours was entitled to perform a balancing act, placing on one side of the scales the weight of his obligations to the lessor and on the other commercial considerations, including his relationships with his sub-tenants, his reputation as a landlord, and the uncertainties of litigation.

This approach corresponds to that adopted by the courts to obligations of employers under health and safety at work legislation to take precautions 'so far as is reasonably practicable' to prevent accidents. In *Marshall v Gotham Co Ltd*,[5] Lord Reid approved the following observations of Asquith LJ (as he then was) in *Edwards v National Coal Board*.[6]

> 'The construction placed by Lord Atkin on the words "reasonably practicable" in *Coltness Iron Co Ltd v Sharp* [1938] AC 90 at 94 seems to me, with respect, right. "Reasonably practicable" is a narrower term than "physically possible" and seems to me to imply that a computation must be made by the owner, in which the quantum of risk is placed on one scale and the sacrifice involved in the measures necessary for averting the risk (whether in money, time or trouble) is placed in the other; and that if it be shown that there is a gross disproportion between them - the risk being insignificant in relation to the sacrifice - the defendants [ie employers] discharge the onus on them.'

Lord Reid considered that an obligation to take 'practicable' precautions is higher than an obligation to take 'reasonably practicable' precautions:

> 'I think it enough to say that if a precaution is practicable it must be taken unless in the whole circumstances that would be unreasonable.'

The policy considerations which bear on the interpretation of health and safety at work legislation are quite different from those affecting the interpretation of a normal commercial agreement. Nevertheless, it is thought that the cases on the health and safety at work legislation are not entirely irrelevant to the interpretation of an obligation under a commercial agreement to do X 'so far as is reasonably practicable'. In particular, it is thought that a person under such an obligation or an obligation 'to use reasonable endeavours' is required to undertake significantly less expenditure to perform the obligation than a person obliged to use his 'best endeavours'.

4 (1986) Times, 13 November.
5 [1954] AC 360 at 373,
6 [1949] 1 KB 704 at 712.

An important judgment of Templeman J (as he then was) in *Rackham v Peek Foods Ltd*[7] marks the limits of a 'best endeavours' obligation. The shareholders in a property company called Roeday entered into an agreement to sell their shares to Consolidated Commercial, a company listed on the London Stock Exchange, and Consolidated's merchant bank, Bates. The sale agreement was conditional on the approval of Consolidated's shareholders, and Consolidated and Bates covenanted to use their best endeavours to procure the fulfilment of that condition. Consolidated's directors issued a circular to their shareholders recommending that they vote in favour of the acquisition of Roeday at an extraordinary general meeting, and Bates supported that recommendation. However, before the extraordinary general meeting was held, the government announced measures to restrain lending to property companies and to increase the tax on their profits. The extraordinary general meeting was postponed and the directors of Consolidated issued a second circular stating that they could no longer recommend the Roeday acquisition. Templeman J held that there was no breach of the 'best endeavours' undertaking:

> 'In my judgment, Bates and the directors of Consolidated were not under a duty to recommend the purchase of Roeday if Bates and the directors of Consolidated both genuinely and reasonably believed that the purchase of Roeday was not in the interests of their shareholders of Consolidated. There is overwhelming evidence ... that Bates and the directors of Consolidated believed that the purchase of Roeday ... could not be beneficial to and might be a disaster for the shareholders of Consolidated. In my judgment in these circumstances Bates and the directors of Consolidated were bound so to advise the shareholders of Consolidated and to use their influence and their powers to ensure that the acquisition of Roeday was not approved ... there was no breach of the "best endeavours" covenant if the directors of Consolidated and Bates gave proper advice. On its true construction the "best endeavours" covenant did not oblige the directors of Consolidated or Bates to give advice which they genuinely believed to be bad advice.'

This decision was followed by Vinelott J in *John Crowther Group plc v Carpets International plc*[8] where he held that–

> 'any obligation to use reasonable endeavours to procure the passing of the resolution ceases if an offer plainly more in the interests of the company is made before that resolution is passed.'

A similar decision was reached by the Court of Session in *Dawson International plc v Coates Patons plc.*[9]

The formula 'take all reasonable steps and exercise all due diligence' is used in many statutes to set out a defence to criminal liability,

7 [1990] BCLC 895.
8 [1990] BCLC 460.
9 [1990] BCLC 560.

for example, section 39 of the Consumer Protection Act 1987. In *Tesco Supermarkets Ltd v Nattrass*,[10] the formula was considered by the House of Lords in the context of the Trade Descriptions Act 1968, and it was held that, in the case of a company, it imposed a twofold duty: to set up an efficient system for the avoidance of offences under that Act, and a proper operation of the system. If that duty were satisfied, the company was not responsible for a failure on the part of a junior manager.[11]

'Such consent not to be unreasonably withheld'

If a clause prohibits A from doing something without B's prior written consent, is there an implied term that B will not unreasonably withhold his consent? In *Price v Bouch*[12] Millett J stated:

> 'There is no principle of law that, whenever a contract requires the consent of one party to be obtained by the other, there is an implied term that such consent is not to be unreasonably refused. It all depends on the circumstances.'

He held that the fact that the committee whose consent was required was bound to act honestly and not for some improper motive was a ground for holding that there was no implied term either that it would not unreasonably refuse consent or that, if it refused consent, it would give its reasons.[13]

This statement by Millett J was approved by the Court of Appeal in *Cryer v Scott Bros (Sudbury) Ltd.*[14] That concerned a covenant in a transfer of registered land which required the transferees to submit any building plans to the transferors' surveyor for approval before building work was begun. The Court of Appeal endorsed a distinction which Megarry J had made in *Clerical Medical and General Life Assurance Society v Fanfare Properties Ltd*,[15] between a matter requiring 'a general and unrestricted consent' (eg a covenant precluding the carrying on without consent of any trade upon the premises) and covenants which require the approval of a specific matter, as when the title has to be approved, or plans of a building have to be submitted for approval. In the latter class of case, Megarry J

10 [1972] AC 153, [1971] 2 All ER 127, HL.

11 By contrast, in *Riverstone Meat Co Pty Ltd v Lancashire Shipping Co Ltd* [1961] AC 807 the House of Lords (reversing the Court of Appeal and the judge at first instance) held that an obligation under the Hague Rules of 'due diligence on the part of the carrier to make the ship seaworthy' had the effect of making the carrier/shipowner responsible for the negligence of an independent contractor engaged to repair the ship.

12 (1986) 53 P & CR 257.

13 See also *Re Londonderry's Settlement* [1965] Ch 918 and *Imperial Group Pension Trust Ltd v Imperial Tobacco Ltd* [1991] IRLR 66.

14 (1986) 55 P & CR 183, CA.

15 (1981) unreported.

stated that 'the Courts will not permit the party whose approval is required to misuse the requirement by refusing to approve a title or plans which are free from any tenable objection.' The Court of Appeal held that the covenant in issue was subject to an implied proviso that approval of the plans would not be unreasonably withheld. This implication was necessary to give business efficacy.

In the light of this, a party whom an agreement requires to obtain the other party's consent before taking certain action, should request the inclusion of the following provisions:

(a) that the other party will not unreasonably withhold consent;

(b) that, if he withholds consent or makes it subject to conditions, he will provide a written statement of his reasons;

(c) that consent will be deemed to have been given unless a notice stating that it is refused is served on or before a specified date.

If possible, the clause should also state the grounds on which consent may be withheld and place the burden of proving reasonableness on the party whose consent is required. See also the section on Assignment in Chapter 18.

'Negotiation' and 'determination'

Parties often have to provide that a particular aspect of a transaction will be settled or agreed after the contract is signed. The aspect may relate to an event which will occur, if at all, only some time after the contract is entered into; or there may not be enough time before the signing to draft provisions to cover the point. In this situation the parties face the problem of whether leaving the point open will cause not only the clause providing for it to be settled later, but also the rest of the contract, to be void for uncertainty. There are three main ways in which a matter, for example the price payable under the contract, can be left open for later resolution.

The first method is to provide for determination by an independent expert, for example, a valuer. The problem here is whether the contract can be enforced if the agreed machinery cannot be operated, for example, because one of the parties will not appoint the expert. *Sudbrook Trading Estate Ltd v Eggleton*[16] arose out of a lease which gave the lessees an option to purchase the freehold reversion 'at such a price not being less than £12,000 as may be agreed upon by two valuers one to be nominated by the lessor and the other by the lessee and in default of such agreement by an umpire appointed by the valuers.' The lessees exercised their option, but the lessors refused to appoint a valuer. An unbroken line of authority stretching back to 1807 established a rule that, where a contract specified a

16 [1983] 1 AC 444.

particular method of fixing the price, and that method had not for any reason been implemented, the court would neither order specific performance to compel the parties to operate the agreed machinery, nor substitute its own machinery to ascertain the price. The rule was also regarded as settled law in Australia, Canada and some of the states in the United States of America. However, the House of Lords rejected it as unjust and inappropriate in modern conditions. Lord Diplock, in particular, could not consider it 'fit for survival in a civilised system of law'.

The House of Lords replaced the rule by this general principle: where the price-fixing mechanism is a 'subsidiary and non-essential' term of the contract, then, if it breaks down, whether because one of the parties refuses to operate it or for any other reason, the court will substitute its own machinery.[17] Lord Fraser of Tullybelton said this:

> '...the clause should be construed as meaning that the price was to be a fair price. On the other hand where an agreement is made to sell at a price to be fixed by a valuer who is named, or who, by reason of holding some office such as auditor of a company whose shares are to be valued, will have special knowledge relevant to the question of value, the prescribed mode may well be regarded as essential. Where, as here, the machinery consists of valuers and an umpire, none of whom is named or identified, it is in my opinion unrealistic to regard it as an essential term. If it breaks down there is no reason why the court should not substitute other machinery to carry out the main purpose of ascertaining the price in order that the agreement may be carried out.'

Lord Scarman said:

> 'I would unhesitatingly conclude that the parties intended that the lessee should pay a fair and reasonable price to be determined as at the date when he exercised the option. The valuation formula was introduced into the contract merely as a convenient way of ascertaining the price at that future time.'

The House of Lords ordered specific performance of the contract constituted by the exercise of the lessee's option and an enquiry as to the fair value of the freehold reversion.

Lord Fraser also approved this statement which Templeman LJ (as he then was) had made in the Court of Appeal regarding a term that is essential:

> 'Where an agreement which would otherwise be unenforceable for want of certainty or finality in an essential stipulation has been partly performed so that the intervention of the court is necessary in aid of a grant that has already taken effect, the court will strain to the utmost to supply the want of certainty even to the extent of providing a substitute machinery.'

17 The argument of Mr Peter Millett QC at 465 to 466E is very helpful in showing the basis of the new principle.

The second method of dealing with an open matter is to provide that it will be determined in accordance with a stated formula, but without providing any machinery for operating the formula. In *Brown v Gould*[18] a clause in a lease gave the lessee an option to renew it and provided for the new lease to be 'at a rent to be fixed having regard to the market value of the premises at the time of exercising this option taking into account to the advantage of the tenant any increased value of such premises attributable to structural improvements made by the tenant . . .'. The tenant, having substantially rebuilt the premises, exercised the option. The landlord contended that the option to renew was void for uncertainty. Megarry J stated, in effect as a general principle, that–

> 'The court is reluctant to hold void for uncertainty any provision that was intended to have legal effect.'[19]

Megarry J held that, if an option provides for the price or rent to be determined according to a stated formula, without specifying any machinery for working out the formula, the court had jurisdiction to determine the price or rent. The option was therefore valid.

The third method is to provide for the outstanding point to be negotiated and agreed between the parties after the contract is entered into. The problem here is the Court of Appeal's decision in *Courtney and Fairbairn Ltd v Tolaini Bros (Hotels) Ltd.*[20] The court (Lord Denning MR, Lord Diplock and Lawton LJ) rejected a statement of Lord Wright in *Hillas & Co Ltd v Arcos Ltd*[1] that, if there is good consideration, English law will recognise a contract to negotiate. The Court of Appeal held that such a contract is too uncertain to have any binding force; and that no court could estimate the damages because no one could tell whether the negotiations would have been successful or would have fallen through or, if successful, what the result would have been. *Courtney v Tolaini Bros* has been applied by the Court of Appeal in *Mallozi v Carapelli SpA*[2] and *Walford v Miles.*[3] In the latter case the Court of Appeal (Dillon and Stocker LJJ, Bingham LJ dissenting) held that an agreement by A with B to continue negotiations with B and not to negotiate with any third party was not a valid contract under English law.

However, in *Neilson v Stewart*[4] the House of Lords confined the principle in *Courtney v Tolaini* to a term which is 'essential' to the

18 [1972] Ch 53, [1971] 2 All ER 1505.
19 See also *Royal Life Insurance v Phillips* (1990) 61 P & CR 182 in which Nolan J held that a letter marked 'subject to contract' and 'without prejudice', but clearly intended to have legal effect, was effective to trigger a rent review.
20 [1975] 1 All ER 716, [1975] 1 WLR 297.
1 [1932] All ER Rep 494 at 505.
2 [1976] 1 Lloyd's Rep 407.
3 (1991) Independent, 15 January.
4 (1991) unreported.

implementation of the contract. The case arose out of an informal letter agreement for the sale by one director to another director of his 50% interest in the relevant company. The sale document provided that the director would transfer his shares for £50,000 which he would then lend back to the company. The document stated:

> 'payment shall be deferred for a period of one year, after which time, payment shall be negotiated to our mutual agreement and satisfaction.'

Lord Jauncey of Tullichettle, who delivered the main speech, quoted the following passage from the judgment of Lord Guthrie in *Dempster Ltd v Motherwell Bridge and Engineering Co Ltd*[5] in which a contract for the sale of steel over a period of three years was upheld, although it provided for 'the prices to be mutually settled at a later and appropriate date':

> 'The matter for decision must always be whether the parties have not got beyond the stage of negotiation, or whether there is a concluded bargain. In the usual case, the price to be paid is one of the essential matters on which agreement is necessary before either party is bound. If they have not agreed upon the actual sum, or on a method of deciding that sum, there is not the consensus in idem requisite before a contract can be completed. But if they agree that the question of price shall be deferred, and agree on the things to be done to meet the immediate needs of the situation, there is consensus in idem, and each can require the other to do what he has undertaken to do for the price settled. In such circumstances the matter of price is not "vital to the arrangement between them", to use the words of Lord Buckmaster in *May and Butcher Ltd v R*.[6]

Lord Jauncey of Tullichettle said that the question was whether the time and manner of repayment of the loan 'were essential to the taking effect of the contract as a whole'. He held that they were not. It was clear that the parties intended that the transfer of shares and the subsequent loan-back should take place as soon as possible; and that they contemplated that this would take place long before the time and manner of repayment of the loan fell to be considered by them. Moreover, Lord Jauncey held that agreement as to the time and manner of repayment of the loan was not essential even to the part of the contract that dealt with the loan. He cited various authorities which show that, under Scottish law, every loan carries with it an obligation of the borrower to repay. If the contract contains provisions for repayment, those provisions, he said, will prevail. If, however, the contract contains no provisions or if for some reason the provisions turn out to be ineffectual, then the obligation to repay on demandrevives. It followed that it was not essential that the parties

5 1964 SC 308.
6 [1934] 2 KB 17.

should agree about the period of the loan because, in the absence of agreement in the contract, a loan is repayable at any time on demand.[7] Nor was payment of interest an essential condition of the contract of loan. An interest-free loan, Lord Jauncey observed, is perfectly valid; and, if nothing is said about interest, it becomes a question of construction whether the parties intended that none should be payable or that the Scottish rule of law requiring payment of legal interest should apply.[8]

A similar approach was adopted by the Court of Appeal in *Didymi Corpn v Atlantic Lines and Navigation Co.*[9] This arose out of a charter-party which provided that, if the actual performance of the vessel did not meet certain specifications, 'the hire shall be equitably decreased by an amount to be mutually agreed between owners and charterers'. It also provided that, if the vessel maintained a better speed and/or consumption than specified, the owners would receive an increase of hire 'such increase to be calculated in the same way as the reduction' referred to previously. The owners alleged that the vessel had maintained a better speed and consumption than that stipulated and claimed against the charterers. The charterers argued that the clause was void for uncertainty and relied on *Courtney v Tolaini Bros*. However, applying *Sudbrook Trading Estate v Eggleton*, the Court of Appeal held, in effect, that *Courtney v Tolaini Bros* is only relevant to an essential term of the contract or where the question is whether any contract has been entered into at all. That case is inapplicable to 'a subsidiary and non-essential question of how a contractual liability to make payment according to a specified objective standard is to be quantified'. Bingham LJ stressed that the clause represented a commercial bargain made between commercial men. In his judgment, Nourse LJ emphasised that the clause fixed an objective standard:

> 'I would certainly accept that, if there had been a simple agreement for a decrease in the hire to be agreed between the owners and charterers themselves, then the prescribed mode of agreement would have been essential and the agreement would have failed. But that is not the agreement which the parties have made. A purely objective standard has been prescribed. The parties can only agree upon an equitable decrease. ... Accordingly, the parties having agreed upon an objective standard, it seems to me that the identity of those to whom the agreement is referred, albeit that they are the parties themselves, is of no real importance.'

Nourse LJ approved the following observation in the judgment at first instance of Hobhouse J:

7 Compare *Aldous v Cromwell* (1868) LR3 QB 573, and the comments of Pickford LJ in *Bradford Old Bank v Sutcliffe* [1918] 2 KB 833 at 840.
8 See also *British Steel Corpn v Cleveland Bridge Co* [1984] 1 All ER 504 at 511.
9 [1988] 2 Lloyd's Rep 108.

'The words "to be mutually agreed" are directory or mechanical and do not represent the substance of the provision. The substantive provision is that there shall be an equitable decrease in the hire.'

However, an option in a lease to call for a further term 'at a rental to be agreed (but such rental shall not in any event exceed the rental hereby reserved)' was upheld by the Court of Appeal in *Corson v Rhuddlan Borough Council*.[10] The Court of Appeal held that the presence of the words 'to be agreed by the parties' is not fatal to the existence of an enforceable contract if it is otherwise plain, upon the construction of the whole of the document in its context, including of course those words, that there was a clear contractual intention of the parties to be bound by the clause. Applying the decision of a strong Court of Appeal in *Foley v Classique Coaches*,[11] the court implied a term that the rent for the new lease would be a fair rent, subject to an upper limit equal to the rent payable under the existing lease. The effect of implying a fair rent term (although not stated by the court in these terms) was to create an objective standard and to enable the provision for agreement by the parties to be treated as a subsidiary and non-essential term.[12] In other words, the implied term brought the case within the principles which the Court of Appeal had applied in *The Didymi*. An important factor in *Corson* was the commercial nature of the agreement, although the lease was to a golf club. The case represents, perhaps, the furthest that a court will go in upholding a clause providing for a point to be agreed between the parties; and the judgments in *Brown v Gould* and *The Didymi* indicate that Megarry J and Nourse LJ respectively might well have considered the option invalid.

In the light of these cases, it is thought that the *Courtney v Tolaini Bros* principle can be disapplied where there is:

(a) a commercial contract all the other provisions which are sufficiently certain to be enforceable;

(b) a provision that the amount of a payment shall be determined according to a specified standard which is purely objective; and

(c) a clause which provides for the parties to negotiate and agree the amount of the payment on the basis of the specified standard; the clause should be expressed to be a 'subsidiary and non-essential' term and there should be a statement that the obligation to pay the amount ascertained according to the specified standard will not be impaired by a failure of the parties to negotiate or reach agreement.

The cases referred to above are all concerned with questions of quantification; for example, as to the amount of a fair rent or of

10 (1989) 59 P & CR 185.
11 [1934] 2 KB 1.
12 See also *Malcolm v University of Oxford* (1990) Times, 19 December.

an equitable reduction. It is thought, however, that the principle underlying these cases implies that the terms of a document which a party is to execute at a later date can be left for determination by reference to a standard which is purely objective: for example–

> The terms of the licence shall be fair and reasonable, having equal regard to the interests of A and those of B.

Consultation

In public law a duty to 'consult' has a clear meaning; and it is thought that a contractual obligation to consult would not normally be void for uncertainty (although it might not be enforceable by specific performance and damages could be difficult to assess). In *R v Secretary of State for Social Services, ex p Association of Metropolitan Authorities*[13] Webster J said:

> '...in any context the essence of consultation is the communication of a genuine invitation to give advice and a genuine consideration of that advice. In my view it must go without saying that to achieve consultation sufficient information must be supplied by the consulting to the consulted party to enable it to tender helpful advice. Sufficient time must be given by the consulting to the consulted party to enable it to do that, and sufficient time must be available for such advice to be considered by the consulting party. Sufficient, in that context, does not mean ample, but at least enough to enable the relevant purpose to be fulfilled. By helpful advice, in this context, I mean sufficiently informed and considered information or advice about aspects of the form or substance of the proposals, or their implications for the consulted party, being aspects material to the implementation of the proposal as to which the Secretary of State [who, in that case, had the duty to consult] might not be fully informed or advised and as to which the party consulted might have relevant information or advice to offer.'

It is implicit that the person obliged to consult must do so 'with a receptive mind';[14] see also the observations about fettering of discretion made by Ackner LJ (as he then was) in *R v Secretary of State for the Environment, ex p Brent London Borough Council.*[15] Nor, it is thought, is a duty to consult discharged until the person under the duty has given proper consideration to the views expressed by those consulted.[16]

Burden of proof

An issue which commercial agreements seldom address is which party shall bear the burden of proof. In the context of legislation, this

13 [1986] 1 All ER 164 at 167.

14 *Agricultural Horticultural and Forestry Industry Training Board v Aylesbury Mushrooms Ltd* [1972] 1 All ER 280 at 284.

15 [1983] 3 All ER 321 at 352–354.

16 Compare the duty to consider a tender implied in *Blackpool and Fylde Aero Club v Blackpool Borough Council* [1990] 3 All ER 25, [1990] 1 WLR 1195.

question has produced difficult problems of interpretation. *Nimmo v Alexander Cowan & Sons Ltd*[17] was concerned with section 29(1) of the Factories Act 1961 which provided:

> 'There shall, so far as is reasonably practicable, be provided and maintained safe means of access to every place at which any person has at any time to work....'

The House of Lords divided three to two on the question of whether the burden of proof rested with the plaintiff or the defendant. The majority held that, if the plaintiff proved that the place was not safe, it was for the defendant to excuse himself by proving that it was not reasonably practicable to make it safe.

When a similar point arose in *R v Hunt*,[18] the House of Lords held that, where a linguistic construction did not indicate clearly on whom the burden of proof should lie, the court might look to other considerations, such as the mischief at which the provision was aimed and practical considerations such as, in particular, the ease or difficulty for the respective parties of discharging the burden of proof. Lord Ackner said that, if the result of holding that the prosecution had the burden of proof to establish that a controlled drug had *not* been excepted by regulations would make prosecutions particularly difficult with the consequence that the purpose of the legislation would be significantly frustrated, then this would be a relevant consideration to weigh against the grammatical form of the legislation.

Broadly similar considerations apply to an action on a contract. The plaintiff has to prove the existence of the contract, the breach and his loss; but, in the absence of an express provision, the defendant has the burden of proving that the case falls within an exception or exclusion in the contract on which he relies; and, if the plaintiff counters by invoking an exception to that exception, the burden of proof lies on him in that respect.[19] For example, if A undertakes with B not to disclose certain information unless it comes into the public domain otherwise than as a result of a breach of another agreement to which B is a party, B would have to prove that A disclosed the information; the burden would then pass to A to prove that the information was in the public domain at the time of the disclosure; and the burden would revert to B to prove that the information came into the public domain through a breach of the other agreement.

Certain facts can be very difficult to prove. If A Co undertakes with B that A Co will not 'knowingly' permit its employees to do

17 [1968] AC 107, [1967] 3 All ER 187.
18 [1987] AC 352, [1987] 1 All ER 1.
19 *The Glendarroch* [1894] P 226, CA; see also the statement of Lord Denning MR in *Bremer Handelsgesellschaft MbH v Mackprang Jr* [1979] 1 Lloyd's Rep 221 at 223, that at common law a party who relies on an exception clause has the burden of proof.

certain things, B is faced with two problems in enforcing the undertaking. First, which officer or officers of A Co does he have to prove knew of the relevant facts in order to show that A Co 'knowingly' permitted its employees to do the prohibited things? The general rule is that B will have to prove knowledge on the part of A Co's board of directors, or its managing director, if any, or perhaps other senior officers to whom the directors have delegated some part of their management functions, if those officers have been given full discretion to act independently of instructions from the directors.[20] However, in *Evans v Employers Mutual Insurance Association Ltd*[1] the Court of Appeal held that, if evidence establishes that the duty of investigating facts has been delegated in the ordinary course of a company's business to a subordinate employee, the company is bound by his knowledge in the same way as by the knowledge of its board of directors. In that case, a clerk in an insurance company noticed, but failed to call attention to, a serious discrepancy between the information given on a claim form and that given in the proposal for the relevant policy. The clerk's knowledge was attributed to the insurance company which was held, by paying some items with knowledge of the discrepancy, to have waived its right to repudiate liability on the other items.

The second problem arising from an undertaking in the form described above is whether B needs to prove actual knowledge or whether it is enough if he proves constructive knowledge; that is, that a responsible officer of A Co wilfully shut his eyes to the obvious or wilfully and recklessly failed to make such enquiries as an honest and reasonable man would make.[2]

In such cases the difficulties which a party will have in proving the relevant facts significantly reduces his ability, in practical terms, to enforce the contract. Accordingly, a clause which lightens his burden of proof will correspondingly increase the contract's value to him.[2a]

Expert's certificate

Of such clauses, the most common type is a provision that a certificate given, or a determination made, by a party as to certain facts will

20 See the observations of Lord Reid in *Tesco Supermarkets Ltd v Nattrass* [1972] AC 153 at 171F; *The Lady Gwendolen* [1965] P 294 at 343–345 and 355–356; and *Grand Champion Tankers Ltd v Norpipe A/S* [1984] AC 563 at 571E–F.

1 [1936] 1 KB 505.

2 Compare *Baden, Delvaux and Lecuit v Société General pour Favoriser le Developpement du Commerce et de l'Industrie en France SA* [1983] BCLC 325; *Agip (Africa) Ltd v Jackson* [1990] Ch 265; on appeal (1991) Financial Times, 18 January; and *Eagle Trust plc v SBC Securities Ltd* (1991) Times, 14 February.

2a But see Unfair Contract Terms Act 1977, s 13(1)(c).

be 'prima facie evidence' or 'conclusive evidence' of those facts. Banking documents often provide that a certificate signed by an officer of the bank as to the amount owing by the customer or the amount of certain expenses which the bank has incurred shall be prima facie or conclusive evidence.

A provision which states that a certificate shall be 'prima facie' evidence shifts on to the other party the burden of proving that the certificate is incorrect. Providing that a certificate shall be 'conclusive' evidence no doubt makes the certificate harder to attack, but not completely immune from challenge. In *Burgess v Purchase & Sons (Farms) Ltd*[3] Nourse J (as he then was) drew a distinction between a speaking valuation (one which sets out reasons) and a non-speaking valuation:

> 'A non-speaking valuation made of the right property by the right man and in good faith cannot be impugned, although it may still be possible, in the case of an uncompleted transaction, for equitable relief – as opposed to damages – to be refused to the party who wishes to sustain the valuation. On the other hand, ... a speaking valuation which demonstrates that it has been made on a fundamentally erroneous basis can be impugned. In such a case the completion of the transaction does not necessarily defeat the party who wishes to impugn the valuation.'

However, this distinction between speaking and non-speaking valuations was rejected by the Court of Appeal (Dillon and Balcombe LJJ) in *Jones v Sherwood Computer Services plc.*[4] Dillon and Balcombe LJJ both quoted the statement of Lord Denning MR in *Campbell v Edwards*:[5]

> 'If two persons agree that the price of property should be fixed by a valuer on whom they agree, and he gives that valuation honestly and in good faith, they are bound by it. Even if he has made a mistake they are still bound by it. The reason is because they have agreed to be bound by it. If there were fraud or collusion, of course, it would be very different. Fraud or collusion unravels everything.'

However, Dillon and Balcombe LJJ considered that a valuation or an expert's certificate could be set aside for a mistake which meant that the expert had done something different from what he was appointed to do. Dillon LJ said this:

> 'On principle, the first step must be to see what the parties have agreed to remit to the expert, this being, as Lord Denning said in *Campbell v Edwards* [1976] 1 All ER 785, [1976] 1 WLR 403 a matter of contract. The next step must be to see what the nature of the mistake was, if there is evidence to show that. If the mistake was that the expert departed from his instructions in a material respect – eg if he valued the wrong

3 [1983] Ch 216, [1983] 2 All ER 4.
4 [1989] EGCS 172.
5 [1976] 1 WLR 403 at 407.

number of shares, or valued shares in the wrong company, or if, as in *Jones v Jones* [1971] 1 WLR 840, the expert had valued machinery himself whereas his instructions were to employ an expert valuer of his choice to do that – either party would be able to say that the certificate was not binding because the expert had not done what he was appointed to do.'

Dillon LJ made two further important points. The distinction between speaking and non-speaking valuations or certificates is invalid:

> 'The real question is whether it is possible to say from all the evidence which is properly before the court (and not only from the valuation or certificate itself) what the valuer or certifier has done and why he has done it.'

Second, he seems to have rejected the proposition that, even where a contract provides that an expert's certificate shall be final and conclusive, the certificate can be set aside if the expert makes a mistake of law. The contract in issue provided that 'the Accountants and the Expert (if any) shall act as experts and not as arbitrators and their or his determination shall be conclusive and final and binding for all purposes'. Dillon LJ noted that the matters which the accountants and the expert were to determine were capable of giving rise to issues of law or mixed fact and law because they all involved issues as to the true meaning or application of wording in the relevant clause of the contract. He said:

> 'I cannot read the categorical wording of paragraph 7 as meaning that the determination of the accountants or of the expert shall be conclusive final and binding for all purposes "unless it involves a determination of an issue of law or mixed fact and law in which case it shall only be binding if the Court agrees with it".'

This part of Dillon LJ's judgment is scarcely reconcilable with *Re Davstone Estate Ltd's Lease*[6] in which a clause providing for an expert's determination to be conclusive on a matter involving a question of interpretation was held to be contrary to public policy.

It is thought that a clause which purports to make a certificate 'conclusive' even if based on a material misinterpretation of the contract under which it is issued would be contrary to public policy since 'the true construction of the contract is to be decided by the courts and by no one else'.[7] This principle was recently reasserted by the Court of Appeal in *R v Spens*,[8] in which it held that the interpretation of the City Code on Take-overs and Mergers is a question of law for the judge, not an issue of fact for the jury.

6 [1969] 2 Ch 378, [1969] 2 All ER 849.
7 Denning LJ in *Lee v Showmen's Guild of Great Britain* [1952] 2 QB 329 at 344 and Lord Diplock in *Pioneer Shipping Ltd v BTP Tioxide* [1982] AC 724 at 736.
8 (1991) Independent, 8 February.

A clause would be ineffective to the extent that it purports to provide that a certificate issued dishonestly will be valid.

An interesting, and authoritative, decision in this context is that of Buckley J (later Lord Wrenbury) in *Re Caratal (New) Mines Ltd)*.[9] That concerned the predecessor of section 378(4) of the Companies Act 1985 which provides that at a meeting at which a special resolution is proposed, a declaration by the chairman that the resolution is carried is, unless a poll is demanded, 'conclusive evidence of the fact without proof of the number or proportion of the votes recorded in favour of or against the resolution'. Buckley J stated that the declaration of the chairman in that case was not conclusive because he had counted votes given by proxy, and these could not be included because there had not been a poll. Similarly, in a public law context, there is a presumption that, even if a statute provides that a certificate or determination by an administrative authority is to be 'final and conclusive', Parliament did not intend that result to apply in the event that the administrative authority makes an error of law in the course of reaching its decision on matters of fact or administrative policy.[10]

The second, and less common, type of clause concerned with the burden of proof is a provision that it is for a particular party to prove certain facts or that certain facts will be presumed unless the contrary is proved. For example, section 11(5) of the Unfair Contract Terms Act 1977 provides that it is for those claiming that a contract term satisfies the requirement of reasonableness laid down by that Act to show that it does. The City Code on Take-overs and Mergers reinforces its definition of 'persons acting in concert' by stating that six sets of parties will be presumed to be persons acting in concert with each other, unless the contrary is established; so a company is presumed to be acting in concert with its pension fund and a fund manager with a person whose investments he manages on a discretionary basis. A clause of this type might be used where warranties are given by several persons, each 'to the best of his knowledge, information and belief'. The clause could provide that, if it is shown that one warrantor knew that a warranty was incorrect, each of the other warrantors shall be presumed also to have known of that, unless he proves to the contrary.

Irrevocable authorities

A common problem is how to ensure that a particular act will be done or a particular document will be executed if the party whom

9 [1902] 2 Ch 498.
10 *R v Registrar of Companies, ex p Central Bank of India* [1986] QB 1114, [1986] 1 All ER 105.

the agreement obliges to take that step fails to do so. Often the most effective method of ensuring performance is for the agreement to authorise another person to take the necessary action on behalf of the party responsible (call him A) if he fails to perform. To be effective the authority has to be irrevocable in the sense first, that any purported revocation of it by A will be ineffective, and second, that it will continue in force notwithstanding events, for example A's bankruptcy or winding up, which would normally terminate an agent's authority to act for A.

In principle, three conditions have to be satisfied for an authority to be irrevocable. First, the person to whom the authority is given has to be party to the contract by which the authority is conferred. Second, the authority must be given to secure the performance by A of an obligation which he has to the person authorised (and not a different person) or to secure any interest in property which A has granted to the person authorised. Third, the person to whom the authority is given has to provide consideration. The classic statement of the principle was formulated by Wilde CJ in *Smart v Sandars*:[11]

> 'Where an agreement is entered into on a sufficient consideration, whereby an authority is given for the purpose of securing some benefit to the donee of the authority, such an authority is irrevocable. This is what is usually meant by an authority coupled with an interest, and which is commonly said to be irrevocable.'

On this principle, an authority given by a sub-underwriter to the lead underwriter to complete an application on the sub-underwriter's behalf for any shares which have to be taken up by him is irrevocable as between the sub-underwriter and the lead underwriter; it also seems that, if the sub-underwriting letter authorises the lead underwriter to communicate its terms to the issuing company, the authority given by the sub-underwriter may be irrevocable as between him and the issuing company.[12] Another example is a power of attorney contained in an equitable mortgage for the mortgagee to execute a legal mortgage.[13] It seems essential for the authority to make some reference to the obligation or interest in property which it is intended to secure.[14]

The common law principle is expressed in section 4(1) of the Powers of Attorney Act 1971. In *Barrows v HM Chief Land Registrar*,[15] Whitford J treated the common law principle and section 4(1) as co-extensive:

11 (1848) 5 CB 895 at 917.
12 *Re Olympic Fire and General Reinsurance Co Ltd* [1920] 2 Ch 341.
13 *Barclays Bank Ltd v Bird* [1954] Ch 274.
14 *Frith v Frith* [1906] AC 254.
15 (1977) Times, 20 October.

'Where a power of attorney is expressed to be irrevocable and is given to secure–

(a) a proprietary interest of the donee of the power; or
(b) the performance of an obligation owed to the donee,

then, so long as the donee has that interest or the obligation remains undischarged, the power shall not be revoked–

(i) by the donor without the consent of the donee; or
(ii) by the death, incapacity or bankruptcy of the donor or, if the donor is a body corporate, by its winding up or dissolution.

In that case Whitford J also held that a power of attorney in a debenture by which the borrowing company authorises *a receiver* appointed by the bank to execute conveyances of the property charged by the debenture is outside both the common law rule and section 4:

'A power may be irrevocable without consent, by death, incapacity, winding up or otherwise, but only if it was granted to secure a proprietary interest of the donee or the performance of an obligation owing to the donee. Neither of these conditions would normally be fulfilled under a debenture where the receiver is appointed by the debenture holder. There is certainly no question of the powers with which I am concerned having been granted to secure an interest of, or the performance of an obligation owing to the plaintiff receivers.'

However, in *Sowman v David Samuel Trust Ltd*[16] Goulding J left the point open. It is thought that the problem can be avoided by giving the power to the bank, with a right for it to appoint substitutes. Section 4(2) of the 1971 Act seems to indicate that a 'substitute' is in the same position, as regards irrevocability, as the original attorney. However, this may apply only where there is an appointment of a substitute in the full sense of a person who replaces the original appointee as attorney so that the original appointee no longer possesses any authority. A person to whom the original appointee sub-delegates or sub-contracts the power is, perhaps, more properly regarded as a sub-agent than a replacement or substitute attorney.

It is to be noted that section 4(1) requires a power of attorney to state expressly that it is irrevocable. Moreover, under section 5(3), if the power of attorney is expressed to be both irrevocable and to be given by way of security, then a person dealing with the person authorised is protected (unless he knows that the power was not in fact given by way of security) against the risk that, unknown to him, the power has been revoked by agreement between the person who granted it and the person authorised.

16 [1978] 1 All ER 616 at 623–4.

'Due', 'owing' and 'payable'

The different meanings of these words often create uncertainty.

In general, an amount cannot be said to have become 'due' until the date on which it is payable, since it is then that payment actually becomes enforceable.[17] But there is no hard and fast definition and, if there is any possibility of uncertainty, it is better to use some such phrase as 'immediately due and payable'.

'Owing' appears to have no clear meaning. If it is intended to mean 'presently payable' those words (or 'due for payment') should be used instead. If that meaning is not intended, it will often be necessary to add some clarifying words, eg 'owing, whether due for payment then or later'.

The meaning of 'payable' depends almost entirely on the context in which it is used.

'Due and payable' and 'immediately payable' clearly mean that that debt is presently enforceable. On the other hand a reference to 'all sums which become or may become payable under this Agreement' will cover sums payable at a later date and sums payable only in certain events.

'And' and 'or'

Federal Steam Navigation Co Ltd v Department of Trade and Industry[18] shows the importance of using 'and' and 'or' correctly. An Act provided that if a British ship registered in the United Kingdom discharged oil into the sea–

> 'the owner or master of the ship'

would be guilty of an offence. The Department of Trade and Industry prosecuted both the owner and the master and they were both convicted. They appealed on the ground that the language of the section required the Crown to elect whether to prosecute the owner or the master and could not prosecute both. The two senior Law Lords, Lord Reid and Lord Morris of Borth-y-Gest, considered that the appeal should have been allowed. Lord Reid said:

> '"Or" can never mean "and". The dictionaries have been searched in vain for any trace of any usage by which "or" has a conjunctive meaning. It is true that in some authorities it has been stated that "or" can be held or construed to mean "and". In my judgment that is quite wrong.'

Lord Wilberforce and Lord Salmon were of the contrary opinion. The fifth Law Lord, Lord Simon of Glaisdale, said that, at the

17 See, for example, *Potel v IRC* [1971] 2 All ER 504 at 513.
18 [1974] 2 All ER 97, [1974] 1 WLR 505.

conclusion of the counsels' argument, he had been of the same opinion as Lord Reid and Lord Morris of Borth-y-Guest, but that, on reading in draft the speeches prepared by Lord Wilberforce and Lord Salmon, he became convinced that the latter were correct.

'Substantial'

'Substantial part' is a term which often appears in a variety of contexts. The best-known example is, perhaps, a clause in a loan stock trust deed or loan agreement which prohibits the issuer or borrower from selling or disposing of 'the whole or a substantial part of its assets'.[19]

Some light is thrown on 'substantial' by a series of cases on rent legislation where the courts have considered the phrase 'a substantial portion of the whole rent' or 'a substantial part of the whole rent'. In *Palser v Grinling*[20] Viscount Simon gave this guidance:

> 'What does "substantial portion" mean? It is plain that the phrase requires a comparison with the whole rent, and the whole rent means the entire contractual rent payable by the tenant in return for the occupation of the premises together with all the other covenants of the landlord. "Substantial" in this connection is not the same as "not unsubstantial", ie, just enough to avoid the de minimis principle. One of the primary meanings of the word is equivalent to considerable, solid, or big. It is in this sense that we speak of a substantial fortune, a substantial meal, a substantial man, a substantial argument or ground of defence. Applying the word in this sense, it must be left to the discretion of the judge of fact to decide as best he can according to the circumstances in each case, the onus being on the landlord. If the judgment of the Court of Appeal in *Palser's* case were to be understood as fixing percentages as a legal measure, that would be going beyond the powers of the judiciary. To say that everything over 20 per cent of the whole rent should be regarded as a substantial portion of that rent would be to play the part of a legislator. If Parliament thinks fit to amend the statute by fixing percentages, Parliament will do so. Aristotle long ago pointed out that the degree of precision that is attainable depends on the subject-matter. There is no reason for the House to differ from the conclusion reached in these two cases that the portion was not substantial, but this conclusion is justified by the view taken on the facts, not by laying down percentages of general application.'

The House held that £14 did not represent a substantial proportion of a total of £175 nor £23 a substantial proportion of a total of £280.

19 In *Commercial Union Assurance Co Ltd v T G Tickler Ltd* (4 March 1959, unreported) Dankwerts J (as he then was) rejected an argument by Sir Milner Holland QC that an event of default in these terms in a loan stock trust deed was void for uncertainty.

20 [1948] 1 All ER 1 at 11.

In *Artillery Mansions Ltd v Macartney*[1] the Court of Appeal held that £15 was not a substantial portion of the total rent of £185. In *Woodward v Docherty*,[2] the Court of Appeal set aside the county court judge's finding that £70 per annum was the part of the rent attributable to the use of furniture, and assessed the figure at £40 instead. Scarman LJ, delivering the court's judgment, said that he did not think that the Court of Appeal could reverse the judge's finding that £70 a year was a substantial part of a rent of about £520 per year – 'though it was, I think, very near the borderline'. However, the Court of Appeal held that £40 was not a substantial part of the rent of £520. In *Mann v Cornella*[3] the Court of Appeal rejected a claim that, if 9.12 per cent of the rent represented the charge for furniture, that was a substantial part of the whole rent.

In *R v Monopolies and Mergers Commission, ex p South Yorkshire Transport Ltd*,[4] Otton J rejected a contention by the MMC that a 'substantial part of the United Kingdom' in section 64(3) of the Fair Trading Act 1973 means a not insubstantial part. The correct approach, he said, was to ask whether the area was substantial in the light of its area, its population and its economic activity as a proportion of the United Kingdom as a whole.

Geographical expressions

Depending on the context, 'England' normally includes Wales and the Isles of Scilly. 'Great Britain' means England, including Wales and Scotland. 'The United Kingdom' means Great Britain and Northern Ireland. 'The British Isles' means the United Kingdom, the Channel Islands (ie Jersey, Guernsey, Alderney and Sark) and the Isle of Man.[5]

'State' denotes an entity which meets the public international law criteria of statehood, while 'country' tends to mean an area with its own private international law legal system, such as the state of Delaware.[6] 'Territory' can mean an area in which a state's jurisdiction is practically and normally exercised, although it is not recognised as having *de jure* jurisdiction in that area.[7]

1 [1949] 1 KB 164, [1948] 2 All ER 875.
2 [1974] 2 All ER 844, [1974] 1 WLR 966.
3 (1980) 254 Estates Gazette 403.
4 (1991) Times, 9 April.
5 See Interpretation Act 1978 and, as regards Great Britain, the Union with Scotland Act 1706; also 8 Halsbury's Laws 404 and 802.
6 8 Halsbury's Laws 403; Dicey and Morris *The Conflict of Laws* (1987) p 27.
7 *Schtraks v Government of Israel* [1962] AC 556, [1962] 3 All ER 529; Ian Brownlie *Principles of Public International Law* (1990) at pp 115–116; note also the language of the State Immunity Act 1978, s 21(a).

CHAPTER 13

REPRESENTATIONS AND WARRANTIES

A wide variety of agreements commonly contain representations and warranties. An agreement by which an issuing house agrees to sponsor or underwrite a new issue of shares contains representations and warranties, for example, that the statements in the listing particulars or prospectus are true and do not omit a material fact and that the shares will be validly allotted and issued. There will also be warranties about the company's latest audited accounts, that there has been no material adverse change since the date of those accounts and that no litigation or claim involving the company is pending. Similar financial representations and warranties appear in loan agreements. An agreement for the sale of a company will contain far more extensive representations and warranties about the company being sold. A contract may well contain a representation and warranty by the contractor as to the correctness of the information contained in its tender and related documents. All such agreements attempt to give the statements concerned the status of both representations and warranties.

Broadly speaking, a representation is a pre-contractual statement of fact which was made by one party to the contract to another party and which has induced the other party to enter into the contract, whereas a warranty is a statement incorporated in a contract as one of its terms.

There are significant differences between the rights which exist in respect of misrepresentation and those relating to breach of warranty. One of the main differences was described by Slade LJ in *Harlingdon & Leinster Enterprises Ltd v Christopher Hull Fine Art Ltd*:[1]

> 'If a party to a contract wishes to claim relief in respect of a misrepresentation as to a matter which did not constitute a term of the contract, his claim will fail unless he is able to show that he relied

1 [1990] 1 All ER 737, 751–752.

> on this representation in entering into the contract; in general, however, if a party wishes to claim relief in respect of a breach of *a term* of the contract (whether it be a condition or warranty) he need prove no actual reliance.'

However, in certain cases of misrepresentation, notably those involving actions by investors on prospectuses, the burden of proof can be modest.

There are two main remedies for misrepresentation. The first is rescission of the contract, but this may cease to be available if the plaintiff delays in bringing proceedings or an innocent third party acquires an interest in the subject matter of the contract. The second main remedy is damages. Under the Misrepresentation Act 1967, a party to a contract is entitled to damages if he entered into it after a misrepresentation was made to him by another party, unless the other party proves that he had reasonable grounds on which to base the representation. In any other case of non-fraudulent misrepresentation, damages are at the discretion of the court and can only be awarded as an alternative to rescission and, moreover, only if rescission would otherwise have been available.

The amount recoverable as damages for misrepresentation is normally that which is needed to put the plaintiff in the position in which he would have been had he not entered into the contract, not in the position in which he would have been had the representation been true. The point is that damages for misrepresentation cannot compensate for loss of a bargain or loss of profit. In *Swingcastle Ltd v Alastair Gibson*,[2] the House of Lords held that a person who had lent money at a high rate of interest in reliance of a negligent valuation of the property on which the loan was secured could not recover from a negligent valuer damages in respect of interest at the high contractual rate that he had been entitled to be paid by the borrower. Damages had to be assessed on the basis that the lender should be placed in the position that he would have been in if he had received a competent report from the valuer and had consequently made no loan. The fallacy of the lender's claim to recover the high contractual interest was that they were trying to obtain from the valuer compensation for the borrower's failure.[3] For example, A buys a company from B for £1 million and is induced to do so by a negligent statement made by B. Had the statement been correct, the market value of the shares purchased by A would have been £1.2 million. In fact, their value is £900,000. A can recover only £100,000.

By contrast, the remedy for a breach of warranty is damages, and normally rescission or termination is unavailable. The amount recoverable is the sum required to put the plaintiff in the position

2 [1991] 2 WLR 1091.
3 See also *Naughton v O'Callaghan* [1990] 3 All ER 191.

which he would have been if the warranty had been correct.[4] So, in the example given above, if the representation had been incorporated as a term of the contract, damages of £300,000 would have been recoverable.

Broadly speaking, there are similar remoteness of damage tests as to which types of loss are recoverable in respect of misrepresentation and breach of warranty. However, an important difference exists with regard to damages recoverable under section 2(1) of the Misrepresentation Act 1976 for a misrepresentation not made on reasonable grounds. In *Royscot Trust Ltd v Rogerson*,[5] the Court of Appeal held that the measure of such damages is that for damages for fraudulent misrepresentation, and not for negligence, so that unforeseeable losses are recoverable provided that they are not too remote. It therefore seems that there is more scope to recover damages in respect of a section 2(1) representation than for a breach of warranty, in respect of which the 'reasonable contemplation' limit will apply.[6]

A representation or warranty can serve two subsidiary purposes. It can estop the person who made it from denying that the stated fact existed, but this is subject to the three conditions specified by Diplock J in *Lowe v Lombank Ltd*[7] being fulfilled: the representation has to be 'clear and unambiguous'; the person making it must have meant it to be acted on by the representee or, at any rate, so conducted himself that a reasonable man in the representee's position would take the representation to be true and believe that it was meant that he should act on it; and the representee must have in fact believed it to be true and must have been induced by that belief to act on it. In *Woodhouse A C Israel Cocoa Ltd SA v Nigerian Produce Marketing Co Ltd*,[8] the House of Lords approved and commented on the statement of Bowen LJ in *Low v Bouverie*[9] that the requirement for a representation to be unambiguous 'does not necessarily mean that the language must be such that it cannot possibly be open to different constructions, but that it must be such as will be reasonably understood in a particular sense by the person to whom it is addressed.' Lord Salmon said:

> 'It is reasonably easy to draft a letter containing a representation, the true meaning of which is clear and unequivocal. I would classify such a letter as "alpha". It is, however, quite another matter to be able to draft a letter, or anything else, which is not only clear and unequivocal but is also incapable of having extracted from it some possible meaning other than its true meaning. I would classify such a letter, if it exists, as "alpha plus". As I understand Bowen LJ's judgment, all he was saying

4 *Smith Kline & French Laboratories Ltd v Long* [1988] 3 All ER 887 at 891.
5 (1991) Times, 3 April.
6 See 12 Halsbury's Laws 1174 to 1176.
7 [1960] 1 All ER 611, [1960] 1 WLR 196.
8 [1972] AC 741, [1972] 2 All ER 271.
9 [1891] 3 Ch 82.

was that the language upon which an estoppel is founded must comply with what I call the "alpha" standard but that it need not come up to "alpha plus".'

A more direct and effective way to create an estoppel is to include an express acknowledgment of the relevant fact by the party to be bound. Like a representation, the acknowledgment has to be unambiguous and grounded upon fact. However, unlike a representation, there is no requirement for the other party to have believed the statement; nor, it seems, does the other party need to have acted on the basis of the statement, apart from entering into the agreement that contains it.[10]

In addition, a representation or warranty, for example, that a person is absolutely entitled to certain property free from any adverse interests or rights can assist a purchaser of the legal title in establishing that he had no notice of an equitable interest which existed, so that he purchases the property free of that interest.

The main problems in attempting to give a statement the status of an actionable representation is the difficulty of proving that the statement was the reason, or one of the reasons, which induced the representee to enter into the contract or that he in fact placed any reliance on it. The usual method of dealing with this problem is to include in the contract an acknowledgment by A first that, before the contract was entered into, he made representations to B in the terms set out in the contract, and second, that B was induced by *each* of those representations to enter into the contract and that B entered into the contract in reliance on *each* of those statements. It is open to doubt whether a court would give effect to such an acknowledgment if it were the sole evidence of inducement in the case of a representation which was clearly immaterial, for example, that the company being sold is in possession of all its statutory books. In *Museprime Properties Ltd v Adhill Properties Ltd*,[11] Scott J held that any misrepresentation which in fact induces a person to enter into a contract entitles him to rescind it, and the question of whether it was material, in the sense that it would have induced a reasonable person to enter into the contract, is relevant only to the onus of proof. That case also indicates that damages are recoverable for an immaterial misrepresentation if it induced the plaintiff to enter into the contract.[12]

A less common way of trying to ensure that a statement becomes an actionable representation is to provide that it forms 'the basis'

10 *Colchester Borough Council v Smith* [1991] 1 All ER 29, [1991] 2 WLR 540; *Amalgamated Investment and Property Co Ltd v Texas Commerce International Bank Ltd* [1982] QB 84.
11 (1990) 61 P & CR 111.
12 But see Treitel *The Law of Contract* at pp 260 and 263.

of the contract. In *Dawsons Ltd v Bonnin*,[13] the House of Lords held, by a majority of three to two, that a clause in an insurance policy which stated that the proposal form should be the basis of the contract had the effect of allowing the insurers to disclaim liability on the ground that one of the statements contained in the proposal form was incorrect, without having to prove that the statement was material. In fact, it had no importance. Viscount Haldane said:

> '... when answers ... are declared to be the basis of the contract this can only mean that their truth is made a condition exact fulfilment of which is rendered by stipulation foundational to its enforceability.'

In other words, if a clause provides that a statement by A shall be the basis of the contract, the truth of that statement is a condition precedent to B's obligations.[14] However, it is not clear that a basis clause will entitle B to damages (as distinct from rescission or termination) if the statement proves incorrect.

'Repeating representations and warranties' feature in some contracts. In an agreement for the acquisition of a company, where payment of the price and transfer of the shares is to take place some time after the agreement is signed, the representations and warranties will be deemed to be repeated at completion with reference to the facts then existing. Similarly, representations and warranties in finance documents are deemed to be repeated when each advance is made and also at the start of each interest period, when the bank makes its funding arrangements in the inter-bank market. If there is merely a clause which provides that the original representations and warranties are 'deemed to be repeated' at a later date, it is arguable that the statements were, in fact, not repeated and that, if they were, there was no actual reliance. It is therefore preferable to provide for a certificate by a director of the representing party to the effect that the representations and warranties set out in the agreement are correct as at the date of the certificate. The certificate may be signed by the director for and on behalf of the relevant company, and there is no reason why it should not contain a clause excluding personal liability on his part. Moreover, it is thought that such a clause would satisfy the requirement of reasonableness under the Unfair Contract Terms Act 1977 unless the director signs the certificate dishonestly or recklessly.

In practice, agreements normally deal with the uncertainties which arise under the general law in relation to representations and warranties by making specific provision in the event that any of the statements labelled as representations and warranties proves to

13 [1922] 2 AC 413.

14 Compare the decision of the House of Lords in *Bank of Nova Scotia v Hellenic Mutual War Risks Association (Bermuda), The Good Luck* (1991) Times, 17 May, about the effect of a breach of a promissory warranty under the Marine Insurance Act 1906.

be incorrect. There will normally be a right to terminate if this happens, unless the contract has been completed, for example, by the shares in the relevant company being transferred to the purchaser. Second, but less often, there will be provisions as to how damages are to be calculated; for example, in the case of an agreement for the acquisition of a company, this could be by reference to the difference between the company's actual net asset value and its net asset value had the warranty been correct, giving the vendor making the warranty credit for any understatement of assets or overstatement of liabilities.

The wording of representations and warranties requires some care. A generalised warranty that a company's accounts 'are true and accurate and have been prepared in accordance with generally accepted accounting principles' is probably less effective than a specific warranty that–

> the company's audited balance sheet as at 31 December 1990 and its audited profit and loss account for the financial year ended on that date, the related auditors' report and the directors' report for that year comply with all requirements of the Companies Act 1985 and all applicable accounting standards, as defined in section 256 of that Act.

Similarly, a warranty that 'no material litigation is pending by or against the Company' might well not be construed as warranting that the company was not being investigated by an official body, for example, the European Commission in connection with article 85 of the Treaty of Rome.

Often an agreement provides for a Schedule or disclosure letter to make disclosures for the purpose of qualifying the representations and warranties contained in the agreement. In *Levison v Farin*,[15] Ralph Gibson J (as he then was) considered the following warranty:

> 'Save as disclosed the vendors hereby jointly and severally warrant to and undertake with the purchasers that between the balance sheet date and the completion date ... the overall financial position of the company will not have changed adversely in any material way allowing for normal trade fluctuations.'

The company that was being sold produced knitwear designed by the main director/vendor. During the negotiations for the sale, the vendors disclosed to the purchaser that this main director had had an illness and that she had not designed a spring/summer collection. Ralph Gibson J held that this was not effective disclosure for the purpose of or with reference to the clause:

> 'I do not say that the facts made known by disclosure of the means of knowledge in the course of negotiation could never constitute disclosure for such a clause as this but I have no doubt that a clause in this form

15 [1978] 2 All ER 1149.

> is primarily designed and intended to require a party who wishes by disclosure to avoid a breach of warranty to give specific notice for the purpose of the agreement, and a protection by disclosure will not normally be achieved by merely making known the means of knowledge which may or do enable the other party to work out certain facts and conclusions.'

Similarly, in the case of a contract for the sale of land, Millett J held that, if the vendor knows of an encumbrance, he cannot rely on a condition in the sale contract which provides that the property is sold subject to any matters which might be disclosed on a search unless he makes 'full and frank disclosure' of the encumbrance to the purchaser.[16]

However, in a straightforward house sale a purchaser can be treated as having himself received a disclosure letter which the estate agents send to his solicitors but which his solicitors do not pass on to him.[17]

16 *Rignall Developments Ltd v Halil* [1988] Ch 190, [1987] 3 All ER 170.
17 *Strover v Harrington* [1988] Ch 390, [1988] 1 All ER 769.

CHAPTER 14

ARITHMETICAL EXPRESSIONS AND EXPRESSIONS OF TIME

Arithmetical expressions

Many financial and commercial agreements have to contain provisions describing arithmetical concepts.

Simple concepts can be expressed as follows:

$A + B$	the aggregate of A and B
$A - B$	the amount by which A exceeds B or the amount by which B falls short of A If it is possible either that A and B could be equal or that B could exceed A, the following wording should be used instead: the amount, if any, by which A exceeds B or B exceeds A.
$A \times B$	an amount found by multiplying A by B
$A \div B$	an amount (expressed to 3 places of decimals) found by dividing A by B or a fraction of which the numerator is A and the denominator B.

A formula is better for an arithmetical concept which is not straightforward. For example:

A Note's subscription price is:

$$P \times \frac{1 + \frac{(R \times D)}{360}}{1 + \frac{(Y \times D)}{360}}$$

where:

P is the Note's face amount;

R is the rate of interest on the Note;

Y is the yield specified in the offer for the Note and expressed to four decimal places; and

D is the number of days in the Note's tenor.

Examples of statutory formulae can be found in sections 35(2) and 38(2) of the Capital Gains Tax Act 1979 and sections 197B and 590B of the Income and Corporation Taxes Act 1988.

Expressions of time

Some care needs to be taken in drafting time limits. One issue relates to limits expressed in terms of numbers of 'months'. An additional problem can arise in relation to a period expressed to run from 'the date of this Agreement'.

Section 61 of the Law of Property Act 1925 defines 'month' as a calendar month, and this definition applies to all deeds, contracts and other instruments governed by English law, unless the context otherwise requires. The common law rule had been that 'month' meant a calendar month only in bills of exchange and other commercial documents and otherwise meant a lunar month or 28 days.[1] In the case of legislation the Interpretation Act 1978 provides that 'month' means calendar month.

In *Dodds v Walker*[2] the House of Lords described the rules for calculating a period of one month or of a specified number of months where a calendar month definition applies. Lord Diplock said:

> 'It is also clear under a rule that has been consistently applied by the courts since *Lester v Garland* (1808) 15 Ves 248, [1803–13] All ER Rep 436 that, in calculating the period that has elapsed after the occurrence of the specified event such as the giving of a notice, the day on which the event occurs is excluded from the reckoning. It is equally well established ... that when the relevant period is a month or a specified number of months after the giving of a notice the general rule is that the period ends on the corresponding date in the appropriate subsequent month, ie the day of that month that bears the same number as the day of the earlier month on which the notice was given.
>
> The corresponding date rule is simple ... except in a small minority of cases, ... all that the calculator has to do is to mark in his diary the corresponding date in the appropriate subsequent month. Because the number of days in five months of the year is less than in the seven others the inevitable consequence of the corresponding date rule is that one month's notice given in a 30-day month is one day shorter than one month's notice given in a 31-day month and is three days shorter if

1 See, for example, *Hart v Middleton* (1845) 2 Car & Kir 9 at 10.
2 [1981] 2 All ER 609, [1981] 1 WLR 1027; compare art 36 of the 1932 Geneva Convention on Bills of Exchange.

it is given in February. Corresponding variations in the length of notice reckoned in days occurs where the required notice is a plurality of months.'

Lord Diplock then referred to notices given on the 31st of a 31-day month and expiring in a 30-day month or in February, and notices expiring in February and given on the 30th or 29th (except in leap years) of any other month of the year. In these cases, Lord Diplock stated that 'the period given by the notice ends on the last day of the month in which the notice expires'.

Lord Russell of Killowen gave two examples of a four-month notice. If served on 28 September, time would begin to run at midnight 28–29 September and would end at midnight 28–29 January. If the notice were served on 30 October, time would begin to run on 30–31 October and would end at midnight 28 February–1 March (or midnight 29 February–1 March in a leap year).

These rules were applied by the Court of Appeal in *Riley Investments Ltd v Eurostile Holdings Ltd.*[3] The Landlord and Tenant Act 1954 requires a tenant's application for a new tenancy to be made 'not less than two nor more than four months after the giving of the landlord's notice under section 25'. The landlord's notice was given on 23 March and the tenant's application was made on 23 May. The Court of Appeal held that the tenant's notice was good; the dates *less* than two months after 23 March were 24 March to 22 May (inclusive).

Hogg Bullimore & Co v Co-Operative Insurance Society Ltd[4] arose out of section 25(1) of the 1954 Act, which provides that a notice by a landlord terminating a tenancy is invalid 'unless given not more than 12 nor less than 6 months before the date of termination specified therein'. The landlord's notice was served on 2 April and specified 2 October as the date of termination. Whitford J held that the notice was valid.

In *Re Figgis*[5] Megarry J had to consider a commorientes clause in a will by which the testator gave his house to his wife 'if she shall survive me and be living at the expiration of a period of three months from my death'. The testator died on 9 January at about 5.00am and his wife on 9 April at about 11.00am. In a decision which is difficult to reconcile with *Riley Investments v Eurostile Holdings*, Megarry J held that the period of three months ended at midnight on the date of the wife's death so that the gift of the house did not take effect in her favour.

Similar rules apply to a provision requiring a person to take certain steps within a specified number of days 'from' or 'after' the occurrence of a particular event. The day on which the event occurs is excluded (see 45 Halsbury's Laws 1134), unless the period is a specified number of days 'commencing on' or 'beginning with' the date of the

3 [1985] 3 All ER 181, [1985] 1 WLR 1139.
4 (1984) 50 P & CR 105.
5 [1969] 1 Ch 123, [1968] 1 All ER 999.

occurrence. The formula 'beginning from' normally excludes the date of the occurrence.[6]

The decision of the House of Lords in *Afovos Shipping COSA v Pagnan*[7] establishes the general principle that 'where a person under an obligation to do a particular act has to do it on or before a particular date he has the whole of that day to perform it'. The House of Lords held that even where the obligation is to make a remittance to the credit of a bank account and the remittance is not received by the bank's close of business on the due date, there is no default until midnight.

However, a provision which requires 'at least' or 'not less than' a specified number of days' notice to be given is often construed as requiring that number of 'clear' days, excluding not only the date on which the notice is served but also that on which it expires.[8]

Banking documents normally contain special provisions about the duration of periods expressed in terms of months, to ensure that such periods can only end on days on which banks and financial markets are open in the relevant financial centres. In the absence of such provision, the position is unclear, except in the case of a bill or promissory note falling within the Bills of Exchange Act 1882. In such a case, section 14(1) of that Act provides that a maturity date which would fall on a non-business day is postponed to the following business day. Subject to that, the position is unclear in the absence of express words. Under a charter which provides for payment of the hire in advance and entitles the owners to withdraw the vessel 'failing the punctual and regular payment of the hire', hire which falls due on a Sunday must be paid on the previous Friday.[9] However, in *Pritam Kaur v Russell & Sons Ltd*,[10] the Court of Appeal laid down a rule that, where a statute prescribes a period for doing an act which can only be done if the court office is open, and the period expires on a Sunday or other day on which the court office is closed, the act may be done on the next day when the office is open.

A trap arises from the rule that a clause specifying a period of 'six months from the date hereof' or 'three years commencing on the date of this Agreement' operates by reference to the date which happens to have been inserted at the commencement of the agreement even where that is not the date of true execution: the parties are

6 *Hammond v Haigh Castle & Co Ltd* [1973] 2 All ER 289; *Trow v Ind Coope (West Midlands) Ltd* [1967] 2 QB 899, [1967] 1 All ER 19; affd [1967] 2 All ER 900, CA; see also Order 3, rule 2, Rules of the Supreme Court.

7 [1983] 1 All ER 449, [1983] 1 WLR 195.

8 See, for example, *Re Hector Whaling Ltd* [1936] 1 Ch 208 on what is now section 378(2) of the Companies Act 1985.

9 *Mardorf Peach & Co Ltd v Attica Sea Carriers Corpn of Liberia* [1977] AC 850, [1977] 1 All ER 545.

10 [1973] QB 336, [1973] 1 All ER 617.

taken to have agreed that the deed or document should operate from its apparent date.[11]

Accordingly, in clauses of this type it is better to avoid such expressions as six months from 'the date hereof' and instead to refer to a period from a specified date typed into the deed or document before execution. In the case of a deed containing clauses the operation of which depends on the date that is specified, this practice also avoids the argument that, since the date of the deed controls the way in which its provisions operate, the date is a material part of the deed (contrary to the normal position) and can therefore be inserted after execution only under a power of attorney executed as a deed.

Inclusive/exclusive

A time provision should make it clear whether it is inclusive or exclusive of the first and last days by reference to which it is defined.

The following are ambiguous:

By	–	use 'on or before' instead
From	–	use instead either 'after' or 'from and excluding'. If it is intended to include the date referred to, use 'from and including'
Until	–	use 'to and including' or 'to but excluding'; *The Kiel*[12] illustrates the problems which can arise from 'until'
Between	–	state whether the period is to be inclusive or exclusive of the first day and the last day.

Excluded middle

Examples of common traps are:

whether before or after the date of this Agreement

the Vendor shall remain a director for two years if the profits are less than £5 million, and for four years if they are more than £5 million.

'Forthwith'

A clause may require a party to take certain action 'forthwith' after a particular event occurs. Although 'forthwith' is often regarded as synonymous with 'absolutely immediately', it may in certain contexts mean 'within a reasonable time', if no harm can result from this less stringent interpretation.[13] In *Sameen v Abeyewickrema*[14] the Privy

11 *Styles v Wardle* (1825) 4 B&C 908.
12 (1991) Financial Times, 8 March.
13 *Hillingdon London Borough Council v Cutler* [1968] 1 QB 124, [1967] 2 All ER 361, CA.
14 [1963] AC 597, [1963] 3 All ER 382.

Council considered a provision in the Civil Procedure Code of Ceylon which required an appellant, when his petition of appeal was received by the court, 'forthwith' to lodge a notice of security for the respondent's costs. Lord Dilhorne LC, delivering the advice, said:

> 'In many cases it may well be that unless the notice is filed the same day it cannot be said to be filed "forthwith," but it may be filed forthwith even though not filed the same day. Their Lordships do not propose to attempt to define "forthwith". The use of that word clearly connotes that the notice must be filed as soon as practicable, but what is practicable must depend upon the circumstances of each case.'

In *R v Secretary of State for Social Services, ex p Child Poverty Action Group*[15] the Court of Appeal construed a requirement that the DHSS ensure that a claim 'shall be submitted forthwith to an adjudication officer for determination' as not arising until the department was in possession of not only the claim form but the basic information necessary to enable the claim to be determined; however, once that information was available, the Department had to submit the claim 'as soon as reasonably possible'.

Even the word 'immediately' has been construed as meaning 'with all reasonable speed considering the circumstances of the case'.[16] There is also Court of Appeal authority for the proposition that 'as soon as possible' is stricter than 'as soon as reasonably practicable'.[17]

It may be that 'directly' has a firmer meaning than 'forthwith'. In *Duncan v Topham*[18] it was held that 'directly' means speedily, or at least as soon as practicable and not just 'within a reasonable time'. But that case shows that 'directly' does not mean 'instantaneously'.

In *R v Stratford-on-Avon District Council, ex p Jackson*[19] the Court of Appeal considered a provision requiring an application for judicial review to be made 'promptly and in any event within three months'. It held that the essential requirement was that the application had to be made 'promptly' and the fact that the application had been made within three months did not necessarily mean that this requirement had been met. In *Bank of Nova Scotia v Hellenic Mutual War Risks Association (Bermuda) Ltd The Good Luck*[20] the House of Lords declined to give 'promptly' a lax intepretation.

15 [1990] 2 QB 540, [1989] 1 All ER 1047.

16 *R v Inspector of Taxes, ex p Clarke* [1974] QB 220, [1972] 1 All ER 545, CA: see also *Hughes v Viner* [1985] 3 All ER 40.

17 *R v Dartmoor Prison Board of Visitors* [1986] 2 All ER 651 at 662.

18 (1849) 8 CB 225.

19 (1986) 51 P & CR 76.

20 (1991) Times, 17 May; contrast Lord Wilberforce's interpretation of the advice clause in *Bremer Handelsgesellschaft mbH v Vanden Avenne-Izegem PUBA* [1978] 2 Lloyd's Rep 109 at 113.

CHAPTER 15

CONDITIONS PRECEDENT AND TERMINATION CLAUSES

Conditions precedent

Conditions precedent clauses often have great business importance.[1] Care should be taken to make sure that a party is given the protection which he assumes he is getting and that there is no possible set of circumstances in which the clause might 'backfire' and operate against him.

The following list shows common defects of such clauses.

(a) The condition is so vague that it makes the entire agreement void for uncertainty. In *Lee-Parker v Izett (No 2)*[1a] a condition in a contract for the sale of a house that 'This sale is subject to the purchaser obtaining a satisfactory mortgagee' was void for uncertainty and also made the entire contract void. By contrast, in Scotland the Outer House has held that a condition precedent that 'detailed planning permission to the satisfaction of the purchaser shall be granted to the purchaser' required the purchaser to act reasonably.[2]

(b) The agreement does not expressly oblige the relevant party to ensure (or use reasonable endeavours to ensure) that the specified condition (eg the obtaining of an export licence or a landlord's consent) is satisfied. However, such an obligation may be implied: see, for example, the decision of the Court of Appeal in *Kyprianou v Cyprus Textiles Ltd*;[3] contrast the House of Lords' decision in *Czarnikow Ltd v Rolimpex*[4] that a clause requiring a seller to 'obtain' an export licence did not import an obligation to maintain it in force.

1 See Lord Goff of Chieveley's analysis of conditions precedent in *Bank of Nova Scotia v Hellenic Mutual War Risks Assn* [1991] 2 WLR 1279 at 1293–1296.
1a [1972] 2 All ER 800, [1972] 1 WLR 775.
2 *Gordon District Council v Wimpey Homes Holdings Ltd* 1988 SLT 481.
3 [1958] 2 Lloyd's Rep 60.
4 [1979] AC 351, [1972] 2 All ER 1043.

(c) No cut-off date is specified by which the condition has to be satisfied. A cut-off date should always be included to prevent the parties remaining under a contingent commitment indefinitely. Usually the appropriate party should be empowered to grant a single extension or several extensions. It is thought that, unless expressly stated, a power to grant an extension cannot be granted after the deadline has passed. An express power to grant an extension after the deadline is helpful where an unexpected contingency prevents a deadline being met; otherwise there has to be, in effect, a new agreement.

(d) The clause states that certain provisions are to come into force when a particular party has received certain documents meeting certain criteria. This leaves open the question of whether a document meets the required criteria and so whether the relevant provisions have come into force. A more satisfactory formula is: (1) to state that the provisions will come into force when a party notifies the other parties that it has received the required documents; (2) to make that notice conclusive; (3) to impose on the party concerned an express obligation to give that notice as soon as practicable after it has received all the necessary documents.

(e) The agreement as a whole is expressed to be made conditional on the matters concerned. Clearly this cannot be the case, since the clause which itself sets out the pre-conditions must necessarily come into force as soon as the agreement is signed. Similarly any governing law and jurisdiction clauses which the agreement contains. The formula 'This Agreement shall come into force when...' therefore leaves it unclear which clauses are of immediate effect and which are conditional. Instead, the clauses in each category should be specified. The provisions which need to be brought into force immediately normally include the general definitions clause and the clause on notices, and usually the representations and warranties since these speak, as of the date on which the agreement is signed. If there is a provision that all legal and other expenses connected with the agreement are to be paid by one party, this may need to be brought into force immediately, in which case it should be stated that the provision applies even if the specified conditions are not satisfied.

Termination clauses

Some agreements are signed on the basis that they will come into force immediately but will cease to operate if certain conditions are not met by a particular date. Other agreements give one party a right of termination if the other party commits certain breaches or it becomes clear that certain warranties made by the other party were not correct.

Termination clauses should be viewed in the light of general contract law principles. English law has three categories of contractual term. A 'condition' is a term a breach of which entitles the other party to treat himself as excused from further performance of the contract. A 'warranty' is a term a breach of which entitles the innocent party to damages, but not to treat himself as excused from its performance. An 'innominate' or 'intermediate' term is one a breach of which may entitle the innocent party to treat himself as excused from further performance or may entitle him only to damages, depending on the nature and consequences of the breach. This classification was laid down in the landmark judgment of Diplock LJ in *Hong Kong Fir Shipping Co Limited v Kawasaki Kisen Kaisha Ltd*,[5] as explained by the House of Lords in *Bunge Corpn v Tradax SA*.[6] Essentially, the difference between a condition and an innominate term is that *any* breach of a condition, irrespective of the gravity of the breach's results, entitles the innocent party to excuse himself from further performance; but a breach of an innominate term only does this if it has the effect of depriving the other party of substantially the whole benefit which it was the intention of the parties that he should obtain from the contract.[7]

A further point is that, when in the context of a breach of contract one speaks of 'termination', what is meant is no more than that the innocent party or, in some cases, both parties, are excused from further performance. The innocent party may then claim damages.[8] In *Johnson v Agnew*[9] the House of Lords approved the following statement of principle of Dixon J in *McDonald v Dennys Lascelles Ltd*:[10]

> 'When a party to a simple contract, upon a breach by the other contracting party of a condition of the contract, elects to treat the contract as no longer binding upon him, the contract is not rescinded as from the beginning. Both parties are discharged from the further performance of the contract, but rights are not divested or discharged which have already been unconditionally acquired. Rights and obligations which arise from the partial execution of the contract and causes of action which have accrued from its breach alike continue unaffected. When a contract is rescinded because of matters which affect its formation, as in the

5 [1962] 2 QB 26, [1962] 1 All ER 474.
6 [1981] 2 All ER 513 at 540.
7 The position is broadly similar under Articles 25, 49(1)(a) and 64(1)(a) of the 1980 Vienna Convention on the International Sale of Goods.
8 A good example of this is *Berger & Co Inc v Gill & Duffus SA* [1984] AC 382: see Lord Diplock's comments at 390H to 391E, 392D, 394G to 396B.
9 [1980] AC 367 at 396.
10 (1933) 48 CLR 457 at pp 476–477.

> case of fraud, the parties are to be rehabilitated and restored, so far as may be, to the position they occupied before the contract was made. But when a contract, which is not void or voidable at law, or liable to be set aside in equity, is dissolved at the election of one party because the other has not observed an essential condition or has committed a breach going to its root, the contract is determined so far as it is executory only and the party in default is liable for damages for its breach.'[11]

The contract itself is not 'terminated' or 'rescinded' in the sense of ceasing to exist. A clause excluding or limiting liability will remain in effect, although whether it actually covers the breach which has occurred is a question of interpretation.[12] An arbitration clause also remains in effect.[13] Nor does termination extinguish a party's right to be paid a sum on a date after the termination if the right was 'unconditionally acquired' before termination.[14]

To reflect the common law position, it is thought that normally a termination clause should state–

(a) that the parties shall be relieved from future performance of their obligations under the agreement;

(b) that any rights or obligations including prospective ones (and perhaps also contingent ones) to which a party has become entitled or subject before the termination of the agreement shall remain effective;

(c) that termination will not affect any right to damages which the party serving the termination notice may have in respect of the default giving rise to the termination or any other right to damages which either party may have in respect of any breach occurring before termination;

(d) that certain clauses of the agreement, for example, definitions governing law, jurisdiction and confidentiality shall remain in effect after termination. If the agreement contains indemnities, it is advisable to add a specific reference to these.

11 The first half of this statement was again approved by the House of Lords in *Bank of Boston Connecticut v European Grain and Shipping Ltd* [1989] AC 1056, 1098–1099.

12 *Photo Production Ltd v Securicor Transport Ltd* [1980] AC 827, [1980] 1 All ER 556, HL.

13 *Heyman v Darwins Ltd* [1942] AC 356, [1942] 1 All ER 337.

14 *Bank of Boston Connecticut v European Grain and Shipping Ltd* [1989] AC 1056 at 1009.

CHAPTER 16

AMENDMENTS

Many agreements are concerned with altering the terms of earlier documents. The traditional practice, still followed in the case of loan stock trust deeds, is to describe the amending document as a supplemental deed or agreement and to refer to the document being amended as 'the Principal Deed' or the 'Principal Agreement'. If further amendments might be made in subsequent years, the first amending document is described as 'this First Supplemental Trust Deed' or 'this First Supplemental Agreement'.

If an amending agreement is all one-way, in the sense that A makes concessions but receives nothing in return from the other parties, normal practice would be for the agreement to be executed as a deed to prevent A from arguing that it is not binding on him for lack of consideration. However, in *Anangel Atlas Cia Naviera SA v Ishikawajima-Harima Heavy Industries Co Ltd (No 2)*,[1] Hirst J rejected a claim that an agreement merely to embody and define a previously ill-defined understanding was not capable of constituting consideration, where the agreement was 'all one-way', the only limitations having been volunteered by one of the parties. Hirst J said this:

> 'Where parties clarify a previous ill-defined understanding in precise terms, defining both its scope and limitations, there is clearly consideration moving from both the sides, and it is immaterial that the main beneficiaries of the agreement themselves volunteered the limitations.'

This is in line with the modern approach described by Lord Hailsham of St Marylebone in *Woodhouse Ltd v Nigerian Produce Ltd*:[2]

> 'The buyers asked for a variation in the mode of discharge of a contract of sale. If the proposal ... was accepted and acted upon, I venture to

1 [1990] 2 Lloyd's Rep 526.
2 [1972] AC 741 at 757–758.

think that the vendors would have been bound by their acceptance at least until they gave reasonable notice to terminate, and I imagine that a modern court would have found no difficulty in discovering consideration for such a promise. Businessmen know their own business best even when they appear to grant an indulgence, and in the present case I do not think that there would have been insuperable difficulty in spelling out consideration...'

In *Williams v Roffey Bros & Nicholls (Contractors) Ltd*[3] Russell LJ said:

> 'Consideration there must still be but in my judgment the courts nowadays should be more ready to find its existence so as to reflect the intention of the parties to the contract where the bargaining powers are not unequal and where the finding of consideration reflects the true intention of the parties.'

Purchas LJ considered that the modern approach to the question of consideration is that where there are benefits derived by each party to a contract of variation, even though one party does not suffer a detriment, this is not fatal to establishing consideration.

The special status of composition agreements was described by Sir George Jessel MR in *Couldery v Bartrum*.[4] A composition agreement is one by which an insolvent person's creditors agree to accept a percentage of the amounts owing to them in full satisfaction of their debts, but Sir George Jessel's observations are equally applicable to a pure rescheduling, that is an agreement which postpones the repayment dates without any write-off:

> 'According to English Common Law a creditor might accept anything in satisfaction of his debt except a less amount of money. He might take a horse, or a canary, or a tomtit if he chose, and that was accord and satisfaction; but, by a most extraordinary peculiarity of the English Common Law, he could not take 19s 6d in the pound; that was nudum pactum. Therefore, although the creditor might take a canary, yet, if the debtor did not give him a canary together with his 19s 6d, there was no accord and satisfaction; if he did, there was accord and satisfaction. That was one of the mysteries of English Common Law. ... But, that being so, there came a class of arrangements between creditors and debtors, by which a debtor who was unable to pay in full offered a composition of something less in the pound. Well, it was felt to be a very absurd thing that the creditors could not bind themselves to take less than the amount of their debts ... and, as every debtor had not a stock of canary-birds or tomtits, or rubbish of that kind, to add to his dividend, it was felt desirable to bind the creditors in a sensible way by saying that, if they all agreed, there should be a consideration

3 [1990] 1 All ER 512 at 524.

4 (1881) 19 ChD 394. Jessel's speech in the House of Commons on the Bankruptcy Bill of 1868 had prompted Gladstone to offer him the Solicitor-Generalship.

imported from the agreement constituting an addition to the dividend, so as to make the agreement no longer nudum pactum, but an agreement made for valuable consideration; then there would be satisfaction. Consequently, if the creditors came in and all agreed inter se to take 10s in the pound, the agreement inter se supplied the additional consideration which was supposed to be necessary, and the debts were satisfied – so satisfied, that, if one of the creditors obtained an unfair advantage, a Court of Equity actually interfered, and allowed the debtor to recover back the surplus from him, because he was not entitled to take from the debtor anything more than the composition. The principle upon which the creditor was made to repay was, that his debt was satisfied, and that he had no right to take an unfair advantage.'

A deed is not normally required to vary another deed.[5] This is so even where the original document is a lease which had to be made by deed under section 52 of the Law of Property Act 1925. It used to be possible for a power of attorney executed as a deed to be extended by a simple letter,[6] and this is thought to remain the position, although the Powers of Attorney Act 1971 now requires a power of attorney to be granted by a deed.

A typical amending clause

The following illustrates the normal method of making amendments:

Clause to be amended
3 (1) The aggregate amount payable for the shares is £3 million, payable as follows:–

(a) £1 million on the date of this Agreement;
(b) £1 million on 30th June 1992;
(c) £1 million on 31st December 1992.

(2) The instalment mentioned in subclause 1(c) shall become immediately payable if the instalment mentioned in subclause (1)(b) is not paid on 30th June 1992.

(3) From and including the date of this Agreement the outstanding amount of the instalments mentioned in subclause (1)(b) and (c) shall carry interest at a rate per annum equal to the base lending rate of the Surrey Bank plc plus 4 per cent.

Amendments
1 (1) Clause 3 of the Principal Agreement is amended as follows.

(2) In subclauses (1)(b) and (2) '30th June' is replaced by '15 March'.

5 *Mitas v Hyams* [1951] 2 TLR 1215; *Plymouth Corpn v Harvey* [1971] 1 All ER 623, [1971] 1 WLR 549.
6 *Reckitt v Barnett, Pembroke and Slater Ltd* [1929] AC 176.

(3) In subclause (3) after 'interest' there is inserted 'until they are paid and as well after as before judgment'.

(4) In subclause (3) 'plus 4 per cent' is omitted.

(5) The following subclause is added:
'(4) The instalment mentioned in subclause (1)(c) shall be reduced by the amount which the Auditors' report states is due to the Purchaser under clause 6 below.'

However, if several amendments are to be made to a particular clause or subclause, it is usually more convenient to set out the new provision in its entirety. If a phrase consisting of, say, more than ten words has to be deleted, it is usual to identify it by a formula such as:

> The words from and including 'the Company' (where those words appear for a second time) to and including 'on demand'.[7]

Care should be taken to ensure that the language of a new provision is consistent with that of the existing agreement into which it is inserted. In particular, the new provision should make use of any relevant defined terms in the existing agreement.

Renumbering

Although it is common to renumber when a clause or subclause is inserted or omitted, this is unnecessary and can be confusing.

A new clause or subclause can be designated with the number of the clause or subclause after which it is inserted and the letter A, B and so on. For example, the Companies Act 1989 inserted a new section (about general commercial companies) after section 3 of the 1985; because the new section was numbered 3A, sections 4 to 747 did not have to be renumbered. Likewise, the three new sections (about written resolutions) inserted after section 381 were numbered 381A, 381B and 381C.

Similar numbering is used for new subsections. For instance, two new subsections have been inserted in section 437 of the Companies Act 1985; after subsection (1) a new subsection (1A) was inserted by the Financial Services Act 1986; after which a new subsection (1B) was added by the Companies Act 1989; meanwhile subsections (2) and (3) kept their original numbering.

At paragraph level, new insertions are designated (aa), (bb) and so on. For example, the new paragraph inserted by the Courts and Legal Services Act 1990 after paragraph (a) in section 54(4) of the Supreme Court Act 1981 was designated (aa), which avoided renumbering paragraphs (b) to (e); and in section 153(4) of the Companies Act 1985 a new paragraph (bb) was inserted by the Financial Services Act 1986 after paragraph (b).

7 Compare Interpretation Act 1978, s 20.

A good example of the statutory technique is section 449 of the Companies Act 1985 which has been amended by the Insolvency Act 1985, the Insolvency Act 1986, the Financial Services Act 1986, the Banking Act 1987 and the Companies Act 1989.

Nor, according to the statutory practice, is renumbering necessary when a provision is deleted. When the Insolvency Act 1986 repealed sections 488 to 650 of the Companies Act 1985, it did not renumber section 651 and the sections following it. There has been no renumbering of the Law of Property Act 1925 to take account of the repeals of sections 40 and 73 by the Law of Property (Miscellaneous Provisions) Act 1989. In section 125 of the 1925 Act the repeal of subsection (1) did not lead to subsections (2) and (3) being renumbered.

Novation

A common type of amendment replaces a party to an agreement by another person. A party's rights can be assigned (subject to the possibility that the amending agreement might thereby become chargeable to stamp duty), but it is normally considered that obligations cannot be assigned.[7] Accordingly, the party to be replaced is released from his obligations, and the party replacing him undertakes to perform them. The following is a typical 'novation' clause. The purpose of subclause (4)(b) is to make it clear that notice of the assignment has been given in accordance with section 136 of the Law of Property Act 1925; and subclause (5)(b) is intended to cover provisions, such as a clause excluding or limiting liability, which do not create 'obligations', but which would nevertheless have been 'binding' on A:

(1) The following has effect for ensuring that B completely replaces A as a party to the Principal Agreement.

(2) A as beneficial owner assigns to B absolutely all A's interests and rights under the Principal Agreement.

(3) The other parties to the Principal Agreement agree–

(a) that, without limiting the generality of that assignment, it entitles B in its own right to exercise all rights of a discretionary nature which the Principal Agreement confers on A, including any right to make a determination; and

(b) that this Agreement constitutes express notice in writing to them of that assignment.

(4) Without prejudice to the next subclause, each of the other parties to the Principal Agreement unconditionally releases A from all its obligations under the Principal Agreement.

7 However, see *Tito v Waddell (No 2)* [1977] Ch 106, [1977] 3 All ER 129, considered in Chapter 2 above.

(5) However, A remains bound by all the provisions of the Principal Agreement which are intended to exclude or restrict the liability of any of the other parties to it for negligence (as defined in section 1 of the Unfair Contract Terms Act 1977) or breach of any fiduciary duty.

(6) B undertakes with each of the parties to the Principal Agreement except A–

(a) to observe, perform and discharge all the obligations which, but for the foregoing release, A would have had under the Principal Agreement; and
(b) to be bound by all the provisions of the Principal Agreement.

(7) All references, whether express or implied, in the Principal Agreement to A shall take effect as references to B.

(8) In this clause 'obligations' includes liabilities and 'rights' includes powers.

(9) This clause takes effect on 1st January 1993.

Effective date

It is important for an amending agreement to specify whether the amendments come into effect when the amending agreement is signed, on a particular date, or when certain conditions are fulfilled. It is also important that the agreement should address how it will affect transactions which are in progress, but not completed, on the date when the amendments come into effect; in a banking context, this includes interest payable for a period, part of which falls before the effective date.

Boiler-plate

A common problem is how fully the 'boiler-plate' of the principal agreement (such as the definitions clause and the clauses about notices, applicable law and submission to jurisdiction) has to be reproduced in the amending agreement. There are three main options.

The first is to include the following in the amending agreement:

> This Agreement shall be read and shall take effect as one with the Principal Agreement.

This is a common statutory formula which makes the definitions and procedural provisions of the principal Act apply to the later Act, 'unless there is some manifest discrepancy, making it necessary to hold that that the later Act has to some extent modified something found in the earlier Act'.[8] However, the formula is rather technical and seldom understood by non-lawyers. One particular result of the formula is that, if the principal agreement contains a clause providing for all the legal expenses connected with that agreement to be borne by one party, that is extended to the legal expenses connected with the amending agreement.

The second option is a clause stating that certain specified provisions of the principal agreement apply for the purposes of the amending agreement as if references in those provisions to the principal agreement were references to the amending agreement. The specified provisions will be the definitions clause, the boiler-plate clauses and, in an international agreement, applicable law and jurisdiction.

The third option is a modified version of the second, but with the applicable law clause and the submission to the jurisdiction of the courts of England (or the other selected state) being set out in full since these provisions would be important in the event of litigation. Similarly, an arbitration clause would be set out in full.

8 See, for example, *Phillips v Parnaby* [1934] 2 KB 299.

CHAPTER 17

SET-OFF AND RIGHT OF RETENTION

The question of whether a party to a contract has a valid right of set-off or retention in respect of amounts which he would otherwise have to pay under the contract is often of practical importance; particularly if the other party becomes insolvent. If A is obliged to pay £1000 to B but has a claim against B for £800, and B is insolvent, A will only be able to obtain full settlement of his claim against B if he can use it to reduce his own debt to £200.

This chapter outlines the three types of set-off available under the general law in the absence of express agreement; considers the grounds on which any express right of set-off or retention can be invalid; and examines how such a right can be affected by the other party to the contract assigning the contract or going into liquidation.

Set-off under the general law

Essentially, set-off is procedural, in the sense of being a defence, normally to a monetary claim, but sometimes to a suit for specific performance if brought in respect of a breach of a payment obligation. In High Court proceedings, the defence of set-off is governed by Order 18, rule 17 of the Rules of the Supreme Court:

> 'Where a claim by a defendant to a sum of money (whether of an ascertained amount or not) is relied on as a defence to the whole or part of a claim made by the plaintiff, it may be included in the defence and set-off against the plaintiff's claim, whether or not it is also added as a counter-claim.'

Three points are notable. First, the rule does not itself define the conditions which a cross-claim must meet in order to constitute a valid set-off. However, the rule expressly provides that the defendant's claim has to be to a sum of money, but does not need to be liquidated. Third, nothing in the rule requires the plaintiff's claim, against which the set-off is asserted, to be to a sum of money.

The general law recognises two types of set-off, in the strict sense of the term, and a third right similar to set-off.[1]

At common law, originally there was, in general, no right of set-off. If a defendant were owed a debt by the plaintiff, the defendant had to commence a separate action and could not set up the plaintiff's debt as a defence to the latter's claim. The Statutes of Set-off were passed in 1729 and 1735 to remedy this. The first statute provided that, if there were mutual debts between a plaintiff and a defendant, one debt might be set against the other. But, under both that statute and the statute of 1735, the claims on both sides had to be liquidated debts or money demands which could be ascertained with certainty at the time of pleading. The Statutes of Set-off were repealed in 1879 and 1883, but subject to a saving for any jurisdiction or principle or rule of law of equity established or confirmed. This saving enables a defendant to assert a right of set-off which he would have had under the repealed statutes.[2] A right of that kind is a legal set-off.

Until the Supreme Court of Judicature Acts 1873 and 1875, courts of equity had the power to prohibit by injunction the enforcement of a common law claim where there was a cross-claim which they regarded as being of an appropriate character. Section 24 of the 1873 Act took away that power and provided instead that such a cross-claim could be raised as a defence. That section's provisions are, in effect, re-enacted in section 49 of the Supreme Court Act 1981. Equitable set-off is principally relevant to claims for damages, since only a liquidated claim qualifies as a legal set-off.

The classic formulation of the criterion for whether a cross-claim constitutes an equitable set-off against a common law claim was that it had to be such as 'impeached' the title to the legal demand.[3] However, a different test was adopted by the House of Lords in *Bank of Boston Connecticut v European Grain and Shipping Ltd*.[4] This test is based on the statement of Lord Hobhouse in *Government of Newfoundland v Newfoundland Rly Co*:[5]

> 'Unliquidated damages may ... be set off as between the original parties, and also against an assignee if flowing out of and inseparably connected with the dealings and transactions which also give rise to the subject of the assignment [ie the debt on which the defendant is being sued].'

1 A bank's right to combine accounts is not a right of set-off which postulates mutual but independent obligations between the two parties, but an accounting right: see Buckley LJ's statement in *Halesowen Presswork and Assemblies Ltd v Westminster Bank* [1971] 1 QB 1 at 46E; also *Bhogal v Punjab National Bank* [1988] 2 All ER 296.

2 See the explanation of Morris LJ (as he then was) in *Hanak v Green* [1958] 2 QB 9 at 17 and 22.

3 *Rawson v Samuel* (1839) 1 Cr & Ph 161; see also the formulation of Goff LJ in *Federal Commerce and Navigation Co Ltd v Molena Alpha* [1978] QB 927 at 981.

4 [1989] AC 1056, [1989] 1 All ER 545.

5 (1888) 13 App Cas 199.

The *Government of Newfoundland* case arose out of a contract between a railway company and the government under which the company agreed to construct a railway line of 340 miles in five years and, having done so, to maintain and operate it. In return, the government agreed to pay the company an annual subsidy for 35 years, the subsidy to be paid in proportionate parts as and when each five-mile section of the line was completed and operating. The company built part of the line, but abandoned the remainder, upon which the government refused to make any further subsidy payments. The company, together with certain assignees of its rights under the contract, brought a petition of right against the government, claiming that the government was bound to continue payment of the subsidy in respect of the five-mile sections of the line which had been completed. The Privy Council held that the government was bound by the terms of the contract to continue these payments as claimed; but that it was entitled, as against both the company and the assignees, to set off against that liability the damage suffered by it as a result of the company's failure to complete the line.

In *BICC plc v Burndy Corpn*[6] the Court of Appeal (Kerr LJ dissenting) held that any set-off (legal or equitable) can be used as a defence to a non-monetary relief in respect of a breach of payment obligation. The case arose out of an agreement dealing with patents in which two companies had a joint interest. The agreement provided that BICC was to be responsible for processing and maintaining the joint rights and that Burndy was to reimburse BICC for the expenses they incurred in doing that. The agreement also provided that a party which failed to fulfil its obligations could be required to assign to the innocent party all its interests in the joint rights. BICC incurred expenses, but Burndy failed to reimburse them within the time fixed by the agreement. BICC then claimed that they were entitled to an assignment of Burndy's interest in the joint patents. They brought an action for the specific performance of the agreement to assign. Burndy's defence was that they were entitled to set off far greater sums due to them from BICC under the agreement. The Court of Appeal held that this legal set-off could be used (a) as a defence to the action against them for specific performance (Kerr LJ dissenting), and (b) together with other facts, as a basis for obtaining equitable relief against forfeiture of their interest in the joint patents.

It used to be thought that a right of set-off could not be waived. However, the decision of Hirst J in *Hong Kong and Shanghai Banking Corpn v Kloeckner & Co AG*[7] establishes that an undertaking to make payment 'without any discount, deduction, off-set, or counter-claim

6 [1985] Ch 232, [1985] 1 All ER 417.

7 [1990] 2 QB 514. See also judgment of Cairns LJ (as he then was) in *Re Agra and Masterman's Bank, ex p Asiatic Banking Corpn* (1867) 2 Ch App 391 at 397.

whatsoever' is valid. By contrast, the statutory set-off which applies in a bankruptcy or a winding up cannot be waived (see below).

'Abatement', the third right, is similar to set-off but is confined to contracts for the sale of goods and for work and labour. When a claim is made for the price of goods sold and delivered with a warranty or for work and labour done, the defendant is entitled to set up against the amount claimed any damages which he has suffered as a result of the plaintiff's breach of the warranty or contract.[8] This principle is given statutory effect by section 53 of the Sale of Goods Act 1979. Subsection (1) provides that where there is a breach of warranty by the seller, or where the buyer elects to treat a breach of condition as a breach of warranty, the buyer is not by reason only of the breach of warranty entitled to reject the goods; but he may–

(a) set up against the seller the breach of warranty in diminution or extinction of the price; or

(b) maintain an action against the seller for damages for breach of warranty.

Subsection (4) provides that the fact that the buyer has set up a breach of warranty in diminution or extinction of the price does not prevent him from suing on the same breach of warranty if he has suffered further damage.

In *Gilbert Ash (Northern) Ltd v Modern Engineering (Bristol) Ltd*[9] Lord Diplock stated that, unlike equitable set-off, abatement is available as of right to a party to a contract for the sale of goods or for work and labour. The court has no discretion to withhold it. A further distinction is that abatement is not a 'mere procedural rule designed to avoid circuity of action but a substantive defence at common law'. Lord Diplock also said that the right to abatement can be excluded by the contract, but that, since it is presumed that neither party intends to abandon any remedy which arises by operation of law, clear words must be used in order to negative the right to abatement.

Contractual set-off and retention

A contract can provide what is, in effect, a right of set-off where such a right would not otherwise be available under the general law. In particular, where there would be no equitable set-off because

8 A benign rule of the common law exempts contracts with solicitors from claims for abatement except where the lawyer's negligence has been such as to deprive his client of 'all possibility of benefit' from the lawyer's services: *Templer v M'Lachlan* (1806) 2 Bos & PNR 136.
9 [1974] AC 689, [1973] 3 All ER 195.

the two claims are not connected with the same transaction, the parties may, by their contract, establish a connection and provide that the claims shall go 'in liquidation' of each other and that 'the balance only be considered as the debt between the parties'.[10]

A similar type of provision is a retention clause which entitles A to withhold payment of sums which would otherwise be due to B if B commits a breach of the agreement. For example, it is common for an agreement for the sale of a private company to provide that the purchaser may withhold all or part of the consideration in the event that the warranties made by the vendor about the financial position of the company being sold prove to be incorrect. Unlike the clause considered in the previous paragraph, a retention clause does not, in terms, liquidate or extinguish the liability to pay the amount concerned.

A set-off or retention clause should deal with the following points:

(a) If cross-claims could arise in different currencies, can these be set off and, if so, what is the exchange rate at which one cross-claim should be translated into the currency of another?

(b) Can a debt payable at a future date be set off against a debt payable at an earlier date and, if so, at what rate is the first debt to be discounted?

(c) Is a liability, the existence of which is contingent (eg a liability under a guarantee for a fixed sum before any default by the principal debtor), eligible for set-off and, if so, on what basis is the liability to be valued?

(d) Is a liability which is certain but the amount of which is unascertained (eg a liability for unliquidated damages) eligible for set-off and, if so, how is the liability to be estimated?

Possible challenges to set-off and retention clauses

There are three main grounds on which a set-off or retention clause can be challenged. The first is as a penalty. The contract which featured in *Gilbert Ash v Modern Engineering*[11] provided:

> 'If the sub-contractor fails to comply with any of the conditions of this sub-contract, the contractor reserves the right to suspend or withhold payment of any monies due or becoming due to the sub-contractor.'

Four of the Law Lords said this was a penalty. Lord Reid pointed out that there was no reference to the amount of the contractor's

10 *Watson v Mid Wales Railway Co* (1867) LR 2 CP 593, 600 as explained in *Government of Newfoundland v Newfoundland Rly Co* (1888) 13 App Cas 199 at 210.

11 [1974] AC 689, [1973] 3 All ER 195.

claim and no requirement that before withholding payment he need even estimate the amount of his claim. Read literally, the provision would entitle the contractor to withhold sums far in excess of any fair estimate of the value of his claims. That would, Lord Reid said, 'simply be to impose a penalty for refusing to admit his claims.' The provision was unenforceable. By contrast, it is thought that a provision would not be a penalty if it entitles a party to withhold only the amount which he reasonably estimates that he is entitled to recover as damages in respect of the other party's breach.

Two other challenges to a retention clause were attempted in *Re Charge Card Services Ltd.*[12] At issue was a clause in a factoring agreement which entitled the factoring company to withhold from the amount which it would otherwise have to pay for the receivables any amount which it might 'in its absolute discretion decide to retain as security' for amounts payable under the agreement by the company selling the receivables. Another clause stated that, if the selling company went into liquidation, the factoring company could require it to repurchase those of the receivables sold by it which were still outstanding. The first ground on which the retention clause was attacked was as a charge on the selling company's book debts which was void for lack of registration under section 395 of the Companies Act 1985. Millett J rejected the claim that the right of retention was a charge. It was, he held, 'conceptually impossible' for a person under an obligation to pay a sum of money to take a charge over that obligation to secure the payment of a debt owing to him by the payee. The second objection was that the retention clause created a right of set-off was wider than that permitted in a liquidation by the relevant legislation. Millett J rejected that argument also, but it is clear from his judgment that a set-off or retention clause is ineffective in a party's liquidation to the extent that the clause purports to confer rights wider than those available under the insolvency legislation.

Effect of assignment

If a party has a valid right of set-off against the other party to the contract, can he also assert that right against a person who takes an assignment[13] from the other party of the benefit of the contract? The classic statement of principle is that of James LJ (as he then was) in *Roxburghe v Cox*:[14]

> 'Now an assignee of a chose in action ... takes subject to all rights of set off and all other defences which were available against the assignor,

12 [1987] Ch 150, [1986] 3 All ER 289.

13 This includes the crystallisation of a floating charge: *George Barker (Transport) Ltd v Eynon* [1974] 1 All ER 900, [1974] 1 WLR 462.

14 (1881) 17 ChD 520 at 526.

> subject only to this exception, that after notice of an assignment of a chose in action the debtor cannot by payment or otherwise do anything to take away or diminish the rights of the assignee as they stood at the time of the notice. That is the sole exception.'

This principle applies to both an equitable assignment and a legal assignment under section 136 of the Law of Property Act 1925. Although the section uses the phrase 'subject to equities', it is clear that it leaves open to the debtor proper legal and equitable defences.[14] An important point is that section 136 does not enable a bona fide purchaser of the legal title to a chose in action to acquire a title free of equities (for example, a prior equitable charge) of which he has no notice.[15]

In *Business Computers Ltd v Anglo-African Leasing Ltd,*[16] Templeman J (as he then was) said:

> 'The result of the relevant authorities is that a debt which accrues due before notice of an assignment is received, whether or not it is payable before that date, or a debt which arises out of the same contract as that which gives rise to the assigned debt, or is closely connected with that contract, may be set off against the assignee. But a debt which is neither accrued nor connected may not be set off even though it arises from a contract made before the assignment.'

It is thought that this statement requires qualification in the light of *Bank of Boston Connecticut v European Grain and Shipping Ltd*[17] in which the House of Lords approved (at 1102G) the statement of Lord Hobhouse in the *Government of Newfoundland* case[18] that there is no universal rule that claims arising out of the same contract may be set against one another in all circumstances. It is therefore considered that only two categories of debt can safely be regarded as eligible for set-off against an assignee:

(a) a debt owed by B to A which, before A receives notice that B has assigned A's debt to B, has 'accrued due'; this means that B's debt must have crystallised into an actual debt, as opposed to a contingent liability, not that it must have fallen due for payment; B's debt must, however, be payable before the debt of A which B has assigned;[19]

(b) a debt from B to A which has not 'accrued due' before A receives notice that B has assigned A's debt to him but which flows out of, and is inseparably connected with, the same transaction

14 See the judgment of Hobhouse J in the *European Grain* case [1987] 1 Lloyd's Rep 239 at 252, approved in the House of Lords at [1989] AC 1056 at 1110H.
15 *Pfeiffer GmbH v Arbuthnot Factors Ltd* [1988] 1 WLR 150 at 162.
16 [1977] 2 All ER 741 at 748.
17 [1989] AC 1056.
18 (1888) 13 App Cas 199 at 212.
19 *Re Pinto Leite & Nephews* [1929] 1 Ch 221.

as A's debt; the main example is a claim by A against B for unliquidated damages which is 'inseparably connected' with the transaction giving rise to the debt owed by A which B has assigned.

In addition, where a contract limits a party's payment obligations to a net sum after deducting an amount which would otherwise be due from the other party, it is clear that an assignee can recover no more than the net sum, regardless of whether, at the time of the assignment, he had notice of the provision for net payment.[20] Although this is not a case of set-off, it seems likely that even sums which 'accrue due' after the notice of assignment are deductible in computing the net amount payable to the assignee.

It follows that the safest method of ensuring that a party will have a valid right of set-off, which will also be effective against an assignee, is to include a clause in the following form:

> Each party acknowledges that any claim which the Purchaser may have under clause 6 in respect of the Warranties, and the claims of the Vendor under clause 4 in respect of the consideration for the Sale Shares, will flow out of, and be inseparably connected with, the same transaction; accordingly, these claims may be set off against each other, and this includes a claim that a party has for an amount which has not accrued due before he receives notice that the claim against him has been assigned.

In a bankruptcy or liquidation the validity of such a provision is subject to the relevant insolvency legislation: see below.

When a petition is presented for an administration order, section 10 of the Insolvency Act 1986 protects the company's property against steps being taken 'to enforce any security' over it. If the petition is successful, section 11 continues this protection while the administration order remains in force. Sections 10 and 11 also prohibit the commencement or continuation of proceedings against the company. It is thought that these sections do not prevent a defendant to an action by a company in administration pleading as a defence a set-off or abatement which has arisen in the ordinary course of events; but that they may well preclude the assertion of a contractual right of set-off or retention expressly designed to provide security. The judgment of Sir Nicolas Browne-Wilkinson V-C in *Bristol Airport plc v Powdrill*[1] indicates that the court will adopt a wide interpretation of these sections if that is necessary to prevent the clear policy of the provisions about administrations from being frustrated, provided that the words concerned are fairly capable of such an interpretation.[2]

20 *Mangles v Dixon* (1852) 3 HLC 702.

1 [1990] Ch 744 at 758–761, also the decision of Hasman J in *Exchange Travel Agency Ltd v Triton Property Trust plc* [1991] 12 LS Gaz R 33.

2 There is also a statement by Millett J in *Re Charge Card Services Ltd* [1987] Ch 150 at 177A-B, equating a contractual right of set-off to 'a security'.

Liquidation and bankruptcy set-off

Where a company is being wound up in England,[3] set-off is governed by rule 4.90 of the Insolvency Rules 1986 made under the Insolvency Act of that year. The rule does not apply in an administration or an administrative receivership, where the position is governed by the general law principles previously considered. Rule 4.90 does not merely confer a right to set-off, but also imposes a mandatory requirement for set-off between debts to which it applies; and this requirement cannot be dissapplied by a contract between the parties.[4]

A debt is not within rule 4.90 unless it satisfies three requirements:

(a) it must arise out of 'mutual credits, mutual debts or other mutual dealings' between the company and the creditor which took place before the company went into liquidation;

(b) the debt must be one for which the creditor is proving in the liquidation or, it seems, for which he would be entitled to prove but for the set-off; in other words, rule 4.90 does not apply to a debt in respect of which a creditor relies on his security;

(c) the debt must be 'due' at the time at which the account which the rule requires falls to be taken.

'Mutual dealings' has a wide meaning and covers most transactions between the company in liquidation and the creditor which may give rise to rights or liabilities between them.[5] However, 'mutual dealings' does not cover a transaction in which property is made over for a special, or specific, purpose.[6]

Where rule 4.90 applies, three things have to be done. First, an account has to be taken of what is due from the company in liquidation to the creditor and from the creditor to the company. Second, there has to be a set-off. Third, the net balance, if adverse to the company, is provable in the liquidation or, if adverse to the creditor, must be paid by him to the liquidator.

It seems clear that a debt payable at a future date is within the set-off under rule 4.90.[7] It also seems from the judgment of Lord

3 The English courts have jurisdiction to wind up a company incorporated abroad: *Re A Company (No 00359 of 1987)* [1988] Ch 210, [1987] 3 WLR 339.
4 *National Westminster Bank Ltd v Halesowen Presswork & Assemblies Ltd* [1972] AC 785, [1972] 1 All ER 641.
5 See 3(2) Halsbury's Laws 535.
6 *National Westminister Bank v Halesowen Press Work* [1972] AC 785.
7 See *Re Pinto Leite & Nephews* [1929] 1 Ch 221 at 236 and the report of the Review Committee on Insolvency Law and Practice (1982) (Cmnd 8558) paragraph 1352.

Hardwicke LC in *Re Prescot, ex p Prescot*[8] that, where a debt payable at a future date is owed by the company in liquidation, only its discounted present value is brought into the set-off account, but that, where such a debt is owed by a creditor, the full face value is set off.

It also seems that both a liability, the very existence of which is still contingent when the company goes into liquidation, and a liability which is then certain but the amount of which is then unascertainable, are within the rule, provided that this condition is satisfied: that by the time the account required by the rule has to be taken, the liability has matured into 'a quantified money claim' in the natural course of events, that is to say, without any fresh agreement, but solely by virtue of a contract already existing at the date of the commencement of the winding up.[9]

It has been suggested that a creditor is entitled to set off an unmatured contingent liability at its value estimated under rule 4.86. However, the judgment of Millett J in *Re Charge Card Services Ltd* contains repeated statements to the effect that a creditor can only set off a contingent liability of the company in liquidation if, by the time he claims the set-off, the liability has matured into a quantified money claim as a result of the contingency having occurred.[10]

Therefore, where a contract gives rise to a liability the existence of which is contingent or the amount of which may remain unascertained for some time, there should be a mechanism which will ensure that, if the party under the liability goes into liquidation, the liability will 'mature into a quantified money claim' at the latest shortly after the liquidation commences in order for it to be available for set-off under rule 4.90.

Paragraph (3) of rule 4.90 excludes from the set-off certain debts due from the company in liquidation. These are debts in respect of which the creditor had notice 'at the time they became due' that a meeting of creditors had been summoned under section 98 of the Insolvency Act 1986 or that a winding-up petition was pending. It is thought that this reference in paragraph (3) to a debt becoming 'due' has a different meaning from the word 'due' in paragraph (2) where it means 'mature into a quantified money claim'. It seems that paragraph (3) only excludes a debt (a) which arises under a contract entered into by the creditor with the company, or (b) which the creditor buys in from a third party, in either case, after the

8 (1753) 1 Atk 230.

9 *Re Charge Card Services Ltd* [1987] Ch 150 rejecting the opinion of Peter Gibson J in *Carreras Rothman Ltd v Freeman Mathews Treasure Ltd* [1985] Ch 207 at 230 that a liability cannot be set off if its existence was still contingent at the commencement of the liquidation.

10 Ibid at 180B, 182E, 187H, 190D and 190F.

creditor has notice that a section 98 meeting has been summoned or that a petition is pending.[11]

Section 323 of the Insolvency Act 1986 makes similar provision in a bankruptcy as that made by rule 4.90 in a liquidation.

11 This is based on the view expressed by letter by the Department of Trade and Industry (see *Insolvency* by Peter Totty and Michael Jordan, Longman E9.28) that the rule was not intended to change the law: compare the exclusion in section 31 of the Bankruptcy Act 1914. The notion that the word 'due' must necessarily have the same meaning in paragraph (3) as in paragraph (2) is untenable in the light of the statement of the House of Lords in *Payne v Barratt Developments* [1985] 1 All ER 257 at 260F that, 'The rule that the same word occurring more than once in an enactment should be given the same meaning wherever it occurs is a guide which must yield to indications of contrary intention.'

CHAPTER 18

BOILER-PLATE

This chapter considers common 'boiler-plate' clauses which can have considerable practical importance.

Force majeure

It is common for a contract to provide that a particular party, or each party, shall not have any liability for a failure to perform which is caused by an external event beyond its control. A clause of this type in a commercial contract is usually called a 'force majeure' clause. In 1988, the European Commission issued a notice[1] as to the meaning of 'force majeure' in Community legislation, particularly regarding agriculture. However, in English law 'force majeure' is not a term of art. An agreement which is otherwise precise and contains the phrase 'subject to force majeure' is a valid and enforceable contract; but it is void for uncertainty if it contains the phrase 'subject to force majeure *clauses*', since these vary widely from contract to contract.[2]

Force majeure clauses have to be considered against the background of the doctrine of frustration. A force majeure clause may cover events to which the doctrine of frustration does not apply; and, if an event occurs to which the doctrine does apply, the clause may provide for consequences different to those which would ensue under the doctrine, for example, by keeping the contract in existence, while protecting the party who cannot perform against a claim for damages. The classic formulation of the doctrine is that by Lord Radcliffe in *Davis Contractors Ltd v Fareham UDC*:[3]

1 Commission notice C(88) 1696: see Appendix below.
2 *British Electrical and Associated Industries (Cardiff) Ltd v Patley Pressings Ltd* [1953] 1 All ER 94, [1953] 1 WLR 280.
3 [1956] AC 696 at 729 see also the observations of Lord Diplock and Lord Roskill in *Pioneer Shipping v BTP Tioxide*; [1982] AC 724 at 744B and 752A.

'...frustration occurs whenever the law recognises that without default of either party a contractual obligation has become incapable of being performed because the circumstances in which performance is called for would render it a thing radically different from that which was undertaken by the contract. Non haec in foedera veni. It was not this that I promised to do.'[4]

The following points were made by Bingham LJ in *The 'Super Servant Two'*.[5] The question is whether the contract is, on its true construction, wide enough to apply to the new situation: if it is not, then it is at an end. The doctrine of frustration was evolved to mitigate the rigour of the common law's insistence on literal performance of absolute promises. The object of the doctrine is to achieve a just and reasonable result where injustice would result from enforcing a contract in its literal terms after a significant change in circumstances. The essence of frustration is that it should not be due to the act or the election of the party seeking to rely on it; and a frustrating event must take place without blame or fault on the side of that party. Frustration brings the contract to an end forthwith and automatically. Since the effect of frustration is to kill the contract and discharge the parties from liability under it, the doctrine is not to be lightly invoked and must be kept within very narrow limits.

An important point is that a contract is not frustrated because it has become considerably more expensive or onerous for a party to perform it:

'...it is not hardship or inconvenience or material loss itself which calls the principle of frustration into play. There must be as well such a change in the significance of the obligation that the thing undertaken would, if performed, be a different thing from that contracted for.'[6]

It also seems that a contract is not frustrated if the event in issue still leaves a party with sufficient means to satisfy that contract although not all his outstanding contracts and he elects to use those means to satisfy his other contracts.[7]

The following is a typical force majeure clause:

(1) Subject to subclause (3), the Contractor shall have no liability for a consequence of any of the following events if that event and consequence was neither preventable nor foreseeable:–

(a) a flood, storm or other natural event; or
(b) any war, hostilities, revolution, riot or civil disorder; or
(c) any destruction, breakdown (permanent or temporary) or malfunction of, or damage to, any premises, plant, equipment or

4 Compare the force majeure exemption in Article 79 of the Vienna Convention on the International Sale of Goods.
5 [1990] 1 Lloyd's Rep 1.
6 Lord Radcliffe in *Davis Contractors Ltd v Fareham UDC* [1956] AC 696 at 729.
7 *The 'Super Servant Two'* [1990] 1 Lloyd's Rep 1.

materials (including any computer hardware or software or any records); or

(d) the introduction of, or any amendment to, a law or regulation, or any change in its interpretation or application by any authority; or

(e) any action taken by a governmental or public authority or an agency of the European Economic Community, including any failure or delay to grant a consent, exemption or clearance; or

(f) any strike, lockout or other industrial action; or

(g) any unavailability of, or difficulty in obtaining any plant, equipment or materials;

(h) any breach of contract or default by, or insolvency of, a third party (including an agent or sub-contractor), other than a company in the same group as the Contractor or an officer or employee of the Contractor or of such a company; or

(i) any other event, whether similar or not to any of the foregoing.

(2) For this purpose an event or the consequence of an event was neither preventable nor foreseeable if and only if the Contractor could not have prevented it by taking steps which it could reasonably be expected to have taken and the Contractor could not, as at the date of this Contract, have reasonably been expected to take the risk of it into account by providing for it in this Contract, by insurance or otherwise.

(3) Subclause (1) does not apply unless the Contractor–

(a) notifies the Owner of the relevant event and consequence as soon as possible after it occurs;

(b) promptly provides the Owner with any further information which the Owner requests about the event (or its causes) or the consequence; and

(c) promptly takes any steps (except steps involving significant additional costs) which the Owner reasonably requires in order to reduce the Owner's losses or risk of losses.

(4) It is for the Contractor to show that a matter is a consequence of an event covered by subclause (1), that the event and the consequence were neither preventable nor foreseeable and that it has satisfied the conditions set out in subclause (3).

Some clauses provide for the contract to be terminated; others for its performance to be suspended; and others for suspension and then termination if performance cannot be resumed after a certain period. However, in the event of the United Kingdom becoming involved in a war, a rule of public policy dissolves unperformed contracts with enemies existing at the outbreak of war and also all contracts which involve intercourse with the enemy or tend to assist the enemy, even though no enemy is a party.[8] This public policy principle may have applied on the outbreak of hostilities against Iraq in January 1991, although there was no declaration of war by the Prime Minister in the House of Commons and the United Kingdom's position was that it was participating in enforcement

8 *Re Badische Co Ltd* [1921] 2 Ch 331 at 374–375.

action on behalf of the United Nations in pursuance of United Nations Security Council Resolutions. A contract cannot be saved from dissolution by a force majeure clause which provides for performance to be suspended for the duration of hostilities.[9]

The force majeure clauses which appear in financial agreements tend to be different from those in contracts for the supply of goods or services. An underwriting agreement for an offering of shares or bonds commonly allows the underwriters to stop the offering going ahead if, in their opinion, there occurs a change in national or international financial, political or economic conditions, or currency exchange rates or exchange controls which is likely materially to prejudice the success of the issue. It seems doubtful whether such a clause could be invoked for a collapse of stock market prices; such a collapse is one of the main contingencies against which an underwriting agreement is intended to protect the issuer. International loan agreements contain provisions which, by a variety of methods, protect a bank which finds itself unable to attract in the interbank market the deposits necessary for it to fund its advances. Other provisions protect a bank against the introduction of a regulation which increases the bank's cost of maintaining the loan or which makes it illegal for the bank to permit the loan to remain outstanding.

A model force majeure clause is set out in the International Chamber of Commerce's booklet on *Force Majeure and Hardship* (Publication No 421, March 1985).

There has been a tendency for the courts to interpret force majeure clauses very strictly; usually, a party invoking such a clause must show legal or physical impossibility and that he has taken all reasonable steps to avoid or mitigate the consequences of the force majeure event.[10]

Confidentiality

A confidentiality clause is common. The following would be normal in an agreement which does not involve a party giving access to know-how or other restricted information.

(1) Each party shall take reasonable precautions to ensure that none of its officers or employees–

(a) discloses any term of this Agreement; or
(b) discloses or uses any confidential information (as defined below) which he acquires in connection with this Agreement or which he has acquired in connection with the negotiations leading up to it;

9 *Ertel Bieber & Co v Rio Tinto Co* [1918] AC 260 and *Clapham SS Co Ltd v Handels-En-Transport-Maatschappij Vulcaan of Rotterdam* [1917] 2 KB 639.

10 See conclusion 5 in the judgment of Bingham LJ in *The 'Super Servant Two'* [1990] 1 Lloyd's Rep 1 at 7; *Channel Island Ferries Ltd v Sealink UK Ltd* [1988] 1 Lloyd's Rep 323; the discussion of the cases arising out of the US soya bean embargo of 1973 in *The Sale of Goods* by Professor P S Atiyah; and Commission Notice C(88) 1696 reproduced in Appendix, below.

except as is reasonably necessary for the performance of that party's obligations under this Agreement or as the other parties agree.

(2) Subclause (1) does not prevent a disclosure which an external lawyer to the party concerned has advised that, in his opinion, the party (or one of its officers or employees) is, or probably is, legally obliged to make.

(3) Nor does subclause (1) prevent a disclosure which is made for a proper purpose–

(a) to a public authority;
(b) to a court of law in the United Kingdom or elsewhere or otherwise in any legal proceeding;
(c) to the senior management of a party's parent undertaking;
(d) to the auditors of, or any lawyer or professional person acting for, a party or its parent undertaking.

(4) If–

(a) a party or any of its officers or employees makes a disclosure under subclause (2) or (3); or
(b) the senior management of a party become aware of facts indicating that any of its officers or employees has or may have disclosed or used information in contravention of this clause;

the party shall–

(i) immediately serve on the other parties a notice specifying the information concerned and the persons to whom it has or may have been disclosed or (as the case may be) the use to which it has or may have been put; and
(ii) promptly provide each of the other parties with any further information which it reasonably requests about that disclosure or use.

(5) The parties acknowledge that, since damages or an account of profits will not be an adequate remedy for a breach of this clause, a party is entitled to an injunction to prevent a breach or a continued breach or, in the case of a breach of subclause (4), to an order for specific performance.[11]

(6) For the purposes of this clause information is 'confidential information' if any party to this Agreement might reasonably be expected to object for whatever reason to its becoming generally known; and 'public authority' means any governmental, regulatory or other public authority, in the United Kingdom or elsewhere, including an authority of the European Economic Community, an authority responsible for the administration or collection of a tax, a professional body or other self-regulating authority, and a stock exchange; also a person appointed by any of the foregoing to carry out an investigation or inquiry.

Quite apart from the competition law implications the judgment of Salmon LJ in *Initial Services Ltd v Putterill*[12] makes it clear that

11 Although a provision of this nature is increasingly common, it is seldom necessary for a confidentiality obligation as in subclause (1): see *A-G v Barker* [1990] 3 All ER 257.
12 [1968] 1 QB 396, [1967] 3 All ER 145.

such a confidentiality clause can be subject to public interest exceptions as well as to the exceptions expressly stated. The example given by Salmon LJ was that of a service contract in which the employee undertakes not to disclose the existence of a contract which the employer has entered into and which required registration under the Restrictive Trade Practices legislation but which the employer has decided not to register. In *Lion Laboratories Ltd v Evans*[13] it was held that the defence of public interest is now well established in actions for breach of confidence and, although there is less authority on the point, also in actions for breach of copyright: the defence is not limited to situations in which there has been serious wrong-doing by the party seeking to prevent disclosure. The judge has to balance the public interest in upholding the right to confidence against some other public interest that will be served by publication of the confidential material: see the explanation given by Lord Griffiths in *A-G v Guardian Newspapers (No 2)*.[14] *Initial Services Ltd v Putterill* suggests that this balancing exercise applies where the obligation not to disclose arises from an express contractual term rather than either an implied contractual term[15] or a general duty of confidence based on loyalty and fair dealing. In particular, the decision of the Court of Appeal in *Finers v Miro*[16] strongly suggests that an express confidentiality clause is overridden if there is a serious prima facie case of fraud against the party it is designed to protect.

If an agreement involves a party providing access to know-how, the clause would impose a higher obligation than that to take 'reasonable precautions' and the exemptions might well be more tightly drawn. In addition, there could well be an obligation to make the information available only to specifically agreed employees and then only after they had signed confidentiality undertakings. There might also be an express indemnity against consequential losses caused by any breach. There would also be provisions requiring the return of documents, tapes and disks on termination of the contract.

'Time of the essence'

A common clause is–

> Time shall be of the essence in relation to this Agreement.

This makes timely performance by A a pre-condition of performance by B. In *Lombard North Central plc v Butterworth*[17] Mustill LJ said:

13 [1985] QB 526, [1984] 2 All ER 417.
14 [1990] 1 AC 109 at 268–269.
15 For example, *Tournier v National Provincial and Union Bank of England* [1924] 1 KB 461. But see the observations of Staughton J (as he then was) in *Libyan Arab Foreign Bank v Bankers Trust Co* [1989] 3 All ER 252 at 285.
16 [1991] 1 All ER 182, [1991] 1 WLR 35.
17 [1987] QB 527, [1987] 1 All ER 267, CA.

> 'Where a promisor fails to give timely performance of an obligation in respect of which time is expressly stated to be of the essence, the injured party may elect to terminate and recover damages in respect of the promisor's outstanding obligations, without regard to the magnitude of the breach.'

Although Mustill LJ referred to 'the injured party', it is clear that a party is entitled to terminate regardless of whether he has suffered, or will suffer, any loss as result of the other party's failure to perform on time.[18]

Lombard plc v Butterworth shows that, if there is a 'time of the essence' provision, damages are recoverable for loss of the whole transaction and can include an amount in respect of future payments to the innocent party which would otherwise have been irrecoverable as a penalty. The case is also notable for a statement by Mustill LJ (at 538E) to the effect that a clause making time of the essence entitles A to terminate if B fails to perform an obligation by the specified time even though a breach of that obligation would not otherwise have amounted to a repudiatory breach by B entitling A to terminate.

Broadly speaking, even without a 'time of the essence' clause time will be considered of the essence in 'mercantile' contracts: this is established by the decisions of the House of Lords in *Bunge Corpn v Tradax SA*[19] and *Compagnie Commerciale Sucres v Czarnikow Ltd.*[20] However, this is by no means an absolute rule. Ultimately, the court may have to make 'a value judgment about the commercial significance of the term in question': see the statement of Kerr LJ quoted in *Compagnie Commerciale Sucres v Czarkinov* at 650. In *United Scientific Holdings Ltd v Burnley Borough Council*[1] the House of Lords held that time was not of the essence in relation to the timetables specified in rent review clauses in two commercial leases. Accordingly, the landlords' failure to comply with the timetable did not cause them to lose their right to a rent review. Lord Salmon said this:

> 'I recognise that the lease relates to what could be fairly described as a commercial transaction. In commercial transactions, provisions as to time are usually but not always regarded as being of the essence of the contract. They are certainly so regarded where the subject matter of the contract is the acquisition of a wasting asset or of a perishable commodity or is something likely to change rapidly in value. In such a case if, eg, the seller fails to deliver within the time specified in the contract, the buyer may be seriously prejudiced. The time provision in

18 See the passage in the judgment of Megaw LJ in *Bunge Corpn v Tradax SA* [1981] 2 All ER 513 at 531F to 532A which was approved by Lord Roskill at 548D and followed by the Court of Appeal in *The Aragon* [1991] 1 Lloyd's Rep 61. See also the speech of Lord Birkenhead LC in *Maclaine v Gatty* [1921] 1 AC 376.

19 [1981] 2 All ER 513 at 542 and 552.

20 [1990] 3 All ER 641 at 649.

1 [1978] AC 904, [1977] 2 All ER 62.

a rent revision clause of the present kind, even in a lease concerning a commercial transaction, is however different in character and I regard it as not being of the essence of the contract unless it is made so expressly or by necessary implication.'

Moreover, even in the context of commodity trading, there can be exceptions to the rule that time is of the essence.[2] The rule can also be excluded by a clause which limits A's remedies in the event of delay by B to demurrage or some other sum.[3]

In *Raineri v Miles*[4] the House of Lords considered the position where time is not of the essence in relation to an obligation. The House rejected an argument that, if time was not of the essence, a clause in a contract for the sale of a house which provided for completion on a specified date could therefore be construed as meaning that completion could take place within a reasonable time after that date. The vendors' failure to complete on the specified date was a breach of contract which entitled the purchaser to damages for any resulting loss. The significance of there being no time of the essence clause was that the vendors' failure to complete did not entitle the purchaser to terminate the contract nor bar the vendors from suing for specific performance.

The decision of the Court of Appeal in *British and Commonwealth Holdings plc v Quadrex Holdings Inc*[5] has considerable practical importance for a contractual obligation as regards which time is not of the essence under the original terms of the contract. The judgment of Sir Nicolas Browne-Wilkinson V-C establishes the following:

(1) The phrase 'time is of the essence of the contract' is capable of causing confusion since the question in each case is whether time is of the essence of the particular contractual term which has been breached. 'There is ... no general concept that time is of the essence of a contract as a whole; the question is whether time is of the essence of a particular term in question.'

(2) Time cannot be of the essence in relation to an obligation which the contract provides is to be performed 'as soon as practicable' after certain pre-conditions are satisfied. In *British and Commonwealth Holdings v Quadrex* the obligation was to complete a purchase of shares in two money-broking companies as soon as practicable after Revenue clearance of a reconstruction

2 *The Honam Jade* [1991] 1 Lloyd's Rep 38.
3 *The Aragan* [1991] 1 Lloyd's Rep 61.
4 [1981] AC 1050, [1980] 2 All ER 145; the decision also applies to other obligations subject to a time limit: *Behzadi v Shaftesbury Hotels Ltd* [1991] 2 All ER 477 at 485 J, [1991] 2 WLR 1251.
5 [1989] QB 842, [1989] 3 All ER 492 as qualified by *Behzadi v Shaftesbury Hotels Ltd*.

scheme had been obtained. Sir Nicolas Browne-Wilkinson V-C stated that 'it is impossible to say that time was originally of the essence of completion since the agreement does not specify a date for completion or fix a time for completion by reference to a formula which subsequently makes the date capable of exact definition.'

(3) In that case, the subject matter of the sale was shares in private companies trading in a very volatile sector and it followed that, if a date for completion had been specified, time would undoubtedly have been of the essence of completion. (There is no reference in the judgment of Sir Nicolas Browne-Wilkinson V-C to the House of Lords decisions in *Bunge Corpn v Tradax SA* which established a general rule of time being of the essence in a mercantile contract.)

(4) Where time was not originally of the essence in relation to a particular contractual obligation, it can be made so, after a default, if the innocent party serves on the defaulting party a notice specifying a deadline for the latter to perform the obligation. However, this is subject to two conditions: (a) the party giving the notice has to be ready, willing and able to complete; (b) the notice when served must limit a reasonable period within which the defaulting party is to perform the obligation.

(5) There used to be a third condition under which a notice making time of the essence could not be served until the default had amounted to 'undue or improper' delay. This condition was rejected by the Court of Appeal in *Behzadi v Shaftesbury Hotels Ltd*,[6] which establishes that such a notice can be served immediately after a default. However, the decision also reasserts the requirement for the notice to fix a period for compliance which is reasonable in all the circumstances.

(6) Any difficulty which the purchaser is having in raising the purchase price is irrelevant to whether the period given by the vendor's notice is reasonable.

In *Delta Vale Properties Ltd v Mills*,[7] the Court of Appeal added a further requirement. A notice making time of the essence must be clear and unambiguous[8] so that when it is received the party in default will know what he is required to do to comply with his obligations. It seems that a notice must state that, if the deadline is not met, the party serving the notice will treat the contract as at an end or will treat himself as entitled to put an end to it.[9] This

6 [1991] 2 All ER 477, [1991] 2 WLR 1251.
7 [1990] 2 All ER 176, [1990] 1 WLR 445.
8 See also *Chancery Lane Developments Ltd v Wades Stores Ltd* (1987) 53 P & CR 306.
9 See the article in [1991] Conv 94 by Associate Professor Butt.

was done by the notice that the Court of Appeal upheld in *British and Commonwealth Holdings v Quadrex*:

> 'On behalf of B & C, I now give you notice that we require you to complete performance of the agreement by no later than 5.00pm on 28th February 1988. For the avoidance of doubt I should make it clear that unless Quadrex completes performance by that time, B & C will treat Quadrex's failure as a repudiation of the Agreement giving rise to all the legal consequences which ensue when one party wrongfully repudiates a contract. Meanwhile B & C remains ready, willing and able to perform its contractual obligations to Quadrex.'

Although 'time of the essence' clauses are commonplace, they should be recognised as potentially oppressive; a slight delay by A in performing an unimportant obligation will entitle B to refuse to perform his obligations. However, if such a clause is included, the judgment in *British and Commonwealth Holdings v Quadrex* indicates that it should be in this form:

> Time is of the essence as regards *every obligation* of the Purchaser under this Agreement.

Anti-waiver clauses

Agreements commonly contain a clause to the following effect:

> (1) The rights of the Bank under this Agreement are cumulative; and nothing in this Agreement excludes or restricts any right which the Bank would have, apart from this Agreement, under the general law or another agreement or document.
>
> (2) Subject to subclause (3), no act, course of conduct, failure or neglect to act or acquiescence on the part of the Bank or a person acting on its behalf shall result in the Bank being taken to have waived, or being precluded (permanently or temporarily) from enforcing or relying on,–
>
> (a) a provision of this Agreement; or
> (b) a breach by another party to this Agreement of an obligation under it or the general law; or
> (c) a right of the Bank under the general law, including a right arising out of a breach such as is described in paragraph (b) above.
>
> (3) Subclause (2) does not apply as between the Bank and another party to the extent that the Bank expressly notifies that party in writing that the Bank waives, or will not enforce or rely on, a specified provision, breach or right; but this is subject to any condition, limitation or other term attaching to the notification, whether expressly or by reasonable implication.
>
> (4) In this clause 'the general law' includes the law of a country

other than England and 'right' includes any power, remedy or proprietary or security interest.

The clause starts by providing that, where in a certain situation the agreement gives a party more than one right, the party is not restricted to exercising only one of them. For example, a bank enforcing a debenture may wish to exercise its mortgagee's power of sale after exercising its power to appoint a receiver.

The clause then provides that the express rights given by the agreement are not to be considered as replacing those which would otherwise be given by the general law. *Capital Finance Co Ltd v Stokes*[10] illustrates a situation in which this clause might arguably be invoked. In that case, a vendor of land took a legal mortgage over it to secure three-quarters of the sale price which was left outstanding as a debt due from the purchasing company; the mortgage became void for lack of registration under the Companies Act; and when the vendor invoked his common law unpaid vendor's lien, the Court of Appeal held that this had been excluded by the legal mortgage.

However, it is unsafe to rely on a general clause of this type, and any particular right which it is important to preserve should be specifically saved. For example, a clause entitling a party to terminate an agreement in certain events might contain the following provision:

> Nothing in this clause excludes or restricts any right which the Lessor would otherwise have under the general law to rescind or terminate this Agreement or to treat itself discharged from further performance of its obligations under this Agreement, whether on the ground of misrepresentation, breach by the Lessee, frustration or otherwise.

In the clause set out at the start of this section, the closing words of subclause (1) are to exclude the doctrine of merger. In its classic form this applies where the parties have signed a contract which is to be carried out by a deed that it requires the parties to execute; on execution of the deed, the contract is 'merged' in it, with the result that any right to sue on the contract is extinguished. In *G Orlik (Meat Products) Ltd v Hastings and Thanet Building Society*[11] Stamp LJ, delivering the judgment of the Court of Appeal, said:

> '...it is axiomatic that, where there is a contract which is afterwards reduced into a deed, then, unless there is something to show that the parties intended to make some term which was *not to be included* in the deed and was, to quote the words of Bowen LJ in *Palmer v Johnson*[12] "... to go on to any ... extent ..." after the execution of the deed, the rights of the parties are governed entirely by the deed.'

10 [1969] 1 Ch 261, [1968] 3 All ER 625, CA.
11 (1975) 29 P&CR 126.
12 (1884) 13 QBD 351 at 357. See also the judgment of Brett LJ in *Leggott v Barrett* (1880) 15 Ch D 306.

However, the doctrine also applies where an oral agreement is followed by a formal written contract which is not a deed and, it is thought, where a skeleton contract, such as heads of agreement, is followed by the complete contract for which it provides. There is also a general rule that, by taking a security of a higher nature in legal valuation than the one he already possesses, a creditor merges his legal remedies on the inferior security: for example, where a creditor who holds an equitable mortgage takes a legal one. However, this rule can be excluded by a contract.[13] Where a security given by a debtor is discharged under the doctrine of merger, a knock-on effect can be to discharge a guarantee for the debtor's liabilities.[14]

In the waivers clause which is set out at the beginning of this section, subclauses (2) and (3) are intended as some protection against inactivity or delay by the bank's management causing erosion of the bank's legal position, particularly under the principles relating to waiver,[15] estoppel and laches. But it is unlikely that a clause of this type gives total protection. Clear acquiescence in a breach might preclude a party from using the clause to argue that its acquiescence had not amounted to a waiver. It is also questionable whether the clause would preserve a party's right to treat itself as discharged from a contract as a result of the other party's breach if it performs some act which clearly shows an intention to go on with the contract and that act is communicated to the other party; for example, the clause would probably not preserve the rights of a buyer under a c.i.f. contract to reject the goods after accepting documents which showed that they had been shipped late. It is most unlikely that such a clause would exclude the doctrine of laches which bars equitable remedies (such as specific performance or rescission) where the plaintiff has delayed seeking relief.[16]

It is also doubtful how far such a provision would dissapply the doctrine of election as explained by Lord Goff of Chieveley in *The Kanchenjunga*:[17]

13 32 Halsbury's Laws 979 to 982.

14 20 Halsbury's Laws 287 and 295.

15 However, conduct can only constitute an estoppel if it amounts to an implied representation; and silence or inaction cannot amount to this unless there is a duty to disclose or act: *Tai Hing Cotton Mill Ltd v Liu Chong Hing Bank Ltd* [1986] AC 80, 110 D–E.

16 By contrast, it may well be that the court will give effect to a clause providing that the Limitation Act 1980 will not apply to any claim which a party may in future come to have under a contract. An agreement not to set up the Limitation Act as a defence to a personal injury claim was upheld by the Court of Appeal, where the agreement was made after the claim had arisen: *Lubovsky v Snelling* [1944] KB 44, [1943] 2 All ER 577.

17 [1990] 1 Lloyd's Rep 391.

'It is a commonplace that the expression "waiver" is one which may, in law, bear different meanings. In particular, it may refer to a forbearance from exercising a right or to an abandonment of a right. Here we are concerned with waiver in the sense of abandonment of a right which arises by virtue of a party making an election. Election itself is a concept which may be relevant in more than one context. In the present case, we are concerned with an election which may arise in the context of a binding contract, when a state of affairs comes into existence in which one party becomes entitled, either under the terms of the contract or by the general law, to exercise a right, and he has to decide whether or not to do so. His decision, being a matter of choice for him, is called in law an election. ... In all cases he has in the end to make his election, not as matter of obligation, but in the sense that, if he does not do so, the time may come when the law takes the decision out of his hands, either by holding him to have elected not to exercise the right which has become available to him, or sometimes by holding him to have elected to exercise it. ... In particular, where with knowledge of the relevant facts a party has acted in a manner which is consistent only with his having chosen one of the two alternative and inconsistent courses of action then open to him – for example, to determine a contract or alternatively to affirm it – he is held to have made his election accordingly, just as a buyer may be deemed to have accepted uncontractual goods in the circumstances specified in s 35 of the [Sale of Goods Act 1979]. ... But of course an election need not be made in this way. It can be communicated to the other party by words or conduct; though, perhaps because a party who elects not to exercise a right which has become available to him is abandoning that right, he will only be held to have done so if he has so communicated his election to the other party in clear and unequivocal terms. ... Once an election is made, however, it is final and binding. ... Moreover it does not require consideration to support it, and so it is to be distinguished from an express or implied agreement, such as a variation of the relevant contract, which traditionally requires consideration to render it binding in English law.

Generally, however, it is a prerequisite of election that the party making the election must be aware of the facts which have given rise to the existence of this new right. This may not always be so....

There are numerous examples of the application of this principle of election in English law. Perhaps the most familiar situation is that which arises when one contracting party repudiates the contract. The effect is that the other contracting party then has a choice whether to accept the repudiation (as it is called) and bring the contract to an end; or to affirm the contract, thereby waiving or abandoning his right to terminate it. If, with knowledge of the facts giving rise to the repudiation, the other party to the contract acts (for example) in a manner consistent only with treating that contract as still alive, he is taken in law to have exercised his election to affirm the contract.'[18]

18 See also *Fercometal SARL v MSC Mediterranean Shipping Co SA* [1989] AC 788 at 805D and E and the Law Commission's Report on the Sale and Supply of Goods (Law Com No 160, Cmnd 137) at 2.40 to 2.52.

Subclause (3) in the above clause restricts the effect of any waiver which the bank decides to give by stating that a waiver can only be relied on by the party to whom it is given; that it is only effective in relation to the particular provision or breach that is 'specified'; and that it is subject to any condition attached to it, whether expressly or by 'reasonable implication'. This expression, it is thought, may allow greater scope for conditions to be implied into a waiver than would be possible under the rather strict rules relating to implied terms in contracts.

Agreements often state that a single or partial exercise of a power will not prevent a further exercise of it. However, it may be preferable to include a positive provision, similar to section 12(1) of the Interpretation Act 1978, that a power can be exercised whenever appropriate (see Chapter 9).

It is also thought doubtful whether such a general negative provision against exhaustion by a partial exercise would always be effective, of itself, to allow a selective exercise of a power; for example, to convert a bank's right to appoint a receiver over certain assets into (i) a right initially to appoint a receiver over some only of the assets, and (ii) a right at a later date to extend the appointment to the remainder. This should be covered expressly.

Amendments

Concerns similar to those underlying waivers clauses lead to the inclusion of provisions which are designed to prevent an agreement being varied informally, for example, by a telephone conversation or a course of dealing. A typical provision is:

> A variation to this Agreement is effective only if each of the parties has agreed to it in writing.

Such a provision would be appropriate for inclusion in an agreement under seal which can be varied by an agreement under hand only[19] or orally.[1]

It is thought, however, that it is doubtful whether such a clause would protect a party against being bound by a variation if the party has engaged in conduct which amounts to a 'clear and unambiguous' representation that it agrees to the variation, it has so conducted itself that a reasonable man would have believed that it was meant that he should act on it and the other party to the contract did in fact act on the representation.[2]

19 *Plymouth Corpn v Harvey* [1971] 1 All ER 623, [1971] 1 WLR 549.
1 *Mitas v Hyams* [1951] 2 TLR 1215.
2 *Lowe v Lombank Ltd* [1960] 1 All ER 611, [1960] 1 WLR 196. Compare article 29(2) of the 1980 Vienna Convention on the International Sale of Goods.

Expenses

Some agreements provide for each party to bear its own expenses – the main category being the legal costs incurred in the negotiation and drafting of the agreement. Others require one of the parties to bear all the expenses, including those connected with anything subsequently arising out of the agreement. A typical provision is:

> The Company shall, on demand, fully indemnify the Bank in respect of all expenses which the Bank has incurred or may later incur in connection with this Agreement or any matter arising out of it, including a request or proposal for a consent, waiver or variation; and, without limiting its generality, this covers all expenses connected with legal advice or legal proceedings relating to this Agreement or a matter arising out of it.

It is thought that the reference to expenses 'incurred' entitles the bank to claim under the indemnity as soon as it has become liable to pay a particular expense, without its being necessary for the bank to have made the payment;[3] contrast the 'pay to be paid' provision in the *The Padre Island (No 2)*.[4] In *Green and Silley Weir Ltd v British Railways Board*[5] Dillon J (as he then was) referred to the different approaches of the common law and equity to contracts of indemnity. At common law a person entitled to an indemnity has no right to sue on it until he has had to pay and has paid money; but in equity, as soon as the fact and extent of his liability had been ascertained, he can obtain a declaration of his right to be indemnified. On the other hand, a clause requiring a party to 'reimburse' the bank may well imply that the bank must first have disbursed the amount claimed back.

If a party's expenses might be significant, the clause should provide for the other party to pay interest if he does not pay the expenses, say, within one week after a demand. The rate of interest should reflect the likely borrowing costs of the party who has incurred the expenses, and to the extent that the rate of interest plainly exceeds that cost it will be irrecoverable as a penalty.

If an agreement will attract stamp duty or registration charges in the United Kingdom or elsewhere, the clause should be extended to cover these items. This is subject to section 117 of the United Kingdom Stamp Duty Act 1891:

> 'Every condition of sale framed with the view of precluding objection or requisition upon the ground of absence or insufficiency of stamp upon any instrument executed after the sixteenth day of May one thousand eight hundred and eighty-eight, and every contract, arrangement, or undertaking for assuming the liability on account of absence or

3 Compare *R v Miller* [1983] 3 All ER 186, [1983] 1 WLR 1056.
4 [1990] 2 All ER 705, [1990] 3 WLR 78, HL.
5 [1985] 1 All ER 237.

insufficiency of stamp upon any such instrument or indemnifying against such liability, absence, or insufficiency, shall be void.'

Entire agreement

A common provision is:

> This Agreement and the documents to be executed under it contain, or will contain, all the terms which the parties have agreed in relation to the transactions provided for by this Agreement and those documents; and none of the parties to this Agreement has been induced to enter into this Agreement or any of those documents by a statement or promise which they do not contain.

The first half of the clause is designed to block an exception to the parol evidence rule. This rule prevents extrinsic evidence (whether oral or of another document) being given to 'add to, vary or contradict' a written contract. However, case law has whittled down the rule and extrinsic evidence is admissible to show that the written contract was not intended to express the whole of the agreement between the parties, for example, where there is an overriding oral promise or the written contract is subject to an oral condition precedent.[6] The Law Commission's Report on the Parol Evidence Rule (Law Com 154, Cmnd 9700 (1986)) indicates (at 2.15) that a clause such as that set out above is of limited effectiveness:

> 'Sometimes parties may include in their contracts a clause to the effect that the whole contract is contained in the document and that nothing was agreed outside it (sometimes called a "merger" or "integration" clause). In particular, it may be provided that nothing said during negotiations is intended to be of any contractual effect unless recorded in the document. Without legislative provision such a clause cannot, we think, have conclusive effect. It may have a very strong persuasive effect but if it were proved that, notwithstanding the clause, the parties actually intended some additional term to be of contractual effect, the court would give effect to that term because such was the intention of the parties. If the parties intended that the additional term should have been recorded in the document, the contract could be rectified. If it had been their intention that the term should be of contractual effect but not be included in the document, the analysis likely to be adopted by the court is that the parties agreed a collateral contract alongside the written one. But if it were proved that the intention of the parties was to make one contract partly in writing and partly orally, the court would give effect to that contract. The parties might have been aware of the integration clause when they agreed the additional terms but have agreed to ignore it, or they might have forgotten about the clause or never read it. Whatever the reason for there being an

6 9 Halsbury's Laws 287.

integration clause and additional terms, the court will give effect to the intention of the parties as it is proved or admitted to have been.'

The second part of the clause set out above is intended to prevent a party claiming damages or rescission on the ground that he entered into the contract in reliance on a representation which is not set out in the contract and which has proved to be incorrect. The Law Commission's Report on the Parol Evidence Rule (page 13, note 49) expresses the view that a provision of this type is caught by section 3 of the Misrepresentation Act 1967 so that its validity depends on the party relying on proving that it shows that it satisfies the requirements of reasonableness as stated in section 11(1) of the Unfair Contract Terms Act 1977. This view is supported by the determination of the House of Lords in *Smith v Bush*[7] to construe the 1977 Act in a manner that leaves no scope for circumvention.

On general principles, it is clear that neither part of the clause would provide a defence to a party who had been dishonest.

Although entire agreement clauses are common, particularly in contracts for the sale of companies, such a clause should be treated with caution. It is often rendered factually incorrect by a side letter. This can be introduced at the last minute, and the parties' advisers may fail to make the necessary amendment to the entire agreement clause. That clause can also be inconsistent with another clause which seeks to preserve the rights of a particular party under any other document (see 'Anti-waiver clauses' above). It should also be appreciated that such an entire agreement clause is double-sided and can operate in an unforeseen way against the party that it is designed to protect.

Notices

A clause about notices usually receives much less attention than the main business terms, but its language becomes important if one of the parties needs to exercise a right which is exercisable only by a written notice. The following clause, which is slightly longer than normal, attempts to deal with two problems which have arisen in practice. The first is a postal strike of the kind which occurred in England in September 1988 and led to the litigation in *Bradman v Trinity Estates plc*.[8] In that case Hoffmann J doubted whether a clause in a company's articles of association which provided that, where a notice was sent by post, delivery should be deemed to be effected 'twenty-four hours after the time when the cover containing the same is posted' applied where 'there is such disruption to the postal service that placing the covers in a letter box cannot reasonably be expected to result in a delivery to the shareholder within 24 hours

7 [1990] 1 AC 831 overruling the Court of Appeal's narrower approach to the Act.
8 [1989] BCLC 757.

or anything like it'. The second case which the clause addresses is where a party, which knows that it is about to be served with, for example, a notice of default, deliberately puts its telex and fax machines out of operation.

In the light of Hoffmann J's observations, it is thought that a clause which deems a notice to have been served a certain time after despatch may be vulnerable if a notice cannot safely be assumed to arrive within that time. In particular, a clause deeming any notice served by post to arrive in all cases within 24 hours of posting is considered suspect.

The following clause is thought more likely to be upheld:

(1) Unless delivered personally, a notice to a party in connection with this Agreement shall be sent by first class pre-paid post (or airmail if sent internationally), telex or fax.

(2) Unless delivered to a party personally, a notice shall be sent to its address which is set out in this Agreement.
However, if the party has notified the serving party of another address [in Great Britain] for the service of notices under this Agreement, the notice shall be sent to that address.

(3) Subject to subclause (4), a notice posted in Great Britain to an address in Great Britain is deemed to have been served at 10.00am on the second business day after the next collection of letters to follow its posting.
Here 'business day' means a day other than a Saturday or Sunday or a public holiday in either the country where the notice is posted or that to which it is sent.

(4) Subclause (3) does not apply to a notice if there is a national or local suspension, curtailment or disruption of postal services which affects the collection of the notice or is such that the notice cannot reasonably be expected to be delivered within two business days after the next collection.

(5) Subject to subclause (6), a notice sent by telex or fax is deemed to have been served–

(a) two hours after despatch, if despatched on a business day before 3.00pm; or
(b) in any other case, at 10.00am on the business day after the date of despatch.

Here 'business day' means a day on which banks are open in the city or other location to which the notice is sent; and the times mentioned are those in that location.

(6) Subclause (5) does not apply–

(a) if before the time at which the notice would otherwise be deemed to have been served, the receiving party informs the sending party that the notice has been received in a form which is unclear in a material respect; and

(b) if the receiving party does that by telephone, it despatches a confirmatory telex or fax within two hours.

[(7) A notice by the Vendors is valid if it is signed by Mr .... for himself and the other Vendors; and a notice to the Vendors or any of them which is served within three months after the date of this Agreement can be validly served by being served on the Vendors' solicitors.]

(8) A party shall not attempt to prevent or delay the service on it of a notice connected with this Agreement.

(9) References in this Agreement to a signed notice include references to such a notice which is sent by fax.

(10) In this clause–

'address' includes a telex or fax number;

'notice' includes a notice under clause (waivers) and also any demand, consent or other communication.

The clause set out above reflects the Court of Appeal's decision in *Hastie & Jenkerson v McMahon*[9] that a plaintiff can serve by fax a document relating to proceedings provided he can prove receipt by the defendant of a clearly legible copy. However, proving this can be difficult and some banks regard a fax as an unsatisfactory medium, to the extent of requiring an indemnity against losses resulting from unauthorised transfers where a customer insists on giving payment instructions by fax.

Where any of the parties is based outside Great Britain, it is necessary to consider whether any modification is required in his case, particularly as regards the provisions about when a notice sent by post is deemed to have been served. The litigation in *Parkstone Ltd v Gulf Guarantee Bank plc*[10] illustrates the problems which can arise from unsatisfactory provisions about notices to overseas persons – in that case the provisions in Table A in the 1948 Companies Act.

Some clauses require a notice sent by telex or fax to be confirmed by letter. If such a requirement is imposed, it should be made clear whether or not non-receipt of a confirmatory letter invalidates the notice. Practical problems may arise if a telex or fax notice is invalidated retroactively.

Assignment

Chapter 2 has considered the practice of defining a party to a contract to include 'its successors and assigns'. This section deals with the

9 [1991] 1 All ER 255, [1991] 1 WLR 1575.
10 [1990] BCLC 850.

clause which states whether or not a party may assign its rights under a contract and, if so, subject to what conditions.

There are three main business options:

(a) complete freedom to assign;

(b) assignment only with the prior written consent of the other party or parties;

(c) assignment only with the prior written consent of the other party or parties, but such consent not to be unreasonably withheld.[11]

There are two main reasons why A would wish to control B's right to assign his rights under the contract. First, B might assign to a person who takes a stricter view of A's obligations, and is more likely to sue on them, than B. The assignee's identity could be particularly significant if the contract requires A to obtain B's permission before entering into certain types of transaction. Similar concerns would arise if the contract gives B access to confidential information. Second, an assignment by B will prevent A setting off against the amount he owes B (or B's assignee) under the contract any debt which is owed to him by B, except a debt which accrues due before A receives notice of B's assignment and a debt which flows out of, and is inseparably connected with the debt owing by A which B assigns.[12] The position is similar if a receiver is appointed under a floating charge over all B's assets.

In the case of leases, but not other contracts, the Landlord and Tenant Act 1988 protects a person bound by a covenant not to assign without the other party's consent if the covenant states that consent is not to be unreasonably withheld. The Act requires the landlord 'within a reasonable time' to give consent, unless it is reasonable to withhold it, and to serve on the tenant a written notice of his decision specifying, additionally, any conditions attached to the consent or, if consent is withheld, the reasons for withholding it. The Act places on the landlord the onus of proving that he has fulfilled these obligations. It may be advisable for a contract to include similar protections for the party seeking consent to assignment; his position can be strengthened further by the clause deeming consent to have been given if the other party does not send an objection notice within, say, 14 days after the application for consent.

An express provision should be included if a party wishes to be able to assign a part or parts of its rights under an agreement. For example, a bank may wish to assign different parts of its loan to several institutions. Similarly, an express provision should be included if a party wishes to be able to create first and second mortgages over its contractual rights.

11 See the section on this in Chapter 12.
12 See Chapter 17.

A common question is whether a prohibition against assignment prevents a party from financing its performance of the contract by creating a charge over the payments it receives. A charge over the right to receive payments under the contract is probably precluded. But if A's contract with B prohibits A from assigning his rights 'under the contract' without B's prior consent, A may nevertheless create security over the amounts paid by B under the contract when they are received in A's bank account. The rights assigned or charged would be A's rights against the bank in respect of the credit balance resulting from B's payments; A's rights as against B come to an end when A's bank receives the payments.

Assignment clauses need to be viewed in the light of modern group structures. A company may reasonably request a clause which allows it to transfer its rights and obligations to another company in the same group, although the other party may wish to restrict this to other group companies with a net tangible worth and net liquid assets at least equal to those of the original party. By the same token, a clause which restricts a company from assigning is of limited value without a clause giving the other party a right to terminate if there is a takeover of that company or a change (not amounting to a takeover) occurring in the effective control of it.

As a general rule, it would not be possible for B to assign or transfer its obligations (as opposed to its rights) under the contract without A's consent; and if B required this facility an express provision would normally be necessary. However, there are certain statutory procedures by which obligations can be transferred, for example sections 427 and 427A of the Companies Act 1985 and section 94 of the Building Societies Act 1986.

Severability

The following is a common damage-limitation clause:

> If any provision of this Agreement is or becomes illegal, void or invalid, that shall not affect the legality and validity of the other provisions.

The purpose of this is to increase the prospect of a court severing any part of the contract which is illegal or invalid from the rest of the contract so as to save the other provisions. But it is unlikely to cause the court to apply the doctrine of severance where the court would have held the entire contract contrary to public policy; or where the objectionable provision cannot be separated from the unobjectionable clauses without remoulding them. However, it is impossible to formulate any set rules and to some extent each case depends on its own circumstances.[13]

13 *Carney v Herbert* [1985] AC 301, [1985] 1 All ER 438.

CHAPTER 19

APPLICABLE LAW

Two issues arise whenever a contract has an international element. Which country's law should be the contract's applicable law? In the courts of which country should any litigation connected with the contract be brought or, if there is an arbitration clause, in which country should the arbitration be held? An international element could exist because the parties are domiciled, or companies incorporated in different countries; or because the subject matter of the contract is located in a country which is different from that of any of the parties, for example, a sale by an English company to a French company of its shares in a Norwegian subsidiary.

The law applicable to a contract is also referred to as the proper law or the governing law. However, the Contracts (Applicable Law) Act 1990 amends some provisions of other Acts which refer to the 'proper law' of a contract to refer to the 'law applicable to a contract'; and the latter term is, perhaps, now the more correct.

At common law, a contract's applicable or proper law governs the contract's interpretation and such issues as whether the contract is void for lack of consideration, whether a clause which confers a benefit on a third party is valid, whether the contract has been validly amended and whether a breach has discharged a party from further performance of his obligations. In addition, the common law rule is that, in an action for damages for breach of contract, the applicable law determines questions of remoteness of damage, whereas the quantification of damage, which according to the applicable law is not too remote, is governed by the law of the country in which the proceedings are brought.[1]

The general rule is that legislation only discharges or modifies obligations under a contract if passed under the contract's applicable

1 *J D'Almeida Araujo Lda v Sir Frederick Becker & Co Ltd* [1953] 2 QB 329, [1953] 2 All ER 288.

law.[2] This is one of the main reasons why an agreement for an international bank loan to the government or state-owned organisation of a country is normally governed by the law of a different country – in the international financial market often England or the State of New York.

The question of which country's law is the applicable law is separate from the question of forum, that is, in which country's courts an action on the contract has to be brought or in which country an arbitration on the contract has to be held. In the European Community the basic rule under the 1968 Brussels Convention (see below) is that an action on a contract is to be brought in either the country of performance of the obligation in question or the country in which the defendant is domiciled. The Brussels Convention has no requirement for proceedings to be brought in the country whose law is the contract's applicable law.

The only significant link between the question of applicable law and that of forum arises under the common law rule where a contract specifies the forum, but not the applicable law. In that case, there is a prima facie inference that the parties intended that the applicable law should be the law of the forum, for example, English law, where the contract provides for disputes to be referred to English courts or arbitration in England.[3] However, for most contracts this link has been severed by the Contracts (Applicable Law) Act 1990 (see below).

Applicable law

The common law rule is that the parties are free to select the applicable law, provided that their choice is bona fide and legal and there is no reason for setting aside the choice on the ground of public policy.[4] A broad statement that the parties' choice 'will be conclusive' was also made by Lord Atkin in *R v International Trustee for Protection of Bondholders AG*.[5] However, it has been doubted whether at common law parties have absolute freedom of choice. In particular, there has not been any clear authority that a choice of English law would be valid where a contract has no connection whatsoever with England, although the assumption underlying a wide range of commercial and financial agreements has been that such a choice would be upheld. This assumption receives some support from observations made by Lord Wilberforce and Lord Diplock in *Compagnie d'Armement Maritime SA v Compagnie Tunisienne*[6] and

2 *Adams v National Bank of Greece SA* [1961] AC 255, [1960] 2 All ER 421, HL.
3 *The Komninos S* (1991) Financial Times, 16 January.
4 Lord Wright in *Vita Food Products Inc v Unus Shipping Co Ltd* [1939] AC 277 at 290.
5 [1937] AC 500 at 529.
6 [1971] AC 572 at 599F and 603F.

also from the observations of Diplock LJ in *Mackender v Feldia AG*.[7]

However, for most contracts entered into on or after 1 April 1991,[8] the common law rule has been replaced by the 1980 Rome Convention on the law applicable to contractual obligations. The Convention is given the force of law in the United Kingdom by the Contracts (Applicable Law) Act 1990. The Act permits reference to be made, in construing the Convention, to the report on it by Professor Mario Giuliano and Professor Paul Lagarde.

Article 3 of the Convention, which is headed 'Freedom of Choice', provides:

> 'A contract shall be governed by the law chosen by the parties. The choice must be express or demonstrated with reasonable certainty by the terms of the contract or the circumstances of the case. By their choice the parties can select the law applicable to the whole or a part only of the contract.'

Article 3 also permits the parties to alter a contract's applicable law.

The Rome Convention applies to most types of contractual commercial obligation, but not the following: obligations arising under a negotiable instrument to the extent that the obligations arise out of the instrument's negotiable character; arbitration agreements and agreements on the choice of court – also individual clauses on these subjects; and the question of whether an agent is able to bind a principal to a third party.

Nor does the Rome Convention apply to the constitution of trusts and the relationship between settlors, trustees and beneficiaries; these questions are dealt with by the 1986 Haig Convention on the law applicable to trusts which will be given effect to in the United Kingdom when the Recognition of Trusts Act 1987 is brought into force. Trusts appear in a variety of commercial contexts, for example, the interests of loan stockholders are usually represented and protected by a trustee; a trust is often used to subordinate one creditor's debt to another's;[9] and a trust is usually the most effective way to deal with the rule that a person cannot enforce a clause intended for his benefit in a contract to which he is not a party.

As regards those contracts to which it applies, the Convention removes any doubts about the validity of a clause providing that the applicable law shall be that of a country with which the contract has no connection.

However, the Convention places some restrictions on the effect of the applicable law. Article 3(3) provides that the fact that the parties have chosen a foreign law shall not, 'where all the other elements

7 [1967] 2 QB 590 at 602A.

8 See the Contracts (Applicable Law) Act 1990 (Commencement No 1) Order 1991: SI 1991/707.

9 Although a subordination trust is, in substance, equitable assignment by way of security or an equitable charge.

relevant to the situation at the time of the choice are connected with one country only', prejudice the application of that country's 'mandatory rules', that is, the rules of the law of that country which cannot be derogated from by contract. Article 7(2) also provides that nothing in the Convention shall restrict the application of the rules of the law of the forum (ie the country in which proceedings are brought) where they are mandatory irrespective of the law otherwise applicable to the contract. The main examples of these 'mandatory rules' are those on competition and restrictive practices, consumer protection and certain rules concerning carriage. Article 16 contains a restrictively worded reservation in favour of public policy in the forum which prevents the applicable law being applied in a particular case if the actual result of doing that in the case in issue would be manifestly incompatible with the forum's public policy.

An important point is that these provisions do not invalidate the applicable law clause as a whole, but merely prevent its application where that would be contrary to certain mandatory or public policy rules of the other relevant jurisdiction.

Article 7(1) of the Convention provides that, when applying the applicable law, effect *may* be given to the mandatory rules of another country with which the situation has a close connection if those rules must be applied whatever the applicable law. However, the United Kingdom has implemented the Convention without this article, and the result may be to preserve the common law rule which invalidates a contract under English law if its performance would be illegal in the country of performance.[10]

Some British legislation expressly applies regardless of a contract's applicable law. Section 27(2) of the Unfair Contract Terms Act 1977 provides for the Act to apply notwithstanding a clause which applies the law of a country outside the United Kingdom if the clause appears to have been imposed for the purpose of evading the Act or if one of the parties dealt as consumer and was habitually resident in the United Kingdom and the steps necessary for making the contract were taken in the United Kingdom by him or on his behalf. Section 347 of the Companies Act 1985 provides that the provisions about directors' service contracts, substantial property transactions involving directors and loans to directors apply whether or not the relevant transaction is governed by the law of the United Kingdom or a part of it.

In the case of an assignment or mortgage of the benefit of a contract,[11] a significant restriction on the effect of its applicable law arises from article 12(2). This provides that the law governing the asset being assigned, rather than the law governing the assignment,

10 *Howard v Shirlstar Container Transport Ltd* [1990] 3 All ER 366, [1990] 1 WLR 1292, CA.

11 Or, it seems, a right against a person which does not arise from a contract.

determines whether the asset is assignable and the relationship between original party A and an assignee of original party B. The asset's governing law also determines the conditions under which the assignment can be invoked against original party A. For example, under English law a debt cannot validly be assigned or mortgaged by the creditor in favour of the debtor.[12] The effect of article 12(2) is that if A's contract with B is governed by English law, a French law mortgage by A in favour of B of A's rights under the contract is ineffective.[13]

As a general principle, the validity of a transfer of title to land or movable property is governed by the law of the country in which the property is situated at the time of the transfer.[14] There is, however, a distinction between contractual issues and the question of whether title has passed. So, a contract for the sale of goods situated in Germany can well be governed by English law so that, for example, English law governs questions of interpretation. However, the purchaser will not acquire a good title to the goods unless the transfer to him is valid under German law. It is thought that the Rome Convention does not enable the parties to exclude the principle by providing that a transfer of land or movable property which would be invalid by the lex situs shall be governed instead by the law applicable to the contract under which the transfer is made.

Subject to these limits, article 8(1) of the Convention provides for a contract's applicable law to determine the validity of the contract and that of any of its provisions.[15] By article 9 a contract is formally valid if it satisfies the formal requirements of its applicable law.[16] Article 10 provides that a contract's stated applicable law shall govern 'in particular': interpretation; performance; within the limits of the powers conferred on the court by its procedural law, the consequences of breach, including the assessment of damages in so far as it is governed by rules of law; the various ways of extinguishing obligations.

Article 1 of the Convention provides for its rules to apply to contractual obligations 'in any situation involving a choice between the laws of different countries'. The official report on the Convention by Professors Giuliano and Lagarde states that the Convention 'is of universal application in the sense that the choice of law which it lays down may result in the law of a State not party to the Convention being applied'. For example, the Convention applies to a choice of New York law in a contract on which a Japanese company

12 *Re Charge Card Services Ltd* [1987] Ch 150 [1986] 3 All ER 289.

13 Unless, perhaps, a French law mortgage possesses none of the features of an English law charge which were described in *Re Charge Card Services Ltd.*

14 *Nelson v Bridport* (1846) 8 BEAV 547 *Hardwick Game Farm v Suffolk Agricultural and Poultry Producers Assn* [1966] 1 All ER 309, 338I; *Winkworth v Christie's Ltd* [1980] Ch 496; *The Anchorline* [1937] 1 Ch 483.

15 Subject to the non-consent defence under article 8(2).

16 Or the law of one of the other countries mentioned in article 9: see also article 14(2).

is suing an English company in the English courts. The Report describes the Convention as 'a uniform measure of private international law which will replace the rules of private international law in force in each of the Contracting States, with regard to the subject matter which it covers and subject to any other convention to which the Contracting States are party'.

The usual form of governing law clause is:

> This Agreement is governed by English law.

Since the Rome Convention, and article 3 in particular, refers to a contract being 'governed' by the law of a particular country, a clause in the above form cannot be said to be inconsistent with the Convention. However, the Convention more frequently refers to 'the law applicable to a contract', and this is the Convention's key term. Accordingly, it may become common for choice of law clauses to state:

> English law is the law applicable to this Agreement.

Whichever formula is used, it is unnecessary to state that an agreement 'shall be construed in accordance with English law'. Both the common law and the Rome Convention require a contract to be interpreted in accordance with its applicable law.

Different applicable laws

The Convention expressly permits different parts of the same contract to be governed by the laws of different countries. This may offer scope to provide for a clause which is unenforceable under English law to be governed by the law of another country. The main examples are provisions against the enforcement of which equity gives relief under the rules against penalties,[17] forfeiture[18] and additional rights being given to a mortgagee as part of the mortgage contract, notably an option to purchase the mortgaged property[19] or a bonus to debenture holders.[20] Although these rules were developed and are maintained for purposes of public policy,[1] it seems possible that they may not be 'mandatory rules' contemplated and protected by articles 3(3) and 7(2) of the Rome Convention. In any event, it is clear that these rules of equity do not qualify as the ordre public

17 *Bridge v Campbell Discount Co Ltd* [1962] AC 600, [1962] 1 All ER 385, HL and *Export Credits Guarantee Department v Universal Oil Co* [1983] 2 All ER 205, [1983] 1 WLR 399.

18 *Jobson v Johnson* [1989] 1 All ER 621, [1989] 1 WLR 1026.

19 *G & C Kreglinger v New Patagonia Meat and Cold Storage Co Ltd* [1914] AC 253 *Nelson v Hannam* [1943] Ch 59, [1942] 2 All ER 680, CA.

20 *Re Rainbow Syndicate Ltd* [1916] WN 178; contrast *Re Cuban Land Co* [1921] 2 Ch 147.

1 See Lord Radcliffe's observations in *Bridge v Campbell Discount Co Ltd* [1962] AC 600 at 622: see also the Law Commission's Working Paper No 99 on Land Mortgages at 3.31 to 3.36.

of the forum which is safeguarded by article 16. On this basis, it may be that, for example, clauses in English law contracts which provide for the rate of interest to increase after a default in payment will be stated to be governed by the law of another jurisdiction in which such provisions are enforceable.

Internationally accepted principles of law governing contractual relations

Subject to the qualification made below, the 1987 decision of the Court of Appeal in *Deutsche Schachtbau-und Tiefbohrgesellschaft mbH v R'as Al-Khaimah National Oil Co*[2] indicates that, where parties do not wish their contract to be governed by the law of any particular country, a provision that the contract shall be governed by–

> 'internationally accepted principles of law governing contractual relations'

will not be rejected by the English courts on the common law ground of uncertainty or public policy. That case arose out of an oil exploration agreement which contained an International Chamber of Commerce arbitration clause. The ICC arbitration rules provided that the parties were free to determine the governing law and that, in the absence of any indication by the parties, 'the arbitrator shall apply the law designated as the proper law by the rule of conflict which he deems appropriate'. In pursuance of that clause, the arbitrators determined that the proper law was 'internationally accepted principles of law governing contractual relations'. It was held that the arbitration clause was governed by Swiss law, and uncontradicted expert evidence was that the arbitration clause was valid under Swiss law. The arbitration was held in Geneva, and the arbitral tribunal held that the defendant should pay $4.6 million to the plaintiff. The latter applied to the English courts for leave to enforce the award as a judgment. The Court of Appeal rejected the defendant's submission that it would be contrary to English public policy to enforce an arbitration award which held that the rights and obligations of the parties were to be determined, not on the basis of any particular national law but upon some unspecified, and possibly ill-defined, internationally accepted principles of law. Sir John Donaldson MR described the 'internationally accepted principles of law governing contractual relations' which the arbitrator applied as 'a common denominator of principles underlying the laws of the various nations governing contractual relations'.

Although another aspect of the Court of Appeal's decision was the subject of a successful appeal to the House of Lords, there was no appeal against the decision that the arbitration award was

2 [1990] 1 AC 295 at 306.

enforceable in England. In *Home and Overseas Insurance Co (UK) Ltd v Mentor Insurance Co (UK) Ltd*[3] Lloyd LJ (with whom Balcombe LJ agreed) indicated his agreement with the decision of the differently constituted Court of Appeal in *DST v Raknoc*. Lloyd LJ said this:

> 'Counsel for Home argued that *DST v Raknoc* was concerned only with the enforcement of a foreign award, and that it has no bearing on the present case, where the contract calls for arbitration in London. But why not? If the English courts will enforce a foreign award where the contract was governed by a "system of 'law' which is not that of England or any other state or is a serious modification of such a law",[4] why should it not enforce an English award in like circumstances?'

The Court of Appeal's decision in *DST v Raknoc* was welcomed by the late Professor Clive Schmitthoff, who noted,[5] that the supreme courts of France and Italy had ruled to the same effect. The decision, nevertheless, has to be treated with caution. In *Amin Rasheed Corpn v Kuwait Insurance Co*[6] Lord Diplock stated that:

> 'contracts are incapable of existing in a legal vacuum. They are mere pieces of paper devoid of all legal effect unless they were made by reference to some system of private law which defines the obligations assumed by the parties....'

Lord Wilberforce also seems to have regarded an internationalised contract 'unattached to any system of law' as impossible. The *Amin Rasheed* case was not cited to the Court of Appeal in *DST v Raknoc*; and the Court of Appeal's decision can only be reconciled with the judgment of Hobhouse J in *Dallal v Bank Mellat*[7] on the basis that Raknoc was a state company.

If a court were to decide that a clause providing for a contract to be governed by 'internationally accepted principles of law governing contractual relations' is not a valid choice of proper law, the common law position is that it would apply as the proper law the system of law with which it determines that the transaction has its closest and most real connection.[8]

It is unclear how far *DST v Raknoc* is compatible with the Rome Convention which under the Contracts (Applicable Law) Act 1990 has replaced the common law rules about the choice of applicable law (although not for an arbitration clause). Article 3 of the Convention provides that a contract shall be governed by 'the law chosen by the parties', and arguably there is an implied limitation to the law of a particular state. However, it is thought the better

3 [1989] 3 All ER 74, [1990] 1 WLR 153.
4 See [1990] 1 AC 315D.
5 [1987] JBL 169.
6 [1984] AC 50 at 65.
7 [1986] QB 441 at 456.
8 *Compagnie d'Armement Maritime SA v Compagnie Tunisienne de Navigation SA* [1971] AC 572, [1970] 3 All ER 71, HL.

view that, when construed in the light of the underlying principle of parties' freedom of choice, article 3 sanctions a choice such as that in *DST v Raknoc*. It is not without significance that one of the authorities mentioned by the Report of Professors Mario Guliano and Paul Lagarde on the Rome Convention (reference to which is permitted by the 1990 Act) for the principle of parties' freedom of contract is the 1977 award of Mr René Jean Dupuy in the arbitration between the California Asiatic Oil Company and the Government of the Libyan Arab Republic. The concession contract in that case stated that it would be governed and interpreted according to the principles of Libyan law to the extent of that which they had in common with principles of international law; and, in the absence of such common points, according to general principles of law. On the other hand, Professor F A Mann has expressed the view that 'for reasons of social policy private persons contracting among themselves should be precluded from choosing a legal system other than a national one'.[9]

If a choice of 'internationally accepted principles of law governing contractual relations' is not a valid choice of applicable law under the Rome Convention, the contract's applicable law would be determined in accordance with article 4 of the Convention. That provides that, if the applicable law has not been chosen by the parties, a contract shall be governed by 'the law of the country with which it is most closely connected'. The article also lays down a general presumption that a contract is most closely connected with the country where the party which is to effect the performance 'which is characteristic of the contract' has, when the contract is entered into, his habitual residence or, in the case of a company, its central administration. There are several exceptions to this; where a contract is entered into in the course of a trade or profession of the party who is to effect characteristic performance, the country with which it is most closely connected is that in which that party's principal place of business is situated or, where the contract provides for that party to perform through a place of business other than in its principal place of business, the country in which that other place of business is situated.

9 Rev belge dr int, 1975, p 565. See also Professor Mann's article in (1987) 36 ICLQ 437 at 448, and *Commercial Arbitration* by Mustill and Boyd at pp 80–82.

CHAPTER 20

JURISDICTION

The parties to a contract with an international element are faced with the decision about the jurisdiction or jurisdictions in which proceedings on the contract may brought. (This assumes they have not provided for arbitration in a particular centre.) Parties normally select the courts of the country of the contract's applicable law. However, two other considerations are relevant: a party may be reluctant to being obliged to sue the other party in the latter's home country; and will probably wish to be able to obtain with the maximum speed and simplicity pre-trial attachment and execution of any judgment in the jurisdiction or jurisdictions in which the other party has substantial assets.

There are two main types of jurisdiction clause. The exclusive clause is designed to bar a party from suing in a jurisdiction other than that specified; and, as a general rule, if a clause provides that the courts of a foreign country shall have exclusive jurisdiction, the English courts will stay proceedings which are commenced in England in breach of the clause. A non-exclusive clause keeps open any right which a party may have to sue in a jurisdiction other than that specified.

The Brussels Convention

Jurisdiction clauses have to be considered in the light of the 1968 Brussels Convention on jurisdiction and the enforcement of judgments in civil and commercial matters. The Brussels Convention has the force of law in the United Kingdom under the Civil Jurisdiction and Judgments Act 1982. The Brussels Convention was amended by the San Sebastian Convention which was signed in 1989 on the accession of Spain and Portugal. To give effect to the San Sebastian Convention, the 1982 Act is amended by the Civil Jurisdiction and Judgments Act 1982 (Amendment) Order 1990 (SI 1990/2591). This Order sets out the text of the Brussels Convention as amended by the San Sebastian Convention relating to the accession of Spain and Portugal.[1]

At present the Contracting States under the Brussels Convention (so far as the United Kingdom is concerned) are Belgium, Germany, France, Italy, Luxembourg, the Netherlands, Denmark, the Republic of Ireland, United Kingdom and Greece. For the purposes of English law, Spain and Portugal become Contracting States when the Civil Jurisdiction and Judgments Act 1982 (Amendment) Order 1990 enters into force.

The Civil Jurisdiction and Judgments Act 1991, when brought into force, will give effect to the 1988 Lugano Convention on jurisdiction and judgments made between the Member States of the European Community and those of the European Free Trade Association. The Lugano Convention will operate in parallel to the Brussels Convention where the defendant is domiciled in an EFTA country. The overall scheme of the Lugano Convention is virtually identical to that of the Brussels Convention as revised by the San Sebastian Convention. The main provision of the Lugano Convention which is relevant in the context of this Chapter, article 17, prorogation of jurisdiction, is identical to that of the corresponding article in the Brussels Convention, except for a slight difference in paragraph (5) which deals with contracts of employment.

The Brussels Convention implements article 220 of the Treaty of Rome which provides for the simplification of formalities governing the reciprocal recognition and enforcement of judgments of courts in the EEC. One of the main objects of the Brussels Convention is, therefore, to bring about 'free movement of judgments' within the EEC.[2] The Convention's second main feature is to lay down common rules of jurisdiction for the courts of each Contracting State with regard to proceedings falling within the scope of the Convention. The reason for this was explained by Bingham LJ in *Re Harrods (Buenos Aires) Ltd*, (1991) Financial Times, 25 January:

> 'If member states were to recognise and enforce each others' judgments virtually on the nod, it was plainly desirable ... to agree on a common basis for accepting jurisdiction, so as to minimise the number of occasions on which state A would have to recognise and enforce a judgment given by state B in circumstances where state A would not itself have accepted jurisdiction.'

The Brussels Convention applies in 'civil and commercial matters'. This term is not defined, but, broadly speaking, it can be regarded

1 A consolidated and updated version of the text of the Brussels Convention appears in OJ No C 189, 28 July 1990, together with reports on that Convention on the accession of Spain and Portugal and on the Lugano Convention. Chapter VI of the latter report contains a useful summary of the judgments of the European Court of Justice between 1976 and 1988 on the Brussels Convention.

2 Contrast *Owens Bank Ltd v Bracco* (1991) Financial Times, 12 April and *EMI Records Ltd v Modern Music Karl-Ulrich Walterbach GmbH* (1991) Times, 27 May.

as excluding matters of public law.[3] The Convention expressly states that it 'shall not extend, in particular, to revenue, customs or administrative matters'. There are other specific exclusions, of which the most important in the present context is arbitration. The effect of this exclusion seems to be to take out proceedings to enforce an arbitration award and proceedings which are closely connected with an arbitration, for example, to obtain ruling on a point of law arising during the arbitration.[3a]

In *Marc Rich & Co v Societa Italiana Impianti*,[4] the Court of Appeal referred to the European Court the question of whether this exclusion applies where one of the issues is whether an arbitration clause was ever incorporated into the contract in issue.

The basic jurisdiction rule of the Brussels Convention is that, in relation to a person domiciled in a Contracting State, the state of domicile is the state on which jurisdiction is primarily conferred. This has two main consequences. The court of domicile cannot refuse jurisdiction on the ground that the courts of another Contracting State are the appropriate forum for the proceedings.[5] The second consequence is that a person domiciled in a Contracting State cannot be sued in another Contracting State unless the case is within one of the exceptions which the Convention provides to its basic rule.

In the case of a defendant who is not domiciled in a Contracting State, the Brussels Convention preserves the jurisdiction of the courts of each Contracting State under its own internal law. In *Re Harrods (Buenos Aires) Ltd*, Bingham LJ approved the following extract from a note by Lawrence Collins:[6]

> 'The Convention was intended to regulate jurisdiction as between the Contracting States. Thus the Convention provides that in principle domiciliaries of a Contracting State should be sued in that State, subject to important and far-reaching exceptions, and not in other Contracting States. Once a court in a Contracting State has jurisdiction it is entitled, vis-à-vis other states, to exercise that jurisdiction and other courts cannot. But the States which were parties to the Convention had no interest in requiring a Contracting State to exercise a jurisdiction where the competing jurisdiction was in a non-Contracting State. The Contracting States were setting up an intra-Convention mandatory system of jurisdiction. They were not regulating relations with non-Contracting States.'[7]

3 *Netherlands State v Ruffer* [1980] ECR 3807, [1981] 3 CMLR 293.

3a *Interdesco SA v Nullifire Ltd* (1991) Financial Times, 3 May shows that an English court will seldom decline on the ground of public policy to enforce a judgment given in another Contracting State.

4 [1989] 1 Lloyd's Rep 548.

5 This was established by *Re Harrods (Buenos Aires) Ltd* (1991) Financial Times, 25 January.

6 (1990) 106 LQR 535.

7 A similar approach was taken by the Court of Appeal in *Owens Bank Ltd v Bracco* (1991) Times, 15 April in deciding that the Convention is concerned with the jurisdiction of the Contracting States inter se and is inapplicable to proceedings for the recognition and enforcement of judgments of non-contracting states.

The general rules about domicile are set out in articles 52 and 53 of the Convention. Essentially, these provide that in proceedings in the courts of state A, those courts apply their own rules to determine whether the defendant is domiciled in state A; and if he is not, they apply the rules of Contracting State B to determine whether he is domiciled in that state. However, to determine the domicile of a company, the courts of state A apply state A's rules of private international law. Section 41 of the 1982 Act sets out the rules for deciding whether an individual is domiciled in the United Kingdom or in a particular part of, or place in, the United Kingdom or in a state other than a Contracting State. Section 42 sets out the main rules about the domicile of companies. An important point is that under section 42 a company is treated as being domiciled in England or another state if–

(a) it was formed under the law of that state and has its registered office or official address there; or

(b) its central management and control is exercised in that state.

This is subject to the qualification that the courts of the relevant state would treat the company as domiciled in that state. For example, a company formed under Panama law is (subject to that qualification) treated as domiciled in Germany, as well as Panama, if its central management and control is exercised in Germany.[8] In *The Rewia*,[9] Sheen J held that a single-vessel company incorporated in Liberia was also domiciled in Germany (because its central management and control was exercised in Hamburg), although the operation and management of the vessel in issue, which was the sole business of the company, was delegated entirely to a company in Hong Kong. Subject to the two main exceptions mentioned below, the Convention's basic rule would normally prevent the Panamanian or Liberian company from being sued in England under a contract, even if the contract were with an English company and were governed by English law.

The first main exception is article 5(1) which provides that a person can be sued on a contract 'in the courts for the place of the performance of the obligation in question'. However, it is often difficult to assign a specific geographical location to an obligation, which may well involve action in more than one country.[10]

The second main exception is article 17. This enables the parties to a contract to agree that the courts of a particular Contracting State are to have jurisdiction to settle disputes connected with the contract. If a clause which is valid under article 17 confers jurisdiction on the English courts, the main results are as follows:

8 *The Deichland* [1990] 1 QB 361, [1989] 2 All ER 1066, CA.
9 [1991] 1 Lloyd's Rep 69.
10 Compare *Medway Packaging Ltd v Meurer Maschinen GmbH & Co KG* [1990] 2 Lloyd's Rep 112, CA.

(1) The general rule that a person domiciled in a Contracting State cannot be sued in another Contracting State is disapplied to the extent of permitting proceedings in England.

(2) If the clause is stated to be for the benefit of only one of the parties, that party retains its right to bring proceedings in any other court which has jurisdiction under the Convention, for example, the courts of the country of the defendant's domicile.

(3) Section 49 of the Civil Jurisdiction and Judgments Act 1982 provides that nothing in the Act shall prevent any court in the United Kingdom from staying or dismissing any proceedings before it, on the ground of forum non conveniens or otherwise, 'where to do so is not inconsistent with the 1968 Convention'. In Re *Harrods (Buenos Aires) Ltd*,[11] Dillon LJ said that section 49 implied that the court would not stay or dismiss proceedings on the ground of forum non conveniens when to do so would normally be inconsistent with the Convention. It is thought that it would be inconsistent with the Convention for an English court to stay on the ground of forum non conveniens proceedings concerning a contract which falls within the Convention's scope and provides for the English courts to have jurisdiction, where the stay would be in favour of proceedings in another Contracting State.[12] By contrast, in *Re Harrods (Buenos Aires) Ltd* Dillon LJ (with whom the other members of the Court of Appeal agreed) said that the Convention does not prevent an English court from staying proceedings against a defendant domiciled in England under a contract providing for the courts of a non-contracting state to have exclusive jurisdiction.

(4) If none of the parties is domiciled in a Contracting State, the clause still excludes the jurisdiction of the courts of any other Contracting State unless the English courts decline jurisdiction. For example, a company incorporated and managed in New York agrees to sell its Italian subsidiary to a company incorporated and managed in New Zealand. Assume that the Italian courts would have jurisdiction because the agreement relates to shares in an Italian company. A clause providing for the English courts to have jurisdiction bars litigation in Italy unless the English courts decline that jurisdiction.

It is considered likely that article 17 allows a clause to confer jurisdiction on the courts of such of two or more specified Contracting States as a particular party may elect, for example, the courts of England or France, at the option of the bank. However, there is

11 (1991) Financial Times, 25 January.
12 But see the comment by Mr Adrian Briggs in (1991) LQR 180, 183 on *365/388 Hagen* (15 May 1990).

more doubt about the validity of a clause which provides for the courts of a specified Contracting State to have 'non-exclusive jurisdiction'.[13]

Royal Bank of Scotland plc v CARIPLO[14] demonstrates the importance of including a clause giving jurisdiction to the English courts where a contract involves a person domiciled in another EC state. Royal Bank of Scotland, acting on the instructions of six Italian banks, had confirmed a number of letters of credit. The instructions stated that claims for reimbursement by RBS should be made to specified banks in New York or Philadelphia. RBS confirmed the letters of credit and paid against the documents that were presented. The Italian importers then received information which led them to believe that they were the intended victims of a fraud. They instructed the Italian banks to freeze the credits. The Italian banks informed RBS that it would not receive reimbursement; and RBS commenced proceedings against them.

Phillips J rejected an argument by RBS that the Italian banks' reimbursement obligation fell to be performed in the United Kingdom with the result that RBS could sue in the United Kingdom under article 5 of the Brussels Convention. Since the request from the Italian banks to RBS to confirm the letters of credit did not contain an article 17 clause giving jurisdiction to the English courts, RBS could not sue in England.

Re a Lawyer's Professional Negligence,[15] a decision of the Regional Court of Appeal in Koblenz, is not without interest. The plaintiff, a German limited partnership, was owed an amount by a Netherlands firm in respect of wine which the plaintiff had sold under standard terms and conditions providing for the courts in Mainz to have jurisdiction. That court queried the validity of the forum clause in the light of article 17. The plaintiff's lawyer had never heard of the Brussels Convention, but four weeks later informed the court that he based his claim that the Mainz court had jurisdiction on 'Title II, Section I, Articles 3, 5(1) and 17' of the Convention. However, the court still expressed doubts about its jurisdiction and the lawyer withdrew the action. Subsequently the Dutch purchaser went bankrupt and the action could not be recommenced in the Netherlands. The German limited partnership therefore commenced proceedings against the lawyer. The Regional Court of Appeal held (a) that the lawyer had been negligent in not being aware of the Brussels Convention; (b) that the Mainz court was wrong in declining jurisdiction since, although the conditions for article 17 were not met and the forum clause was invalid, nevertheless article 5(1) did

13 There is no decided case directly in point, but for an authoritative practitioners' view, see *International Commercial Litigation* by W D Park and S J H Crombie (1990) pp 13–14.

14 (1990) Financial Times, 11 December.

15 [1990] 3 CMLR 415.

confer jurisdiction on the Mainz court; (c) that the action against the lawyer should be dismissed on the ground that, since he had referred to article 5(1), the failure of the Mainz court to accept jurisdiction was not due to the lawyer's negligence but its own error.

This discussion about article 17 has assumed that the contract in issue does not fall within article 12 (insurance matters); article 15 (consumer matters); or article 16 (proceedings about immoveable property, company law, the validity of entries in public registers, patents and trademarks, enforcements of judgments). It is also assumed that the contract is not one of employment. The San Sebastian Convention added a paragraph to article 17 which provides that, in the case of individual contracts of employment, a clause conferring jurisdiction is valid only if entered into after the dispute has arisen or if the employee invokes the clause to sue in courts other than those of the defendant's domicile or those specified in the new version of article 5(1).

Order 11

If a defendant is not present within the jurisdiction of the English courts[16] nor domiciled in a state which is a Contracting State under the Brussels Convention, an action can only be brought against him in the English courts if three conditions are satisfied. First, the case must be one of those which, under Order 11 of the Rules of the Supreme Court, service of a writ out of the jurisdiction of the English courts is permissible. Second, the plaintiff must show that he has 'a good arguable case' on the merits.[17] Third, the court must exercise its discretion under Order 11 to grant leave for a writ to be served out of the jurisdiction. In the present context, the two most important cases permitted by Order 11 are those specified in sub-paragraphs (iii) and (iv) of paragraph 1(1)(d):

> '...the claim is brought to enforce, rescind, dissolve, annul or otherwise affect a contract, or to recover damages or obtain other relief in respect of a breach of a contract, being (in either case) a contract which–
> ...
> (iii) is by its terms, or by implication, governed by English law, or
> (iv) contains a term to the effect that the High Court shall have jurisdiction to hear and determine any action in respect of the contract.'

It is not necessary for a contract to satisfy both sub-paragraphs (iii) and (iv), although, of course, many contracts do. However, to be within sub-paragraph (iii) the whole contract as a single entity must be governed by English law; if a clause is governed by the law of a country other than England, the contract is not within this

16 See *Barclays Bank of Swaziland v Hahn* [1989] 2 All ER 398, HL.
17 See the note in the Supreme Court Practice to Order 11/1/6.

sub-paragraph.[18] Moreover, if there is any room for doubt, Order 11 is construed strictly in favour of the foreign defendant.[19]

Formerly, a plaintiff used to have a heavy burden in satisfying a court that it was proper to exercise its discretion in a case covered by Order 11, Rule 1(d)(iii). However, a different approach is now followed as a result of the decision of the House of Lords in *Spiliada Maritime Corpn v Cansulex Ltd.*[20] That case establishes that, essentially, the principles on which a court will exercise its discretion to grant leave to serve outside the jurisdiction are similar to (although the obverse of) those on which a court will exercise its discretion to stay an action on the ground of forum non conveniens. In both types of case, the fundamental question is to identify the forum in which the case can be suitably tried in the interests of all the parties and for the ends of justice. In Order 11 cases the plaintiff has the burden of proof in persuading the court that England is the appropriate forum; moreover he has to show that England is clearly so. This depends on the particular circumstances of the case, and in *Spiliada* Lord Goff of Chieveley said (at 481) that the fact that English law is the proper law of the contract may be of great importance or it may be of little importance as seen in the context of the whole case. He said that, in determining which is the appropriate forum, the court must first look for 'connecting factors' in the sense of identifying the forum with which the action has 'the most real and substantial connection'. These include not only factors affecting convenience or expense (such as availability of witnesses), but also other factors such as the governing law of the contract and the places where the parties respectively reside or carry on business.

Against this background, it can be seen that the function of a clause providing for the English courts to have jurisdiction in a case not covered by the Brussels Convention is to provide a strong connecting factor with England which will lead to the court's exercising its discretion under Order 11. Clearly the connection with England increases according to whether the clause provides for the English courts to have 'non-exclusive jurisdiction', 'jurisdiction', or 'exclusive jurisdiction'. However, the matter is ultimately one for the court's discretion.[21] It is thought that even a clause providing for the English courts to have 'exclusive jurisdiction' does not completely foreclose or remove the court's discretion under Order 11. This contrasts with a case where the defendant is domiciled in a Contracting State under the Brussels Convention; the effect of article 17 is that a clause providing for the English courts to have jurisdiction will, if valid under that article, exclude the court's power

18 *Armar Shipping Co Ltd v Caisse Algérienne d'Assurance* [1981] 1 All ER 498, [1981] 1 WLR 207, CA.
19 *Newtherapeutics Ltd v Katz* [1991] 2 All ER 151 at 174.
20 [1987] AC 460, [1986] 3 All ER 843.
21 *Kuwait Oil Co v Idemitsu Tankers* [1981] 2 Lloyd's Rep 510.

to stay English proceedings on the ground that another Contracting State is the appropriate forum.

Waiver of forum non conveniens

Where an agreement provides for proceedings to be brought in the courts of a particular jurisdiction, it is common to add a waiver by the parties or one of them (eg the borrower in a financing agreement) of any objection to the specified jurisdiction on the ground of forum non conveniens. This waiver actually amounts to an undertaking not to raise such an objection. However, it is thought that, where the specified jurisdiction is England, the validity of such a waiver or undertaking is questionable.

The decisions of the House of Lords in *National Westminister Bank Ltd v Halesowen Presswork and Assemblies Ltd*[1] and *Johnson v Moreton*[2] establish that, although a person may renounce or waive a right which he has under a statute or a rule of law if the right is entirely for his benefit, this does not apply where there is a public as well as a private interest in the matter concerned.

It is thought that the principle of forum non conveniens contains a public interest element. The principle relates to the discretionary power of the court to permit service out of the jurisdiction which is conferred by Order 11 of the rules of the Supreme Court, and this Order is statutory in nature.[3] More importantly, the principle, as formulated by Lord Goff of Chieveley in *Spiliada*, concerns the forum in which the case can be suitably tried not only for the interests of all the parties, but also 'for the ends of justice'.[4] Furthermore, the speeches of both Lord Goff and Lord Templeman make it clear that, in principle, whether the court exercises its discretion under Order 11 depends not on whether the defendant fails to object, but on whether the plaintiff satisfies the court that England is clearly the appropriate forum.

It is therefore thought that public policy may render unenforceable an undertaking not to oppose on the grounds of forum non conveniens an application for leave under Order 11; and that, even if no such objection is made, the court will not grant leave unless it is satisfied that England is clearly the appropriate forum.

Process agents

A valid clause providing that the English courts shall have jurisdiction is not, of itself, sufficient to enable proceedings to be commenced.

1 [1972] AC 785, [1972] 1 All ER 641.
2 [1980] AC 37, [1978] 3 All ER 37.
3 *Spiliada Maritime Corpn v Cansulex Ltd* [1987] AC 460 at 481.
4 Ibid, 476C, 480G, 483C and 486B.

A writ has to be served. Even where there is a jurisdiction clause which is valid under article 17 of the Brussels Convention, so that Order 11 of the Rules of the Supreme Court permits a writ to be served out of the jurisdiction without leave of the court,[5] there may well be practical difficulties in effecting service in a foreign country; this is particularly so if there is no Civil Procedure Convention in that country providing for service of process of the High Court. To avoid such difficulties, agreements often provide for a party based outside the United Kingdom to appoint a person in England[6] as his agent to receive service of process of the High Court. This is particularly common in international loan agreements and bond issues, where the English process agent is normally an English company with a London office which specialises in this function.

Typical clause

The following (which would normally be preceded by a subclause selecting English law as the applicable law) are common provisions regarding jurisdiction and a process agent:

(1) The courts of England shall have jurisdiction to settle any disputes which may arise out of or in connection with this Agreement.

(2) Subclause (1) is for the benefit of the Bank only; accordingly it retains the right to bring any proceedings relating to this Agreement in any other court which has jurisdiction by virtue of the Convention on jurisdiction and the enforcement of judgments in civil and commercial matters signed at Brussels on 27th September 1968, as amended whether before the date of this Agreement or not ('the Brussels Convention').

(3) Moreover, the Bank may bring any proceedings relating to this Agreement–

(a) in any court which has jurisdiction by virtue of any other convention or provision which is covered by article 57 of the Brussels Convention; or
(b) in any court in a country or territory which is not at the relevant time a Contracting State under the Brussels Convention and in which any property (including intangible property) of the Company is then situated.

(4) Any process connected with proceedings in the English courts which relate to this Agreement shall be deemed to have been validly served

5 Unless other proceedings between the parties concerning the same cause of action are pending in a Convention jurisdiction.
6 However, Order 10, rule 3 of the Rules of the Supreme Court permits the appointment of a person outside the jurisdiction, subject to obtaining leave under Order 11, rule 1 in a case not covered by an article 17 clause giving jurisdiction to the High Court.

on the Company if it is received by XYZ Limited whose present address is ... London ... ('the process agent'); and service or receipt of any such process shall be deemed to have been acknowledged by the Company if it is acknowledged by the process agent.

(5) The previous subclause has effect irrespective of whether, as between the process agent and the Company, the process agent has, or continues to have, any authority to act on the Company's behalf; and no failure or mistake by the process agent (including a failure to notify the Company of the service of any process or to forward any process to the Company) shall invalidate any proceedings or judgment.

(6) Nothing in this clause excludes or limits any right which the Bank may have (whether under the law of any country, an international convention or otherwise) in any jurisdiction with regard to the bringing of proceedings, the service of process, the recognition or enforcement of a judgment or any similar or related matter.

(7) In this clause 'process' includes any document of any kind which falls to be served on or sent to the Company in connection with any stage in any proceedings in the English courts, including proceedings for the recognition or enforcement of a foreign judgment.

Under a common form of clause the party concerned irrevocably appoints the designated company to act as its process agent. However, this is open to technical objections on the ground that the process agent is not a party to the agreement (but this does not matter if there is a separate appointment) and that the appointment cannot be truly irrevocable since it secures no obligation owed by the appointing party to the process agent.[7] It is thought that a provision in the form of subclause (4) above may be preferable; it is simply a contractual term, which normally can only be discharged by agreement with the other parties, that service on the process agent will constitute good service on the party concerned. A similar provision in section 695(1) of the Companies Act 1985 was upheld by the Court of Appeal in *Rome v Punjab National Bank (No 2)*.[8]

Another provision sometimes included states that a judgment given by the English courts may be enforced without review in any other jurisdiction. A clause of this type tends to be controversial; it is unnecessary for the purposes of execution in another Contracting State under the Brussels Convention; and it is unlikely to override any requirements about the enforcement of foreign judgments which may exist in a non-Contracting State.

The effect of a submission to the jurisdiction of the 'British courts' is unclear; literally, this covers not only the courts of England but those in Scotland and Northern Ireland and in colonies such as Hong Kong, Gibraltar and the Falkland Islands. However, in an inter-

7 See 'Irrevocable authorities' in Chapter 12.
8 [1989] 1 All ER 58, [1989] 1 WLR 1211.

national commercial contract, the court will interpret this as meaning the courts of England.[9]

Sovereign immunity

At common law, the doctrine of sovereign immunity prevented the government of a foreign country being sued in the English courts without its consent. The doctrine extended to an organisation which was an arm or emanation of a foreign state, with the position of many central banks being particularly uncertain. The doctrine also prevented execution or attachment over a state's assets in England. It was only in the mid-seventies that the English courts held that the doctrine did not apply to commercial transactions.[10]

Sovereign immunity is now governed by the State Immunity Act 1978. This provides that a state is not immune from proceedings in three main cases: where it has submitted to the jurisdiction of the courts of the United Kingdom (whether after the dispute has arisen or by a prior written agreement); where the proceedings relate to a commercial transaction entered into by the state;[11] where the proceedings relate to a contractual obligation of the state (whether under a commercial transaction or not) which falls to be performed wholly or partly in the United Kingdom. Accordingly, for the purpose of suit, it is unnecessary for a commercial contract to contain an express waiver of sovereign immunity, particularly if there is a clause giving jurisdiction to the English courts.

By contrast, section 13(2) and (3) of the 1978 Act makes it necessary for an agreement to contain a consent by a state to an injunction or order for specific performance being granted against it, to relief being given against it for the recovery of land or other property or for its property being subject to any process for the enforcement of a judgment or arbitration award if these remedies are available against the state. Property which is in use or intended use for commercial purposes is not covered by this immunity,[12] but the Act provides that a central bank's property shall not be regarded as in use for commercial purposes.

Section 2(7) of the 1978 Act provides that the head of a state's diplomatic mission in the United Kingdom (or the person performing his functions) is deemed to have authority to submit to the jurisdiction

9 *The Komninos S* (1991) Financial Times, 16 January.

10 The history of the doctrine in England was outlined by Lord Wilberforce in *I Congreso* [1983] 1 AC 244, [1981] 2 All ER 1064, HL; see also *Buttes Gas and Oil v Hammer (No 3)* [1982] AC 888 at 932D–937A.

11 'Commercial transaction' is defined in section 3(3) to cover any contract for the supply of goods or services, any transaction for the provision of finance and any other transaction which a state enters into otherwise than in the exercise of sovereign authority: see Lord Diplock's comments in *Alcom Ltd v Republic of Columbia* [1984] AC 580 at 601.

12 See *Alcom Ltd v Republic of Columbia* [1984] AC 580, [1984] 2 All ER 6, HL.

of the courts of the United Kingdom. This section also provides that any person who has entered into a contract 'on behalf of and with the authority of a State' is deemed to have authority to effect such a submission in respect of proceedings arising out of the contract. On the other hand, in the case of a section 13(2) consent, only the head of a state's diplomatic mission (or the person performing his functions) is deemed to have authority to give the consent on behalf of the state. It is thought that these provisions do not imply that a submission or consent is invalid if effected by a person who, under the constitutional law of the state concerned has the necessary authority, for example, a foreign counterpart of the Secretary of State or a person expressly authorised by him. At common law, a submission to the jurisdiction of the English courts by a foreign government was only effective if the official making the submission was aware that his government was entitled to sovereign immunity and intended, by the submission, to waive that immunity.[13] It is not clear whether the 1978 Act has abolished this rule in relation to a submission or consent effected by a person who is 'deemed' by the Act to have the necessary authority.

Arbitration

Many commercial agreements provide for disputes to be referred to arbitration. A *Scott v Avery* clause can be added stating that the making of an arbitration award is a condition precedent to any right to bring proceedings in the courts, although the court has power under section 4 of the Arbitration Act 1950 and section 1 of the 1975 Act (as well as an inherent jurisdiction) to stay proceedings in respect of a matter covered by an arbitration clause. It is common for an arbitration clause to exclude the right to appeal to the High Court under section 1 of the Arbitration Act 1979 and the right under section 2 of that Act to apply to the High Court for a determination of a preliminary point of law. However, such an exclusion agreement is only effective in relation to a domestic arbitration agreement if it is entered into after the arbitration commences. For this purpose a 'domestic arbitration agreement' means an arbitration agreement which does not provide for arbitration in a state other than the United Kingdom and none of the parties to which is an individual who is a national of, or habitually resident in, a foreign state or a company incorporated, or whose central management and control is exercised, in a foreign state.

The different arbitral bodies such as the Court of Arbitration of the International Chamber of Commerce and the London Court of International Arbitration have their own forms of arbitration

13 *Baccus SRL v Servicio Nacional del Trigo* [1957] 1 QB 438, [1956] 3 All ER 715, CA.

clause as well as their own rules. A short form clause[14] is as follows:

(1) Any difference which in any way relates to or arises out of this Agreement shall be referred to arbitration by a single arbitrator.

(2) Without limiting its generality, subclause (1) above applies to a difference about–

(a) the existence, validity, termination or discharge, or any variation of this Agreement or of any collateral or related warranty or contract;
(b) any representation or statement which has been made, or is alleged to have been made, in connection with this Agreement.

(3) If–

(a) after a difference has arisen, a party serves the other[s] with a written notice to concur in the appointment of a particular arbitrator; and
(b) that arbitrator is not appointed within 21 days after the notice is served;

the arbitrator shall be appointed by [the President of the Chartered Institute of Arbitrators.]

This subclause also applies if an arbitrator previously appointed declines to act or can no longer act.

(4) The arbitration shall be held in London.

The arbitrator shall have full power to order a party to provide security for costs, regardless of whether the High Court would have power in the circumstances to make such an order.

(5) This subclause excludes the right to appeal or apply to the High Court under section 1(3)(b), 1(5)(b) or 2(1)(b) of the Arbitration Act 1979 in relation to any award under this clause.

(6) In this clause 'difference' includes any dispute and also any claim.

As an alternative to arbitration, an agreement can provide for an issue of fact, usually a valuation, to be determined by an independent, suitably qualified person acting as an expert. For example, the articles of association of a family company may contain a pre-emption article requiring a shareholder to offer his shares to the other shareholders before selling to an outsider and provide that the shares shall be offered at a price which the company's auditors determine to be their fair value. The article will normally state that the auditors shall act 'as experts not as arbitrators', so that the Arbitration Acts 1950–1979 will not apply. Sometimes, however, the parties and the expert himself misunderstand his position and believe that he is in fact an arbitrator.[15]

14 See the discussion in *Commercial Arbitration* by Mustill and Boyd at pp 108–131.
15 *Ipswich Borough Council v Fisons* [1990] Ch 709. See also Chapter 12 above.

CHAPTER 21

NOTARISATION

In some countries, certain documents have taken the form of an instrument drawn up by the notary which contains a declaration by him that the parties signed it before him on a particular date. The instrument, which is also signed and sealed by the notary, is a notarial act in public form or a public instrument. For example, under the Commercial Code of Spain debts evidenced by such a notarised instrument (an esritura publica) rank in a bankruptcy prior to ordinary debts.

Other types of document have to be accompanied by a certificate signed by a notary to the effect that the document was executed before him on a certain date by the persons named in the certificate. Such a certificate is a notarial act in private form. Many powers of attorney for use abroad are supported by such certificates.

If a document is executed before a notary outside the country in which it is to be used, it is normally necessary for the signature of the notary to be verified. This can be done in one of two ways. The notary's signature can be authenticated by the embassy or a consulate of the country in which the document is to be used that is located in the country of the notary: this is called legislation. (For example, a document executed in London for use in Sweden would be legalised by the Swedish Consulate in London.) Alternatively, where a document is executed in a country which has ratified the Hague Convention of 5 October 1961 and is to be used in another such country, the notary's signature can be authenticated by an 'apostille' issued by the Foreign Ministry in the first country. This apostille, which in London is issued by the Foreign and Commonwealth Office, certifies that the notary's certificate has been signed by the notary acting in the capacity of notary public and it bears his seal. Countries party to the 1961 Hague Convention include France, Germany, Israel, Italy, Japan, Luxembourg, the Netherlands, Spain and Switzerland.

APPENDIX 1

STATUTORY AND EC MATERIALS

Law of Property Act 1925
(1925 c 20)

52 Conveyances to be by deed

(1) All conveyances of land or of any interest therein are void for the purpose of conveying or creating a legal estate unless made by deed.

(2) This section does not apply to—

(*a*) assents by a personal representative;
(*b*) disclaimers made in accordance with [sections 178 to 180 or sections 315 to 319 of the Insolvency Act 1986], or not required to be evidenced in writing;
(*c*) surrenders by operation of law, including surrenders which may, by law, be effected without writing;
(*d*) leases or tenancies or other assurances not required by law to be made in writing;
(*e*) receipts [other than those falling within section 115 below];
(*f*) vesting orders of the court or other competent authority;
(*g*) conveyances taking effect by operation of law.

NOTE

The words in square brackets in sub-s (2)(*b*) were substituted by the Insolvency Act 1986, s 439(2), Sch 14, and the words in square brackets in sub-s (2)(*e*) were substituted by the Law of Property (Miscellaneous Provisions) Act 1989, s 1(8), Sch 1, para 2.

56 Persons taking who are not parties and as to indentures

(1) A person may take an immediate or other interest in land or other property, or the benefit of any condition, right of entry, covenant or agreement over or respecting land or other property, although he may not be named as a party to the conveyance or other instrument.

(2) A deed between parties, to effect its objects, has the effect of an indenture though not indented or expressed to be an indenture.

61 Construction of expressions used in deeds and other instruments

In all deeds, contracts, wills, orders and other instruments executed, made or coming into operation after the commencement of this Act, unless the context otherwise requires—

(*a*) 'Month' means calendar month;
(*b*) 'Person' includes a corporation;
(*c*) The singular includes the plural and vice versa;
(*d*) The masculine includes the feminine and vice versa.

NOTE

Commencement of this Act. This Act came into operation on 1 January 1926 by virtue of s 209(2) (repealed).

74 Execution of instruments by or on behalf of corporations

(1) In favour of a purchaser a deed shall be deemed to have been duly executed by a corporation aggregate if its seal be affixed thereto in the presence of and attested by its clerk, secretary or other permanent officer or his deputy, and a member of the board of directors, council or other governing body of the corporation, and where a seal purporting to be the seal of a corporation has been affixed to a deed, attested by persons purporting to be persons holding such offices as aforesaid, the deed shall be deemed to have been executed in accordance with the requirements of this section, and to have taken effect accordingly.

(2) The board of directors, council or other governing body of a corporation aggregate may, by resolution or otherwise, appoint an agent either generally or in any particular case, to execute on behalf of the corporation any agreement or other instrument [which is not a deed] in relation to any matter within the powers of the corporation.

(3) Where a person is authorised under a power of attorney or under any statutory or other power to convey any interest in property in the name or on behalf of a corporation sole or aggregate, he may as attorney execute the conveyance by signing the name of the corporation in the presence of at least one witness, . . . and such execution shall take effect and be valid in like manner as if the corporation had executed the conveyance.

(4) Where a corporation aggregate is authorised under a power of attorney or under any statutory or other power to convey any interest in property in the name or on behalf of any other person (including another corporation), an officer appointed for that purpose by the board of directors, council or other governing body of the corporation by resolution or otherwise, may execute the deed or other instrument in the name of such other person; and where an instrument appears to be executed by an officer so appointed, then in favour of a purchaser the instrument shall be deemed to have been executed by an officer duly authorised.

(5) The foregoing provisions of this section apply to transactions wherever effected, but only to deeds and instruments executed after the commencement of this Act, except that, in the case of powers or appointments of an agent

or officer, they apply whether the power was conferred or the appointment was made before or after the commencement of this Act or by this Act.

(6) Notwithstanding anything contained in this section, any mode of execution or attestation authorised by law or by practice or by the statute, charter, memorandum or articles, deed of settlement or other instrument constituting the corporation or regulating the affairs thereof, shall (in addition to the modes authorised by this section) be as effectual as if this section had not been passed.

NOTE

The words in square brackets in sub-s (2) were substituted by the Law of Property (Miscellaneous Provisions) Act 1989, s 1(8), Sch 1, para 3, and the words omitted from sub-s (3) were repealed by s 4 of, and Sch 2 to, that Act.

76 Covenants for title

(1) In a conveyance there shall, in the cases in this section mentioned, be deemed to be included, and there shall in those several cases, by virtue of this Act, be implied, a covenant to the effect in this section stated, by the person or by each person who conveys, as far as regards the subject-matter or share of subject-matter expressed to be conveyed by him, with the person, if one, to whom the conveyance is made, or with the persons jointly, if more than one, to whom the conveyance is (when the law permits) made as tenants in common, that is to say:

(A) In a conveyance for valuable consideration, other than a mortgage, a covenant by a person who conveys and is expressed to convey as beneficial owner in the terms set out in Part I of the Second Schedule to this Act;

(B) In a conveyance of leasehold property for valuable consideration, other than a mortgage, a further covenant by a person who conveys and is expressed to convey as beneficial owner in the terms set out in Part II of the Second Schedule to this Act;

(C) In a conveyance by way of mortgage (including a charge) a covenant by a person who conveys or charges and is expressed to convey or charge as beneficial owner in the terms set out in Part III of the Second Schedule to this Act;

(D) In a conveyance by way of mortgage (including a charge) of freehold property subject to a rent or of leasehold property, a further covenant by a person who conveys or charges and is expressed to convey or charge as beneficial owner in the terms set out in Part IV of the Second Schedule to this Act;

(E) In a conveyance by way of settlement, a covenant by a person who conveys and is expressed to convey as settlor in the terms set out in Part V of the Second Schedule to this Act;

(F) In any conveyance, a covenant by every person who conveys and is expressed to convey as trustee or mortgagee, or as personal representative of a deceased person, ... or under an order of the court, in the terms set out in Part VI of the Second Schedule to this Act, which covenant shall be deemed to extend to every such person's own acts only, and may be implied in an assent by a personal representative in like manner as in a conveyance by deed.

(2) Where in a conveyance it is expressed that by direction of a person expressed to direct as beneficial owner another person conveys, then, for the purposes of this section, the person giving the direction, whether he conveys and is expressed to convey as beneficial owner or not, shall be deemed to convey and to be expressed to convey as beneficial owner the subject-matter so conveyed by his direction; and a covenant on his part shall be implied accordingly.

(3) Where a wife conveys and is expressed to convey as beneficial owner, and the husband also conveys and is expressed to convey as beneficial owner, then, for the purposes of this section, the wife shall be deemed to convey and to be expressed to convey by direction of the husband, as beneficial owner; and, in addition to the covenant implied on the part of the wife, there shall also be implied, first, a covenant on the part of the husband as the person giving that direction, and secondly, a covenant on the part of the husband in the same terms as the covenant implied on the part of the wife.

(4) Where in a conveyance a person conveying is not expressed to convey as beneficial owner, or as settlor, or as trustee, or as mortgagee, or as personal representative of a deceased person, . . . or under an order of the court, or by direction of a person as beneficial owner, no covenant on the part of the person conveying shall be, by virtue of this section, implied in the conveyance.

(5) In this section a conveyance does not include a demise by way of lease at a rent, but does include a charge and "convey" has a corresponding meaning.

(6) The benefit of a covenant implied as aforesaid shall be annexed and incident to, and shall go with, the estate or interest of the implied covenantee, and shall be capable of being enforced by every person in whom that estate or interest is, for the whole or any part thereof, from time to time vested.

(7) A covenant implied as aforesaid may be varied or extended by a deed or an assent, and, as so varied or extended, shall, as far as may be, operate in the like manner, and with all the like incidents, effects, and consequences, as if such variations or extensions were directed in this section to be implied.

(8) This section applies to conveyances made after the thirty-first day of December, eighteen hundred and eighty-one, but only to assents by a personal representative made after the commencement of this Act.

NOTE

The words omitted from sub-ss (1)(F), (4) were repealed by the Mental Health Act 1959, s 149(2), Sch 8, Pt I.

81 Effect of covenant with two or more jointly

(1) A covenant, and a contract under seal, and a bond or obligation under seal, made with two or more jointly, to pay money or to make a conveyance, or to do any other act, to them or for their benefit, shall be deemed to include, and shall, by virtue of this Act, imply, an obligation to do the act to, or for the benefit of, the survivor or survivors of them, and to, or for the benefit of, any other person to whom the right to sue on the covenant, contract, bond, or obligation devolves, and where made after the commencement of this Act shall be construed as being also made with each of them.

(2) This section extends to a covenant implied by virtue of this Act.

(3) This section applies only if and as far as a contrary intention is not expressed in the covenant, contract, bond, or obligation, and has effect subject to the covenant, contract, bond, or obligation, and to the provisions therein contained.

(4) Except as otherwise expressly provided, this section applies to a covenant, contract, bond, or obligation made or implied after the thirty-first day of December, eighteen hundred and eighty-one.

[(5) In its application to instruments made after the coming into force of section 1 of the Law of Property (Miscellaneous Provisions) Act 1989 subsection (1) above shall have effect as if for the words "under seal, and a bond or obligation under seal," there were substituted the words "bond or obligation executed as a deed in accordance with section 1 of the Law of Property (Miscellaneous Provisions) Act 1989"].

NOTE

Sub-s (5) was added by the Law of Property (Miscellaneous Provisions) Act 1989, s 1(8), Sch 1, para 5.

136 Legal assignments of things in action

(1) Any absolute assignment by writing under the hand of the assignor (not purporting to be by way of charge only) of any debt or other legal thing in action, of which express notice in writing has been given to the debtor, trustee or other person from whom the assignor would have been entitled to claim such debt or thing in action, is effectual in law (subject to equities having priority over the right of the assignee) to pass and transfer from the date of such notice—

(*a*) the legal right to such debt or thing in action;
(*b*) all legal and other remedies for the same; and
(*c*) the power to give a good discharge for the same without the concurrence of the assignor:

Provided that, if the debtor, trustee or other person liable in respect of such debt or thing in action has notice—

(*a*) that the assignment is disputed by the assignor or any person claiming under him; or
(*b*) of any other opposing or conflicting claims to such debt or thing in action;

he may, if he thinks fit, either call upon the persons making claim thereto to interplead concerning the same, or pay the debt or other thing in action into court under the provisions of the Trustee Act 1925.

(2) This section does not affect the provisions of the Policies of Assurance Act 1867.

[(3) The county court has jurisdiction (including power to receive payment of money or securities into court) under the proviso to subsection (1) of this section where the amount or value of the debt or thing in action does not exceed the county court limit.]

NOTE

Sub-s (3) was added by the County Courts Act 1984, s 148(1), Sch 2, Pt II, para 4.

Misrepresentation Act 1967
(1967 c 7)

An Act to amend the law relating to innocent misrepresentations and to amend sections 11 and 35 of the Sale of Goods Act 1893 [22 March 1967]

1 Removal of certain bars to rescission for innocent misrepresentation

Where a person has entered into a contract after a misrepresentation has been made to him, and—

(*a*) the misrepresentation has become a term of the contract; or
(*b*) the contract has been performed;

or both, then, if otherwise he would be entitled to rescind the contract without alleging fraud, he shall be so entitled, subject to the provisions of this Act, notwithstanding the matters mentioned in paragraphs (*a*) and (*b*) of this section.

2 Damages for misrepresentation

(1) Where a person has entered into a contract after a misrepresentation has been made to him by another party thereto and as a result thereof he has suffered loss, then, if the person making the misrepresentation would be liable to damages in respect thereof had the misrepresentation been made fraudulently, that person shall be so liable notwithstanding that the misrepresentation was not made fraudulently, unless he proves that he had reasonable ground to believe and did believe up to the time the contract was made that the facts represented were true.

(2) Where a person has entered into a contract after a misrepresentation has been made to him otherwise than fraudulently, and he would be entitled, by reason of the misrepresentation, to rescind the contract, then, if it is claimed, in any proceedings arising out of the contract, that the contract ought to be or has been rescinded the court or arbitrator may declare

the contract subsisting and award damages in lieu of rescission, if of opinion that it would be equitable to do so, having regard to the nature of the misrepresentation and the loss that would be caused by it if the contract were upheld, as well as to the loss that rescission would cause to the other party.

(3) Damages may be awarded against a person under subsection (2) of this section whether or not he is liable to damages under subsection (1) thereof, but where he is so liable any award under the said subsection (2) shall be taken into account in assessing his liability under the said subsection (1).

[3 Avoidance of provision excluding liability for misrepresentation

If a contract contains a term which would exclude or restrict—

(*a*) any liability to which a party to a contract may be subject by reason of any misrepresentation made by him before the contract was made; or
(*b*) any remedy available to another party to the contract by reason of such a misrepresentation,

that term shall be of no effect except in so far as it satisfies the requirement of reasonableness as stated in section 11(1) of the Unfair Contract Terms Act 1977; and it is for those claiming that the term satisfies that requirement to show that it does.]

NOTE
This section was substituted by the Unfair Contract Terms Act 1977, s 8(1).

4 *(Repealed by the Sale of Goods Act 1979, s 63(2), Sch 3.)*

5 Saving for past transactions

Nothing in this Act shall apply in relation to any misrepresentation or contract of sale which is made before the commencement of this Act.

6 Short title, commencement and extent

(1) This Act may be cited as the Misrepresentation Act 1967.

(2) This Act shall come into operation at the expiration of the period of one month beginning with the date on which it is passed.

(3) *(Applies to Scotland only.)*

(4) This Act does not extend to Northern Ireland.

NOTE
Beginning with the day on which it is passed. This Act was passed, ie received the Royal Assent, on 22 March 1967, and, therefore, came into force on 22 April 1967.

Powers of Attorney Act 1971
(1971 c 27)

An Act to make new provision in relation to powers of attorney and the delegation by trustees of their trusts, powers and discretions [12 May 1971]

1 Execution of powers of attorney

(1) An instrument creating a power of attorney shall be [executed as a deed by] the donor of the power.

(2) . . .

(3) This section is without prejudice to any requirement in, or having effect under, any other Act as to the witnessing of instruments creating powers of attorney and does not affect the rules relating to the execution of instruments by bodies corporate.

NOTE

The words in square brackets in sub-s (1) were substituted, and sub-s (2) was repealed, by the Law of Property (Miscellaneous Provisions) Act 1989, ss 1(8), 4, Sch 1, para 6, Sch 2.

2 *(Repealed by the Supreme Court Act 1981, s 152(4), Sch 7.)*

3 Proof of instruments creating powers of attorney

(1) The contents of an instrument creating a power of attorney may be proved by means of a copy which—

- (*a*) is a reproduction of the original made with a photographic or other device for reproducing documents in facsimile; and
- (*b*) contains the following certificate or certificates signed by the donor of the power or by a solicitor [duly certified notary public] or stockbroker, that is to say—
  - (i) a certificate at the end to the effect that the copy is a true and complete copy of the original; and
  - (ii) if the original consists of two or more pages, a certificate at the end of each page of the copy to the effect that it is a true and complete copy of the corresponding page of the original.

(2) Where a copy of an instrument creating a power of attorney has been made which complies with subsection (1) of this section, the contents of the instrument may also be proved by means of a copy of that copy if the further copy itself complies with that subsection, taking references in it to the original as references to the copy from which the further copy is made.

(3) In this section ['duly certificated notary public' has the same meaning as it has in the Solicitors Act 1974 by virtue of s 87(1) of that Act and] 'stockbroker' means a member of any stock exchange within the meaning

of the Stock Transfer Act 1963 or the Stock Transfer Act (Northern Ireland) 1963.

(4) This section is without prejudice to section 4 of the Evidence and Powers of Attorney Act 1940 (proof of deposited instruments by office copy) and to any other method of proof authorised by law.

(5) For the avoidance of doubt, in relation to an instrument made in Scotland the references to a power of attorney in this section and in section 4 of the Evidence and Powers of Attorney Act 1940 include references to a factory and commission.

NOTE

The words in square brackets in sub-ss (1)(*b*) and (3) were inserted by the Courts and Legal Services Act 1990, s 125(2), Sch 17, para 4.

4 Powers of attorney given as security

(1) Where a power of attorney is expressed to be irrevocable and is given to secure—

(*a*) a proprietary interest of the donee of the power; or
(*b*) the performance of an obligation owed to the donee,

then, so long as the donee has that interest or the obligation remains undischarged, the power shall not be revoked—

(i) by the donor without the consent of the donee; or
(ii) by the death, incapacity or bankruptcy of the donor or, if the donor is a body corporate, by its winding up or dissolution.

(2) A power of attorney given to secure a proprietary interest may be given to the person entitled to the interest and persons deriving title under him to that interest, and those persons shall be duly constituted donees of the power for all purposes of the power but without prejudice to any right to appoint substitutes given by the power.

(3) This section applies to powers of attorney whenever created.

5 Protection of donee and third persons where power of attorney is revoked

(1) A donee of a power of attorney who acts in pursuance of the power at a time when it has been revoked shall not, by reason of the revocation, incur any liability (either to the donor or to any other person) if at that time he did not know that the power had been revoked.

(2) Where a power of attorney has been revoked and a person, without knowledge of the revocation, deals with the donee of the power, the transaction between them shall, in favour of that person, be as valid as if the power had then been in existence.

(3) Where the power is expressed in the instrument creating it to be irrevocable and to be given by way of security then, unless the person dealing with the donee knows that it was not in fact given by way of security, he shall be entitled to assume that the power is incapable of revocation except by the donor acting with the consent of the donee and

shall accordingly be treated for the purposes of subsection (2) of this section as having knowledge of the revocation only if he knows that it has been revoked in that manner.

(4) Where the interest of a purchaser depends on whether a transaction between the donee of a power of attorney and another person was valid by virtue of subsection (2) of this section, it shall be conclusively presumed in favour of the purchaser that that person did not at the material time know of the revocation of the power if—

(*a*) the transaction between that person and the donee was completed within twelve months of the date on which the power came into operation; or
(*b*) that person makes a statutory declaration, before or within three months after the completion of the purchase, that he did not at that material time know of the revocation of the power.

(5) Without prejudice to subsection (3) of this section, for the purposes of this section knowledge of the revocation of a power of attorney includes knowledge of the occurrence of any event (such as the death of the donor) which has the effect of revoking the power.

(6) In this section 'purchaser' and 'purchase' have the meaning specified in section 205(1) of the Law of Property Act 1925.

(7) This section applies whenever the power of attorney was created but only to acts and transactions after the commencement of this Act.

6 Additional protection for transferees under stock exchange transactions

(1) Without prejudice to section 5 of this Act, where—

(*a*) the donee of a power of attorney executes, as transferor, an instrument transferring registered securities; and
(*b*) the instrument is executed for the purposes of a stock exchange transaction,

it shall be conclusively presumed in favour of the transferee that the power had not been revoked at the date of the instrument if a statutory declaration to that effect is made by the donee of the power on or within three months after that date.

(2) In this section 'registered securities' and 'stock exchange transaction' have the same meanings as in the Stock Transfer Act 1963.

7 Execution of instruments etc by donee of power of attorney

[(1) If the donee of a power of attorney is an individual, he may, if he thinks fit—
(*a*) execute any instrument with his own signature, and]
(*b*) do any other thing in his own name,

by the authority of the donor of the power; and any document executed or thing done in that manner shall be as effective as if executed or done by the donee with the signature..., or, as the case may be, in the name, of the donor of the power.

(2) For the avoidance of doubt it is hereby declared that an instrument to which subsection (3)... of section 74 of the Law of Property Act 1925 applies may be executed either as provided in [that subsection] or as provided in this section.

(3) This section is without prejudice to any statutory direction requiring an instrument to be executed in the name of an estate owner within the meaning of the said Act of 1925.

(4) This section applies whenever the power of attorney was created.

NOTE

The words in square brackets in sub-ss (1) and (2) were substituted, and the words omitted from those subsections were repealed, by the Law of Property (Miscellaneous Provisions) Act 1989, ss 1(8), 4, Sch 1, para 7, Sch 2.

8, 9 *(S 8 repeals the Law of Property Act 1925, s 129; s 9 amends the Trustee Act 1925, s 25.)*

10 Effect of general power of attorney in specified form

(1) Subject to subsection (2) of this section, a general power of attorney in the form set out in Schedule 1 to this Act, or in a form to the like effect but expressed to be made under this Act, shall operate to confer—

- (*a*) on the donee of the power; or
- (*b*) if there is more than one donee, on the donees acting jointly or acting jointly or severally, as the case may be,

authority to do on behalf of the donor anything which he can lawfully do by an attorney.

(2) This section does not apply to functions which the donor has as a trustee or personal representative or as a tenant for life or statutory owner within the meaning of the Settled Land Act 1925.

11 Short title, repeals, consequential amendments, commencement and extent

(1) This Act may be cited as the Powers of Attorney Act 1971.

(2) The enactments specified in Schedule 2 to this Act are hereby repealed to the extent specified in the third column of that Schedule.

(3) ...

(4) This Act shall come into force on 1st October 1971.

(5) Section 3 of this Act extends to Scotland and Northern Ireland but, save as aforesaid, this Act extends to England and Wales only.

NOTE

Sub-s (3) partly amends the Law of Property Act 1925, s 125(2), and is partly repealed by the Supreme Court Act 1981, s 152(4), Sch 7.

SCHEDULES

SCHEDULE 1

Section 10

FORM OF GENERAL POWER OF ATTORNEY FOR PURPOSES OF SECTION 10

THIS GENERAL POWER OF ATTORNEY is made this day of 19 by AB of I appoint CD of
[*or* CD of and
EF of jointly *or*
jointly and severally] to be my attorney[s] in accordance with section 10 of the Powers of Attorney Act 1971.

IN WITNESS etc.,

Schedule 2 *(Repealing only.)*

Unfair Contract Terms Act 1977
(1977 c 50)

An Act to impose further limits on the extent to which under the law of England and Wales and Northern Ireland civil liability for breach of contract, or for negligence or other breach of duty, can be avoided by means of contract terms and otherwise, and under the law of Scotland civil liability can be avoided by means of contract terms [26 October 1977]

PART I

AMENDMENT OF LAW FOR ENGLAND AND WALES AND NORTHERN IRELAND

Introductory

1 Scope of Part I

(1) For the purposes of this Part of this Act, 'negligence' means the breach—

(*a*) of any obligation, arising from the express or implied terms of a contract, to take reasonable care to exercise reasonable skill in the performance of the contract;
(*b*) of any common law duty to take reasonable care or exercise reasonable skill (but not any stricter duty);
(*c*) of the common duty of care imposed by the Occupiers' Liability Act 1957 or the Occupiers' Liability Act (Northern Ireland) 1957.

(2) This Part of this Act is subject to Part III; and in relation to contracts, the operation of sections 2 to 4 and 7 is subject to the exceptions made by Schedule 1.

(3) In the case of both contract and tort, sections 2 to 7 apply (except where the contrary is stated in section 6(4)) only to business liability, that is liability for breach of obligations or duties arising—

(*a*) from things done or to be done by a person in the course of a business (whether his own business or another's); or
(*b*) from the occupation of premises used for business purposes of the occupier;

and references to liability are to be read accordingly [but liability of an occupier of premises for breach of an obligation or duty towards a person obtaining access to the premises for recreational or educational purposes, being liability for loss or damage suffered by reason of the dangerous state of the premises, is not a business liability of the occupier unless granting that person such access for the purposes concerned falls within the business purposes of the occupier].

(4) In relation to any breach of duty or obligation, it is immaterial for any purpose of this Part of this Act whether the breach was inadvertent or intentional, or whether liability for it arises directly or vicariously.

NOTE

The words in square brackets in sub-s (3) were added by the Occupiers' Liability Act 1984, s 2, and by the Occupiers Liability (Northern Ireland) Order 1987 (SI 1987/1280) (NI 15), art 4.

Avoidance of liability for negligence, breach of contract, etc

2 Negligence liability

(1) A person cannot by reference to any contract term or to a notice given to persons generally or to particular persons exclude or restrict his liability for death or personal injury resulting from negligence.

(2) In the case of other loss or damage, a person cannot so exclude or restrict his liability for negligence except in so far as the term or notice satisfies the requirement of reasonableness.

(3) Where a contract term or notice purports to exclude or restrict liability for negligence a person's agreement to or awareness of it is not of itself to be taken as indicating his voluntary acceptance of any risk.

3 Liability arising in contract

(1) This section applies as between contracting parties where one of them deals as consumer or on the other's written standard terms of business.

(2) As against that party, the other cannot by reference to any contract term—

(*a*) when himself in breach of contract, exclude or restrict any liability of his in respect of the breach; or
(*b*) claim to be entitled—

(i) to render a contractual performance substantially different from that which was reasonably expected of him, or
(ii) in respect of the whole or any part of his contractual obligation, to render no performance at all,

expect in so far as (in any of the cases mentioned above in this subsection) the contract term satisfies the requirement of reasonableness.

4 Unreasonable indemnity clauses

(1) A person dealing as consumer cannot by reference to any contract term be made to indemnify another person (whether a party to the contract or not) in respect of liability that may be incurred by the other for negligence or breach of contract, except in so far as the contract term satisfies the requirement of reasonableness.

(2) This section applies whether the liability in question—

(*a*) is directly that of the person to be indemnified or is incurred by him vicariously;
(*b*) is to the person dealing as consumer or to someone else.

Liability arising from sale or supply of goods

5 'Guarantee' of consumer goods

(1) In the case of goods of a type ordinarily supplied for private use or consumption, where loss or damage—

(*a*) arises from the goods proving defective while in consumer use; and
(*b*) results from the negligence of a person concerned in the manufacture or distribution of the goods,

liability for the loss or damage cannot be excluded or restricted by reference to any contract term or notice contained in or operating by reference to a guarantee of the goods.

(2) For these purposes—

(*a*) goods are to be regarded as 'in consumer use' when a person is using them, or has them in his possession for use, otherwise than exclusively for the purposes of a business; and
(*b*) anything in writing is a guarantee if it contains or purports to contain some promise or assurance (however worded or presented) that defects will be made good by complete or partial replacement, or by repair, monetary compensation or otherwise.

(3) This section does not apply as between the parties to a contract under or in pursuance of which possession or ownership of the goods passed.

6 Sale and hire-purchase

(1) Liability for breach of the obligations arising from—

(*a*) [section 12 of the Sale of Goods Act 1979] (seller's implied undertakings as to title, etc);
(*b*) section 8 of the Supply of Goods (Implied Terms) Act 1973 (the corresponding thing in relation to hire-purchase),

cannot be excluded or restricted by reference to any contract term.

(2) As against a person dealing as consumer, liability for breach of the obligations arising from—

(*a*) [section 13, 14 or 15 of the 1979 Act] (seller's implied undertakings as to conformity of goods with description or sample, or as to their quality or fitness for a particular purpose);

(*b*) section 9, 10 or 11 of the 1973 Act (the corresponding things in relation to hire-purchase),

cannot be excluded or restricted by reference to any contract term.

(3) As against a person dealing otherwise than as consumer, the liability specified in subsection (2) above can be excluded or restricted by reference to a contract term, but only in so far as the term satisfies the requirement of reasonableness.

(4) The liabilities referred to in this section are not only the business liabilities defined by section 1(3), but include those arising under any contract of sale of goods or hire-purchase agreement.

NOTE

The words in square brackets in sub-ss (1)(*a*) and (2)(*a*) were substituted by the Sale of Goods Act 1979, s 63, Sch 2, para 19.

7 Miscellaneous contracts under which goods pass

(1) Where the possession or ownership of goods passes under or in pursuance of a contract not governed by the law of sale of goods or hire-purchase, subsections (2) to (4) below apply as regards the effect (if any) to be given to contract terms excluding or restricting liability for breach of obligation arising by implication of law from the nature of the contract.

(2) As against a person dealing as consumer, liability in respect of the goods' correspondence with description or sample, or their quality or fitness for any particular purpose, cannot be excluded or restricted by reference to any such term.

(3) As against a person dealing otherwise than as consumer, that liability can be excluded or restricted by reference to such a term, but only in so far as the term satisfies the requirement of reasonableness.

[(3A) Liability for breach of the obligations arising under section 2 of the Supply of Goods and Services Act 1982 (implied terms about title etc in certain contracts for the transfer of the property in goods) cannot be excluded or restricted by reference to any such term.]

(4) Liability in respect of—

(*a*) the right to transfer ownership of the goods, or give possession; or

(*b*) the assurance of quiet possession to a person taking goods in pursuance of the contract,

cannot [(in a case to which subsection (3A) above does not apply)] be excluded or restricted by reference to any such term except in so far as the term satisfies the requirement of reasonableness.

(5) This section does not apply in the case of goods passing on a redemption of trading stamps within the Trading Stamps Act 1964 or the Trading Stamps Act (Northern Ireland) 1965.

NOTE

Sub-s (3A) was added, and the words in square brackets in sub-s (4) were inserted, by the Supply of Goods and Services Act 1982, s 17(2), (3).

Other provisions about contracts

8 *(Substitutes the Misrepresentation Act 1967, s 3, and the Misrepresentation Act (Northern Ireland) 1967, s 3.)*

9 Effect of breach

(1) Where for reliance upon it a contract term has to satisfy the requirement of reasonableness, it may be found to do so and be given effect accordingly notwithstanding that the contract has been terminated either by breach or by a party electing to treat it as repudiated.

(2) Where on a breach the contract is nevertheless affirmed by a party entitled to treat it as repudiated, this does not of itself exclude the requirement of reasonableness in relation to any contract term.

10 Evasion by means of secondary contract

A person is not bound by any contract term prejudicing or taking away rights of his which arise under, or in connection with the performance of, another contract, so far as those rights extend to the enforcement of another's liability which this Part of this Act prevents that other from excluding or restricting.

Explanatory provisions

11 The 'reasonableness' test

(1) In relation to a contract term, the requirement of reasonableness for the purposes of this Part of this Act, section 3 of the Misrepresentation Act 1967 and section 3 of the Misrepresentation Act (Northern Ireland) 1967 is that the term shall have been a fair and reasonable one to be included having regard to the circumstances which were, or ought reasonably to have been, known to or in the contemplation of the parties when the contract was made.

(2) In determining for the purposes of section 6 or 7 above whether a contract term satisfies the requirement of reasonableness, regard shall be had in particular to the matters specified in Schedule 2 to this Act; but this subsection does not prevent the court or arbitrator from holding, in accordance with any rule of law, that a term which purports to exclude or restrict any relevant liability is not a term of the contract.

(3) In relation to a notice (not being a notice having contractual effect),

the requirement of reasonableness under this Act is that it should be fair and reasonable to allow reliance on it, having regard to all the circumstances obtaining when the liability arose or (but for the notice) would have arisen.

(4) Where by reference to a contract term or notice a person seeks to restrict liability to a specified sum of money, and the question arises (under this or any other Act) whether the term or notice satisfies the requirement of reasonableness, regard shall be had in particular (but without prejudice to subsection (2) above in the case of contract terms) to—

(*a*) the resources which he could expect to be available to him for the purpose of meeting the liability should it arise; and
(*b*) how far it was open to him to cover himself by insurance.

(5) It is for those claiming that a contract term or notice satisfies the requirement of reasonableness to show that it does.

12 'Dealing as consumer'

(1) A party to a contract 'deals as consumer' in relation to another party if—

(*a*) he neither makes the contract in the course of a business nor holds himself out as doing so; and
(*b*) the other party does make the contract in the course of a business; and
(*c*) in the case of a contract governed by the law of sale of goods or hire-purchase, or by section 7 of this Act, the goods passing under or in pursuance of the contract are of a type ordinarily supplied for private use or consumption.

(2) But on a sale by auction or by competitive tender the buyer is not in any circumstances to be regarded as dealing as consumer.

(3) Subject to this, it is for those claiming that a party does not deal as consumer to show that he does not.

13 Varieties of exemption clause

(1) To the extent that this Part of this Act prevents the exclusion or restriction of any liability it also prevents—

(*a*) making the liability or its enforcement subject to restrictive or onerous conditions;
(*b*) excluding or restricting any right or remedy in respect of the liability, or subjecting a person to any prejudice in consequence of his pursuing any such right or remedy;
(*c*) excluding or restricting rules of evidence or procedure;

and (to that extent) sections 2 and 5 to 7 also prevent excluding or restricting liability by reference to terms and notices which exclude or restrict the relevant obligation or duty.

(2) But an agreement in writing to submit present or future differences to arbitration is not to be treated under this Part of this Act as excluding or restricting any liability.

14 Interpretation of Part I

In this Part of this Act—

'business' includes a profession and the activities of any government department or local or public authority;
'goods' has the same meaning as in [the Sale of Goods Act 1979];
'hire-purchase agreement' has the same meaning as in the Consumer Credit Act 1974;
'negligence' has the meaning given by section 1(1);
'notice' includes an announcement, whether or not in writing, and any other communication or pretended communication; and
'personal injury' includes any disease and any impairment of physical or mental condition.

NOTE

The words in square brackets in the definition of 'goods' were substituted by the Sale of Goods Act 1979, s 63, Sch 2, para 20.

15–25 (*(Pt II) Applies to Scotland only.*)

PART III

PROVISIONS APPLYING TO WHOLE OF UNITED KINGDOM

Miscellaneous

26 International supply contracts

(1) The limits imposed by this Act on the extent to which a person may exclude or restrict liability by reference to a contract term do not apply to liability arising under such a contract as is described in subsection (3) below.

(2) The terms of such a contract are not subject to any requirement of reasonableness under section 3 or 4 . . .

(3) Subject to subsection (4), that description of contract is one whose characteristics are the following—

(*a*) either it is a contract of sale of goods or it is one under or in pursuance of which the possession or ownership of goods passes; and
(*b*) it is made by parties whose places of business (or, if they have none, habitual residences) are in the territories of different States (the Channel Islands and the Isle of Man being treated for this purpose as different States from the United Kingdom).

(4) A contract falls within subsection (3) above only if either—

(*a*) the goods in question are, at the time of the conclusion of the contract, in the course of carriage, or will be carried, from the territory of one State to the territory of another; or
(*b*) the acts constituting the offer and acceptance have been done in the territories of different States; or

(*c*) the contract provides for the goods to be delivered to the territory of a State other than that within whose territory those acts were done.

NOTE

The words omitted from sub-s(2) apply to Scotland only.

27 Choice of law clauses

(1) Where the [law applicable to] a contract is the law of any part of the United Kingdom only by choice of the parties (and apart from that choice would be the law of some country outside the United Kingdom) sections 2 to 7 and 16 to 21 of this Act do not operate as part [of the law applicable to the contract].

(2) This Act has effect notwithstanding any contract term which applies or purports to apply the law of some country outside the United Kingdom, where (either or both)—

(*a*) the term appears to the court, or arbitrator or arbiter to have been imposed wholly or mainly for the purpose of enabling the party imposing it to evade the operation of this Act; or
(*b*) in the making of the contract one of the parties dealt as consumer, and he was then habitually resident in the United Kingdom, and the essential steps necessary for the making of the contract were taken there, whether by him or by others on his behalf.

(3) (*Applies to Scotland only.*)

NOTE

The words in square brackets in sub-s (1) were substituted by the Contracts (Applicable Law) Act 1990, Sch 4, para 4.

28 Temporary provision for sea carriage of passengers

(1) This section applies to a contract for carriage by sea of a passenger or of a passenger and his luggage where the provisions of the Athens Convention (with or without modification) do not have, in relation to the contract, the force of law in the United Kingdom.

(2) In a case where—

(*a*) the contract is not made in the United Kingdom, and
(*b*) neither the place of departure nor the place of destination under it is in the United Kingdom,

a person is not precluded by this Act from excluding or restricting liability for loss or damage, being loss or damage for which the provisions of the Convention would, if they had the force of law in relation to the contract, impose liability on him.

(3) In any other case, a person is not precluded by this Act from excluding or restricting liability for that loss or damage—

(*a*) in so far as the exclusion or restriction would have been effective in that case had the provisions of the Convention had the force of law in relation to the contract; or
(*b*) in such circumstances and to such extent as may be prescribed, by reference to a prescribed term of the contract.

(4) For the purposes of subsection (3)(*a*), the values which shall be taken to be the official values in the United Kingdom of the amounts (expressed in gold francs) by reference to which liability under the provisions of the Convention is limited shall be such amounts in sterling as the Secretary of State may from time to time by order made by statutory instrument specify.

(5) In this section,—

(*a*) the references to excluding or restricting liability include doing any of those things in relation to the liability which are mentioned in section 13 or section 25(3) and (5); and
(*b*) 'the Athens Convention' means the Athens Convention relating to the Carriage of Passengers and their Luggage by Sea, 1974; and
(*c*) 'prescribed' means prescribed by the Secretary of State by regulations made by statutory instrument;

and a statutory instrument containing the regulations shall be subject to annulment in pursuance of a resolution of either House of Parliament.

29 Saving for other relevant legislation

(1) Nothing in this Act removes or restricts the effect of, or prevents reliance upon, any contractual provision which—

(*a*) is authorised or required by the express terms or necessary implication of an enactment; or
(*b*) being made with a view to compliance with an international agreement to which the United Kingdom is a party, does not operate more restrictively than is contemplated by the agreement.

(2) A contract term is to be taken—

(*a*) for the purposes of Part I of this Act, as satisfying the requirement of reasonableness; and
(*b*) (*applies to Scotland only*).

if it is incorporated or approved by, or incorporated pursuant to a decision or ruling of, a competent authority acting in the exercise of any statutory jurisdiction or function and is not a term in a contract to which the competent authority is itself a party.

(3) In this section—

'competent authority' means any court, arbitrator or arbiter, government department or public authority;
'enactment' means any legislation (including subordinate legislation) of the United Kingdom or Northern Ireland and any instrument having effect by virtue of such legislation; and

'statutory' means conferred by an enactment.

30 (*Repealed by the Consumer Safety Act 1978, s 10(1), Sch 3.*)

General

31 Commencement; amendments; repeals

(1) This Act comes into force on 1st February 1978.

(2) Nothing in this Act applies to contracts made before the date on which it comes into force; but subject to this, it applies to liability for any loss or damage which is suffered on or after that date.

(3) The enactments specified in Schedule 3 to this Act are amended as there shown.

(4) The enactments specified in Schedule 4 to this Act are repealed to the extent specified in column 3 of that Schedule.

32 Citation and extent

(1) This Act may be cited as the Unfair Contract Terms Act 1977.

(2) Part I of this Act extends to England and Wales and to Northern Ireland; but it does not extend to Scotland.

(3) (*Applies to Scotland only.*)

(4) This Part of this Act extends to the whole of the United Kingdom.

SCHEDULES

SCHEDULE 1

Section 1(2)

SCOPE OF SECTIONS 2 TO 4 AND 7

1. Sections 2 to 4 of this Act do not extend to—

(*a*) any contract of insurance (including a contract to pay an annuity on human life);

(*b*) any contract so far as it relates to the creation or transfer of an interest in land, or to the termination of such an interest, whether by extinction, merger, surrender, forfeiture or otherwise;

(*c*) any contract so far as it relates to the creation or transfer of a right or interest in any patent, trade mark, copyright [or design right], registered design, technical or commercial information or other intellectual property, or relates to the termination of any such right or interest;

(*d*) any contract so far as it relates—

(i) to the formation or dissolution of a company (which means any body corporate or unincorporated association and includes a partnership); or

(ii) to its constitution or the rights or obligations of its corporators or members;

(*e*) any contract so far as it relates to the creation or transfer of securities or of any right or interest in securities.

2. Section 2(1) extends to—

(*a*) any contract of marine salvage or towage;
(*b*) any charterparty of a ship or hovercraft; and
(*c*) any contract for the carriage of goods by ship or hovercraft;

but subject to this sections 2 to 4 and 7 do not extend to any such contract except in favour of a person dealing as consumer.

3. Where goods are carried by ship or hovercraft in pursuance of a contract which either—

(*a*) specifies that as the means of carriage over part of the journey to be covered, or
(*b*) makes no provision as to the means of carriage and does not exclude that means,

then sections 2(2), 3 and 4 do not, except in favour of a person dealing as consumer, extend to the contract as it operates for and in relation to the carriage of the goods by that means.

4. Section 2(1) and (2) do not extend to a contract of employment, except in favour of the employee.

5. Section 2(1) does not affect the validity of any discharge and indemnity given by a person, on or in connection with an award to him of compensation for pneumoconiosis attributable to employment in the coal industry, in respect of any further claim arising from his contracting that disease.

NOTE

The words in square brackets in para 1(*c*) were inserted by the Copyright, Designs and Patents Act 1988, s 303(1), Sch 7, para 24.

SCHEDULE 2

Sections 11(2), 24(2)

'GUIDELINES' FOR APPLICATION OF REASONABLENESS TEST

The matters to which regard is to be had in particular for the purposes of sections 6(3), 7(3) and (4), 20 and 21 are any of the following which appear to be relevant—

(*a*) the strength of the bargaining positions of the parties relative to each other, taking into account (among other things) alternative means by which the customer's requirements could have been met;
(*b*) whether the customer received an inducement to agree to the term, or in accepting it had an opportunity of entering into a similar contract with other persons, but without having to accept a similar term;
(*c*) whether the customer knew or ought reasonably to have known of the existence and extent of the term (having regard, among other things, to any custom of the trade and any previous course of dealing between the parties);
(*d*) where the term excludes or restricts any relevant liability if some condition is not complied with, whether it was reasonable at the time of the contract to expect that compliance with that condition would be practicable;
(*e*) whether the goods were manufactured, processed or adapted to the special order of the customer.

(Sch 3 repealed in part by the Sale of Goods Act 1979, s 63(2), Sch 3 and by the

SL(R) Act 1981; remainder amends the Supply of Goods (Implied Terms) Act 1973, ss 14, 15 (as originally enacted and as substituted by the Consumer Credit Act 1974; Sch 4 repealing only.)

Civil Jurisdiction and Judgments Act 1982
(1982 c 27)

41 Domicile of individuals

(1) Subject to Article 52 (which contains provisions for determining whether a party is domiciled in a Contracting State), the following provisions of this section determine, for the purposes of the 1968 Convention and this Act, whether an individual is domiciled in the United Kingdom or in a particular part of, or place in, the United Kingdom or in a state other than a Contracting State.

(2) An individual is domiciled in the United Kingdom if and only if—

(*a*) he is resident in the United Kingdom; and
(*b*) the nature and circumstances of his residence indicate that he has a substantial connection with the United Kingdom.

(3) Subject to subsection (5), an individual is domiciled in a particular part of the United Kingdom if and only if—

(*a*) he is resident in that part; and
(*b*) the nature and circumstances of his residence indicate that he has a substantial connection with that part.

(4) An individual is domiciled in a particular place in the United Kingdom if and only if he—

(*a*) is domiciled in the part of the United Kingdom in which that place is situated; and
(*b*) is resident in that place.

(5) An individual who is domiciled in the United Kingdom but in whose case the requirements of subsection (3)(*b*) are not satisfied in relation to any particular part of the United Kingdom shall be treated as domiciled in the part of the United Kingdom in which he is resident.

(6) In the case of an individual who—

(*a*) is resident in the United Kingdom, or in a particular part of the United Kingdom; and
(*b*) has been so resident for the last three months or more,

the requirements of subsection (2)(*b*) or, as the case may be, subsection (3)(*b*) shall be presumed to be fulfilled unless the contrary is proved.

(7) An individual is domiciled in a state other than a Contracting State if and only if—

(*a*) he is resident in that state; and

(*b*) the nature and circumstances of his residence indicate that he has a substantial connection with that state.

42 Domicile and seat of corporation or asssocation

(1) For the purposes of this Act the seat of a corporation or association (as determined by this section) shall be treated as its domicile.

(2) The following provisions of this section determine where a corporation or association has its seat—

(*a*) for the purpose of Article 53 (which for the purposes of the 1968 Convention equates the domicile of such a body with its seat); and
(*b*) for the purposes of this Act other than the provisions mentioned in section 43(1)(*b*) and (*c*).

(3) A corporation or association has its seat in the United Kingdom if and only if—

(*a*) it was incorporated or formed under the law of a part of the United Kingdom and has its registered office or some other official address in the United Kingdom; or
(*b*) its central management and control is exercised in the United Kingdom.

(4) A corporation or association has its seat in a particular part of the United Kingdom if and only if it has its seat in the United Kingdom and—

(*a*) it has its registered office or some other official address in that part; or
(*b*) its central management and control is exercised in that part; or
(*c*) it has a place of business in that part.

(5) A corporation or association has its seat in a particular place in the United Kingdom if and only if it has its seat in the part of the United Kingdom in which that place is situated and—

(*a*) it has its registered office or some other official address in that place; or
(*b*) its central management and control is exercised in that place; or
(*c*) it has a place of business in that place.

(6) Subject to subsection (7), a corporation or association has its seat in a state other than the United Kingdom if and only if—

(*a*) it was incorporated or formed under the law of that state and has its registered office or some other official address there; or
(*b*) its central management and control is exercised in that state.

(7) A corporation or association shall not be regarded as having its seat in a Contracting State other than the United Kingdom if it is shown that the courts of that state would not regard it as having its seat there.

(8) In this section—

'business' includes any activity carried on by a corporation or association, and 'place of business' shall be construed accordingly;
'official address', in relation to a corporation or association, means an address which it is required by law to register, notify or maintain for the purpose of receiving notices or other communications.

45 Domicile of trusts

(1) The following provisions of this section determine, for the purposes of the 1968 Convention and this Act, where a trust is domiciled.

(2) A trust is domiciled in the United Kingdom if and only if it is by virtue of subsection (3) domiciled in a part of the United Kingdom.

(3) A trust is domiciled in a part of the United Kingdom if and only if the system of law of that part is the system of law with which the trust has its closest and most real connection.

Companies Act 1985
(1985 c 6)

[36 Company contracts: England and Wales

Under the law of England and Wales a contract may be made—

(*a*) by a company, by writing under its common seal, or
(*b*) on behalf of a company, by any person acting under its authority, express or implied;

and any formalities required by law in the case of a contract made by an individual also apply, unless a contrary intention appears, to a contract made by or on behalf of a company.]

NOTE
This section was substituted by the Companies Act 1989, s 130(1).

[36A Execution of documents: England and Wales

(1) Under the law of England and Wales the following provisions have effect with respect to the execution of documents by a company.

(2) A document is executed by a company by the affixing of its common seal.

(3) A company need not have a common seal, however, and the following subsections apply whether it does or not.

(4) A document signed by a director and the secretary of a company, or by two directors of a company, and expressed (in whatever form of

words) to be executed by the company has the same effect as if executed under the common seal of the company.

(5) A document executed by a company which makes it clear on its face that it is intended by the person or persons making it to be a deed has effect, upon delivery, as a deed; and it shall be presumed, unless a contrary intention is proved, to be delivered upon its being so executed.

(6) In favour of a purchaser a document shall be deemed to have been duly executed by a company if it purports to be signed by a director and the secretary of the company, or by two directors of the company, and, where it makes it clear on its face that it is intended by the person or persons making it to be a deed, to have been delivered upon its being executed.

A 'purchaser' means a purchaser in good faith for valuable consideration and includes a lessee, mortgagee or other person who for valuable consideration acquires an interest in property.]

NOTE
This section was inserted by the Companies Act 1989, s 130(2).

[258 Parent and subsidiary undertakings

(1) The expressions 'parent undertaking' and 'subsidiary undertaking' in this Part shall be construed as follows; and a 'parent company' means a parent undertaking which is a company.

(2) An undertaking is a parent undertaking in relation to another undertaking, a subsidiary undertaking, if—

(*a*) it holds a majority of the voting rights in the undertaking, or
(*b*) it is a member of the undertaking and has the right to appoint or remove a majority of its board of directors, or
(*c*) it has the right to exercise a dominant influence over the undertaking—
  (i) by virtue of provisions contained in the undertaking's memorandum or articles, or
  (ii) by virtue of a control contract, or
(*d*) it is a member of the undertaking and controls alone, pursuant to an agreement with other shareholders or members, a majority of the voting rights in the undertaking.

(3) For the purposes of subsection (2) an undertaking shall be treated as a member of another undertaking—

(*a*) if any of its subsidiary undertakings is a member of that undertaking, or
(*b*) if any shares in that other undertaking are held by a person acting on behalf of the undertaking or any of its subsidiary undertakings.

(4) An undertaking is also a parent undertaking in relation to another

undertaking, a subsidiary undertaking, if it has a participating interest in the undertaking and—

(*a*) it actually exercises a dominant influence over it, or
(*b*) it and the subsidiary undertaking are managed on a unified basis.

(5) A parent undertaking shall be treated as the parent undertaking of undertakings in relation to which any of its subsidiary undertakings are, or are to be treated as, parent undertakings; and references to its subsidiary undertakings shall be construed accordingly.

(6) Schedule 10A contains provisions explaining expressions used in this section and otherwise supplementing this section.]

NOTE
This section was inserted by the Companies Act 1989, s 21(1).

[259 Meaning of 'undertaking' and related expressions

(1) In this Part 'undertaking' means—

(*a*) a body corporate or partnership, or
(*b*) an unincorporated association carrying on a trade or business, with or without a view to profit.

(2) In this Part references to shares—

(*a*) in relation to an undertaking with a share capital, are to allotted shares;
(*b*) in relation to an undertaking with capital but no share capital, are to rights to share in the capital of the undertaking; and
(*c*) in relation to an undertaking without capital, are to interests—
(i) conferring any right to share in the profits or liability to contribute to the losses of the undertaking, or
(ii) giving rise to an obligation to contribute to the debts or expenses of the undertaking in the event of a winding up.

(3) Other expressions appropriate to companies shall be construed, in relation to an undertaking which is not a company, as references to the corresponding persons, officers, documents or organs, as the case may be, appropriate to undertakings of that description.

This is subject to provision in any specific context providing for the translation of such expressions.

(4) References in this Part to 'fellow subsidiary undertakings' are to undertakings which are subsidiary undertakings of the same parent undertaking but are not parent undertakings or subsidiary undertakings of each other.

(5) In this Part 'group undertaking', in relation to an undertaking, means an undertaking which is—

(*a*) a parent undertaking or subsidiary undertaking of that undertaking, or (*b*) a subsidiary undertaking of any parent undertaking of that undertaking.]

NOTE
This section was inserted by the Companies Act 1989, s 22.

[260 Participating interests

(1) In this Part a 'participating interest' means an interest held by an undertaking in the shares of another undertaking which it holds on a long-term basis for the purpose of securing a contribution to its activities by the exercise of control or influence arising from or related to that interest.

(2) A holding of 20 per cent or more of the shares of an undertaking shall be presumed to be a participating interest unless the contrary is shown.

(3) The reference in subsection (1) to an interest in shares includes—

(*a*) an interest which is convertible into an interest in shares, and
(*b*) an option to acquire shares or any such interest;

and an interest or option falls within paragraph (*a*) or (*b*) notwithstanding that the shares to which it relates are, until the conversion or the exercise of the option, unissued.

(4) For the purposes of this section an interest held on behalf of an undertaking shall be treated as held by it.

(5) For the purposes of this section as it applies in relation to the expression 'participating interest' in section 258(4) (definition of 'subsidiary undertaking')—

(*a*) there shall be attributed to an undertaking any interests held by any of its subsidiary undertakings, and
(*b*) the references in subsection (1) to the purpose and activities of an undertaking include the purposes and activities of any of its subsidiary undertakings and of the group as a whole.

(6) In the balance sheet and profit and loss formats set out in Part I of Schedule 4, 'participating interest' does not include an interest in a group undertaking.

(7) For the purposes of this section as it applies in relation to the expression 'participating interest'—

(*a*) in those formats as they apply in relation to group accounts, and
(*b*) in paragraph 20 of Schedule 4A (group accounts: undertakings to be accounted for as associated undertakings),

the references in subsections (1) to (4) to the interest held by, and the purposes and activities of, the undertaking concerned shall be construed as references to the interest held by, and the purposes and activities of, the group (within the meaning of paragraph 1 of that Schedule).]

NOTE

This section was inserted by the Companies Act 1989, s 22.

[736 'Subsidiary', 'holding company' and 'wholly-owned subsidiary'

(1) A company is a 'subsidiary' of another company, its 'holding company', if that other company—

(*a*) holds a majority of the voting rights in it, or
(*b*) is a member of it and has the right to appoint or remove a majority of its board of directors, or
(*c*) is a member of it and controls alone, pursuant to an agreement with other shareholders or members, a majority of the voting rights in it,

or if it is a subsidiary of a company which is itself a subsidiary of that other company.

(2) A company is a 'wholly-owned subsidiary' of another company if it has no members except that other and that other's wholly-owned subsidiaries or persons acting on behalf of that other or its wholly-owned subsidiaries.

(3) In this section 'company' includes any body corporate.]

NOTE

This section and s 736A post were substituted for the original s 736 by the Companies Act 1989, s 144(1).

[736A Provisions supplementing s 736

(1) The provisions of this section explain expressions used in section 736 and otherwise supplement that section.

(2) In section 736(1)(*a*) and (*c*) the references to the voting rights in a company are to the rights conferred on shareholders in respect of their shares or, in the case of a company not having a share capital, on members, to vote at general meetings of the company on all, or substantially all, matters.

(3) In section 736(1)(*b*) the reference to the right to appoint or remove a majority of the board of directors is to the right to appoint or remove directors holding a majority of the voting rights at meetings of the board on all, or substantially all, matters; and for the purposes of that provision—

(*a*) a company shall be treated as having the right to appoint to a directorship if—
  (i) a person's appointment to it follows necessarily from his appointment as director of the company, or
  (ii) the directorship is held by the company itself; and

(*b*) a right to appoint or remove which is exercisable only with the consent or concurrence of another person shall be left out of account unless no other person has a right to appoint or, as the case may be, remove in relation to that directorship.

(4) Rights which are exercisable only in certain circumstances shall be taken into account only—

(*a*) when the circumstances have arisen, and for so long as they continue to obtain, or
(*b*) when the circumstances are within the control of the person having the rights;

and rights which are normally exercisable but are temporarily incapable of exercise shall continue to be taken into account.

(5) Rights held by a person in a fiduciary capacity shall be treated as not held by him.

(6) Rights held by a person as nominee for another shall be treated as held by the other; and rights shall be regarded as held as nominee for another if they are exercisable only on his instructions or with his consent or concurrence.

(7) Rights attached to shares held by way of security shall be treated as held by the person providing the security—

(*a*) where apart from the right to exercise them for the purpose of preserving the value of the security, or of realising it, the rights are exercisable only in accordance with his instructions;
(*b*) where the shares are held in connection with the granting of loans as part of normal business activities and apart from the right to exercise them for the purpose of preserving the value of the security, or of realising it, the rights are exercisable only in his interests.

(8) Rights shall be treated as held by a company if they are held by any of its subsidiaries; and nothing in subsection (6) or (7) shall be construed as requiring rights held by a company to be treated as held by any of its subsidiaries.

(9) For the purposes of subsection (7) rights shall be treated as being exercisable in accordance with the instructions or in the interests of a company if they are exercisable in accordance with the instructions of or, as the case may be, in the interests of—

(*a*) any subsidiary or holding company of that company, or
(*b*) any subsidiary of a holding company of that company.

(10) The voting rights in a company shall be reduced by any rights held by the company itself.

(11) References in any provision of subsections (5) to (10) to rights held by a person include rights falling to be treated as held by him by virtue of any other provision of those subsections but not rights which by virtue of any such provision are to be treated as not held by him.

(12) In this section 'company' includes any body corporate.]

NOTE
See the note to s 736 ante.

[736B Power to amend ss 736 and 736A

(1) The Secretary of State may by regulations amend sections 736 and 736A so as to alter the meaning of the expressions 'holding company', 'subsidiary' or 'wholly-owned subsidiary'.

(2) The regulations may make different provision for different cases or classes of case and may contain such incidental and supplementary provisions as the Secretary of State thinks fit.

(3) Regulations under this section shall be made by statutory instrument which shall be subject to annulment in pursuance of a resolution of either House of Parliament.

(4) Any amendment made by regulations under this section does not apply for the purposes of enactments outside the Companies Acts unless the regulations so provide.

(5) So much of section 23(3) of the Interpretation Act 1978 as applies section 17(2)(*a*) of that Act (effect of repeal and re-enactment) to deeds, instruments and documents other than enactments shall not apply in relation to any repeal and re-enactment effected by regulations made under this section.]

NOTE
This section was inserted by the Companies Act 1989, s 144(3).

[SCHEDULE 10A

Section 258

PARENT AND SUBSIDIARY UNDERTAKINGS: SUPPLEMENTARY PROVISIONS

Introduction

1. The provisions of this Schedule explain expressions used in section 258 (parent and subsidiary undertakings) and otherwise supplement that section.

Voting rights in an undertaking

2.-(1) In section 258(2)(a) and (*d*) the references to the voting rights in an undertaking are to the rights conferred on shareholders in respect of their shares or, in the case of an undertaking not having a share capital, on members, to vote at general meetings of the undertaking on all, or substantially all, matters.

(2) In relation to an undertaking which does not have general meetings at which matters are decided by the exercise of voting rights, the references to holding a majority of the voting rights in the undertaking shall be construed as references to having the right under the constitution of the undertaking to direct the overall policy of the undertaking or to alter the terms of its constitution.

Right to appoint or remove a majority of the directors

3.—(1) In section 258(2)(*b*) the reference to the right to appoint or remove a majority of the board of directors is to the right to appoint or remove directors holding a majority of the voting rights at meetings of the board on all, or substantially all, matters.

(2) An undertaking shall be treated as having the right to appoint to a directorship if—

(*a*) a person's appointment to it follows necessarily from his appointment as director of the undertaking, or
(*b*) the directorship is held by the undertaking itself.

(3) A right to appoint or remove which is exercisable only with the consent or concurrence of another person shall be left out of account unless no other person has a right to appoint or, as the case may be, remove in relation to that directorship.

Right to exercise dominant influence

4.—(1) For the purposes of section 258(2)(*c*) an undertaking shall not be regarded as having the right to exercise a dominant influence over another undertaking unless it has a right to give directions with respect to the operating and financial policies of that other undertaking which its directors are obliged to comply with whether or not they are for the benefit of that other undertaking.

(2) A 'control contract' means a contract in writing conferring such a right which—

(*a*) is of a kind authorised by the memorandum or articles of the undertaking in relation to which the right is exercisable, and
(*b*) is permitted by the law under which that undertaking is established.

(3) This paragraph shall not be read as affecting the construction of the expression 'actually exercises a dominant influence' in section 258(4)(*a*).

Rights exercisable only in certain circumstances or temporarily incapable of exercise

5.—(1) Rights which are exercisable only in certain circumstances shall be taken into account only—

(*a*) when the circumstances have arisen, and for so long as they continue to obtain, or
(*b*) when the circumstances are within the control of the person having the rights.

(2) Rights which are normally exercisable but are temporarily incapable of exercise shall continue to be taken into account.

Rights held by one person on behalf of another

6. Rights held by a person in a fiduciary capacity shall be treated as not held by him.

7.—(1) Rights held by a person as nominee for another shall be treated as held by the other.

(2) Rights shall be regarded as held as nominee for another if they are exercisable only on his instructions or with his consent or concurrence.

Rights attached to shares held by way of security

8. Rights attached to shares held by way of security shall be treated as held by the person providing the security—

(*a*) where apart from the right to exercise them for the purpose of preserving the value of the security, or of realising it, the rights are exercisable only in accordance with his instructions, and

(*b*) where the shares are held in connection with the granting of loans as part of normal business activities and apart from the right to exercise them for the purpose of preserving the value of the security, or of realising it, the rights are exercisable only in his interests.

Rights attributed to parent undertaking

9.—(1) Rights shall be treated as held by a parent undertaking if they are held by any of its subsidiary undertakings.

(2) Nothing in paragraph 7 or 8 shall be construed as requiring rights held by a parent undertaking to be treated as held by any of its subsidiary undertakings.

(3) For the purposes of paragraph 8 rights shall be treated as being exercisable in accordance with the instructions or in the interests of an undertaking if they are exercisable in accordance with the instructions of or, as the case may be, in the interests of any group undertaking.

Disregard of certain rights

10. The voting rights in an undertaking shall be reduced by any rights held by the undertaking itself.

Supplementary

11. References in any provision of paragraphs 6 to 10 to rights held by a person include rights falling to be treated as held by him by virtue of any other provision of those paragraphs but not rights which by virtue of any such provision are to be treated as not held by him.]

NOTE

This Schedule was inserted by the Companies Act 1989, s 21(2), Sch 9.

Law of Property (Miscellaneous Provisions) Act 1989 (1989 c 34)

An Act to make new provisions with respect to deeds and their execution and contracts for the sale or other disposition of interests in land; and to abolish the rule of law known as the rule in Bain v Fothergill [27 July 1989]

1 Deeds and their execution

(1) Any rule of law which—

(*a*) restricts the substances on which a deed may be written;
(*b*) requires a seal for the valid execution of an instrument as a deed by an individual; or
(*c*) requires authority by one person to another to deliver an instrument as a deed on his behalf to be given by deed,

is abolished.

(2) An instrument shall not be a deed unless—

(*a*) it makes it clear on its face that it is intended to be a deed by the person making it or, as the case may be, by the parties to it (whether by describing itself as a deed or expressing itself to be executed or signed as a deed or otherwise); and
(*b*) it is validly executed as a deed by that person or, as the case may be, one or more of those parties.

(3) An instrument is validly executed as a deed by an individual if, and only if—

(*a*) it is signed—
(i) by him in the presence of a witness who attests the signature; or
(ii) at his direction and in his presence and the prescence of two witnesses who each attest the signature; and
(*b*) it is delivered as a deed by him or a person authorised to do so on his behalf.

(4) In subsections (2) and (3) above 'sign', in relation to an instrument, includes making one's mark on the instrument and 'signature' is to be construed accordingly.

(5) Where a solicitor[, duly certificated notary public] or licensed conveyancer, or an agent or employee of a solicitor[, duly certificated notary public] or licensed conveyancer, in the course of or in connection with a transaction involving the disposition or creation of an interest in land, purports to deliver an instrument as a deed on behalf of a party to the instrument, it shall be conclusively presumed in favour of a purchaser that he is authorised so to deliver the instrument.

(6) In subsection (5) above—

'disposition' and 'purchaser' have the same meanings as in the Law of Property Act 1925
['duly certificated notary public' has the same meaning as it has in the Solicitors Act 1974 by virtue of section 87 of that Act;] and
'interest in land' means any estate, interest or charge in or over land or in or over the proceeds of sale of land.

(7) Where an instrument under seal that constitutes a deed is required for the purposes of an Act passed before this section comes into force, this section shall have effect as to signing, sealing or delivery of an instrument by an individual in place of any provision of that Act as to signing, sealing or delivery.

(8) The enactments mentioned in Schedule 1 to this Act (which in consequence of this section require amendments other than those provided by subsection (7) above) shall have effect with the amendments specified in that Schedule.

(9) Nothing in subsection (1)(*b*), (2), (3), (7) or (8) above applies in relation to deeds required or authorised to be made under—

(*a*) the seal of the county palatine of Lancaster;
(*b*) the seal of the Duchy of Lancaster; or
(*c*) the seal of the Duchy of Cornwall.

(10) The references in this section to the execution of a deed by an individual do not include execution by a corporation sole and the reference in subsection (7) above to signing, sealing or delivery by an individual does not include signing, sealing or delivery by such a corporation.

(11) Nothing in this section applies in relation to instruments delivered as deeds before this section comes into force.

NOTE

In sub-ss (5), (6) the words in square brackets were inserted by the Courts and Legal Services Act 1990, s 125(2), Sch 17, para 20.

2 Contracts for sale etc of land to be made by signed writing

(1) A contract for the sale or other disposition of an interest in land can only be made in writing and only by incorporating all the terms which the parties have expressly agreed in one document or, where contracts are exchanged, in each.

(2) The terms may be incorporated in a document either by being set out in it or by reference to some other document.

(3) The document incorporating the terms or, where contracts are exchanged, one of the documents incorporating them (but not necessarily the same one) must be signed by or on behalf of each party to the contract.

(4) Where a contract for the sale or other disposition of an interest in land satisfies the conditions of this section by reason only of the rectification of one or more documents in pursuance of an order of a court, the contract shall come into being, or be deemed to have come into being, at such time as may be specified in the order.

(5) This section does not apply in relation to—

(*a*) a contract to grant such a lease as is mentioned in section 54(2) of the Law of Property Act 1925 (short leases);
(*b*) a contract made in the course of a public auction; or
(*c*) a contract regulated under the Financial Services Act 1986;

and nothing in this section affects the creation or operation of resulting, implied or constructive trusts.

(6) In this section—

'disposition' has the same meaning as in the Law of Property Act 1925;
'interest in land' means any estate, interest or charge in or over land or in or over the proceeds of sale of land.

(7) Nothing in this section shall apply in relation to contracts made before this section comes into force.

(8) Section 40 of the Law of Property Act 1925 (which is superseded by this section) shall cease to have effect.

3 Abolition of rule in Bain v Fothergill

The rule of law known as the rule in Bain v Fothergill is abolished in relation to contracts made after this section comes into force.

4 Repeals

The enactments mentioned in Schedule 2 to this Act are repealed to the extent specified in the third column of that Schedule.

5 Commencement

(1) The provisions of this Act to which this subsection applies shall come into force on such day as the Lord Chancellor may by order made by statutory instrument appoint.

(2) The provisions to which subsection (1) above applies are—

(*a*) section 1 above; and
(*b*) section 4 above, except so far as it relates to section 40 of the Law of Property Act 1925.

(3) The provisions of this Act to which this subsection applies shall come into force at the end of the period of two months beginning with the day on which this Act is passed.

(4) The provisions of this Act to which subsection (3) above applies are—

(*a*) sections 2 and 3 above; and
(*b*) section 4 above, so far as it relates to section 40 of the Law of Property Act 1925.

NOTE

Commencement. The appointed day for the purposes of sub-ss (1) and (2) above was 31 July 1990; see the Law of Property (Miscellaneous Provisions) Act 1989 (Commencement) Order 1990 (SI 1990/1175).

The date on which the provisions referred to in sub-s (4) came into force was 27 September 1989.

6 Citation

(1) This Act may be cited as the Law of Property (Miscellaneous Provisions) Act 1989.

(2) This Act extends to England and Wales only.

NOTE

Commencement. This section came into force on the day this Act was passed, ie 27 July 1989 (the date of Royal Assent); cf s 5 ante.

Schedule 1: *paras 1–5 amend the Law of Property Act 1925, ss 52, 74, 80 and 81; paras 6, 7 amend the Powers of Attorney Act 1971, ss 1 and 7, and para 8 amends the Solicitors Act 1974, s 22.*

Schedule 2 (*Repealing only.*)

The Insolvency Rules 1986 (SI 1986/1925)

4.90 Mutual credit and set-off

(1) This Rule applies where, before the company goes into liquidation there have been mutual credits, mutual debts or other mutual dealings between the company and any creditor of the company proving or claiming to prove for a debt in the liquidation.

(2) An account shall be taken of what is due from each party to the other in respect of the mutual dealings, and the sums due from one party shall be set off against the sums due from the other.

(3) Sums due from the company to another party shall not be included in the account taken under paragraph (2) if that other party had notice at the time they became due that a meeting of creditors had been summoned under section 98* or (as the case may be) a petition for the winding up of the company was pending.

(4) Only the balance (if any) of the account is provable in the liquidation. Alternatively (as the case may be) the amount shall be paid to the liquidator as part of the assets.

*Insolvency Act 1986, s 98 requires that, in a creditor's voluntary winding up, a creditors' meeting has to be held not later than the 14th day after the winding up resolution is passed.

The 1968 Brussels Convention on Jurisdiction and the Enforcement of Judgments in Civil and Commercial Matters

PREAMBLE

THE HIGH CONTRACTING PARTIES TO THE TREATY ESTABLISHING THE EUROPEAN ECONOMIC COMMUNITY

Desiring to implement the provisions of Article 220 of that Treaty by virtue of which they undertook to secure the simplification of formalities governing the reciprocal recognition and enforcement of judgments of courts or tribunals:

Anxious to strengthen in the Community the legal protection of persons therein established:

Considering that it is necessary for this purpose to determine the international jurisdiction of their courts, to facilitate recognition and to introduce an expeditious procedure for securing the enforcement of judgments, authentic instruments and court settlements:

Have decided to conclude this Convention and to this end have designated as their Plenipotentiaries:

(*Designations of Plenipotentiaries of the original six Contracting States*)

WHO, meeting within the Council, having exchanged their Full Powers, found in good and due form.

HAVE AGREED AS FOLLOWS:

TITLE I
SCOPE

Article 1

This Convention shall apply in civil and commercial matters whatever the nature of the court or tribunal. It shall not extend, in particular, to revenue, customs or administrative matters.

The Convention shall not apply to–

1. The status or legal capacity of natural persons, rights in property arising out of a matrimonial relationship, wills and succession.

2. Bankruptcy, proceedings relating to the winding-up of insolvent companies or other legal persons, judicial arrangements, compositions and analogous proceedings.

3. Social security.

4. Arbitration.

TITLE II
JURISDICTION

Section 1
GENERAL PROVISIONS

Article 2

Subject to the provisions of this Convention, persons domiciled in a Contracting State shall, whatever their nationality, be sued in the courts of that State.

Persons who are not nationals of the State in which they are domiciled shall be governed by the rules of jurisdiction applicable to nationals of that State.

Article 3

Persons domiciled in a Contracting State may be sued in the courts of another Contracting State only by virtue of the rules set out in Sections 2 to 6 of this Title.

In particular the following provisions shall not be applicable as against them–

— in Belgium: Article 15 of the civil code (Code civil—Burgerlijk

Wetboek) and Article 638 of the judicial code (Code judiciarie—Gerechtelijk Wetboek).
- in Denmark: Article 246(2) and (3) of the law on civil procedure (Lov om rettens pleje).
- in the Federal Republic of Germany: Article 23 of the code of civil procedure (Zivilprozeßordnung).
- in Greece, Article 40 of the code of civil procedure (Λῶδικας Πολιτικης Δικονομίας),
- in France: Articles 14 and 15 of the civil code (Code civil),
- in Ireland: the rules which enable jurisdiction to be founded on the document instituting the proceedings having been served on the defendant during his temporary presence in Ireland,
- in Italy: Articles 2 and 4, nos 1 and 2 of the code of civil procedure (Codice di procedura civile),
- in Luxembourg: Articles 14 and 15 of the civil code (Code civil),
- in the Netherlands: Articles 126(3) and 127 of the code of civil procedure (Wetboek van Burgerlijke Rechtsvordering),
- in Portugal: Article 65(1)(c), article 65(2) and Article 65A(*c*) of the code of civil procedure (Código de Processo Civil) and Article 11 of the code of labour procedure (Código de Processo de Trabalho),
- in the United Kingdom: the rules which enable jurisdiction to be founded on:
  (a) the document instituting the proceedings having been served on the defendant during his temporary presence in the United Kingdom; or
  (b) the presence within the United Kingdom of property belonging to the defendant; or
  (c) the seizure by the plaintiff of property situated in the United Kingdom.

Article 4

If the defendant is not domiciled in a Contracting State, the jurisdiction of the courts of each Contracting State shall, subject to the provisions of Article 16, be determined by the law of that State.

As against such a defendant, any person domiciled in a Contracting State may, whatever his nationality, avail himself in that State of the rules of jurisdiction there in force, and in particular those specified in the second paragraph of Article 3, in the same way as the nationals of that State.

Section 2
SPECIAL JURISDICTION

Article 5

A person domiciled in a Contracting State may, in another Contracting State, be sued–

1. In matters relating to a contract, in the courts for the place of performance of the obligation in question; in matters relating to individual contracts of employment, this place is that where the employee habitually carries out his work, or if the employee does not habitually carry out his work in any one country, the employer may also be sued in the courts

for the place where the business which engaged the employee was or is now situated.

2. In matters relating to maintenance, in the courts for the place where the maintenance creditor is domiciled or habitually resident or, if the matter is ancillary to proceedings concerning the status of a person, in the court which, according to its own law, has jurisdiction to entertain those proceedings, unless that jurisdiction is based solely on the nationality of one of the parties.

3. In matters relating to tort, delict or quasi-delict, in the courts for the place where the harmful event occurred.

4. As regards a civil claim for damages or restitution which is based on an act giving rise to criminal proceedings, in the court seised of those proceedings, to the extent that court has jurisdiction under its own law to entertain civil proceedings.

5. As regards a dispute arising out of the operations of a branch, agency or other establishment, in the courts for the place in which the branch, agency or other establishment is situated.

6. As settlor, trustee or beneficiary of a trust enacted by the operation of a statute, or by a written instrument, or created orally and evidenced in writing, in the courts of the Contracting State in which the trust is domiciled.

7. As regards a dispute concerning the payment of remuneration claimed in respect of the salvage of a cargo or freight, in the court under the authority of which the cargo or freight in question–

(*a*) has been arrested to secure such payment, or

(*b*) could have been so arrested, but bail or other security has been given;

provided that this provision shall apply only if it is claimed that the defendant has an interest in the cargo or freight or had such an interest at the time of salvage.

Article 6

A person domiciled in a Contracting State may also be sued–

1. Where he is one of a number of defendants, in the courts for the place where any one of them is domiciled.

2. As a third party in an action on a warranty or guarantee or in any other third party proceedings, in the court seised of the original proceedings, unless these were instituted solely with the object of removing him from the jurisdiction of the court which would be competent in his case.

3. On a counter-claim arising from the same contract or facts on which the original claim was based, in the court in which the original claim is pending.

4. In matters relating to a contract, if the action may be combined with an action against the same defendant in matters relating to rights *in rem* in immovable property, in the court of the Contracting State in which the property is situated.

ARTICLE 6A

Where by virtue of this Convention a court of a Contracting State has jurisdiction in actions relating to liability from the use or operation of a ship, that court, or any other court substituted for this purpose by the internal law of that State, shall also have jurisdiction over claims for limitation of such liability.

SECTION 3
JURISDICTION IN MATTERS RELATING TO INSURANCE

ARTICLE 7

In matters relating to insurance, jurisdiction shall be determined by this Section, without prejudice to the provisions of Articles 4 and 5 point 5.

ARTICLE 8

An insurer domiciled in a Contracting State may be sued–

1. in the courts of the State where he is domiciled, or

2. in another Contracting State, in the courts for the place where the policy-holder is domiciled, or

3. if he is a co-insurer, in the courts of a Contracting-State in which proceedings are brought against the leading insurer

An insurer who is not domiciled in a Contracting State but has a branch, agency or other establishment in one of the Contracting States shall, in disputes arising out of the operations of the branch, agency or establishment, be deemed to be domiciled in that State.

ARTICLE 9

In respect of liability insurance or insurance of immovable property, the insurer may in addition be sued in the courts for the place where the harmful event occurred. The same applies if movable and immovable property are covered by the same insurance policy and both are adversely affected by the same contingency.

ARTICLE 10

In respect of liability insurance, the insurer may also, if the law of the court permits it, be joined in proceedings which the injured party had brought against the insured.

The provisions of Articles 7, 8 and 9 shall apply to actions brought by the injured party directly against the insurer, where such direct actions are permitted.

If the law governing such direct actions provides that the policy-holder or the insured may be joined as a party to the action, the same court shall have jurisdiction over them.

Article 11

Without prejudice to the provisions of the third paragraph of Article 10, an insurer may bring proceedings only in the courts of the Contracting State in which the defendant is domiciled irrespective of whether he is the policy-holder, the insured or a beneficiary.

The provisions of this Section shall not affect the right to bring a counterclaim in the court in which, in accordance with this Section, the original claim is pending.

Article 12

The provisions of this Section may be departed from only by an agreement on jurisdiction–

1. which is entered into after the dispute has arisen, or

2. which allows the policy-holder, the insured or a beneficiary to bring proceedings in courts other than those indicated in this Section, or

3. which is concluded between a policy-holder and an insurer, both of whom are domiciled in the same Contracting State, and which has the effect of conferring jurisdiction on the courts of that State even if the harmful event were to occur abroad, provided that such an agreement is not contrary to the law of that State, or

4. which is concluded with a policy-holder who is not domiciled in a Contracting-State, except in so far as the insurance is compulsory or relates to immovable property in a Contracting State, or

5. which relates to a contract of insurance in so far as it covers one or more of the risks set out in Article 12A.

Article 12A

The following are the risks referred to in point 5 of Article 12–

1. Any loss of or damage to–
   (*a*) sea-going ships, installations situated offshore or on the high seas, or aircraft arising from perils which relate to their use for commercial purposes.
   (*b*) goods in transit other than passengers' baggage where the transit consists of or includes carriage by such ships or aircraft.

2. Any liability, other than for bodily injury to passengers or loss of or damage to their baggage–
   (*a*) arising out of the use or operation of ships, installations or aircraft as referred to in point 1(a) above in so far as the law of the Contracting State in which such aircraft are registered does not prohibit agreements on jurisdiction regarding insurance of such risks:
   (*b*) for loss or damage caused by goods in transit as described in point 1(b) above.

3. Any financial loss connected with the use or operation of ships,

installations or aircraft as referred to in point 1(a) above, in particular loss of freight or charter-hire.

4. Any risk or interest connected with any of those referred to in points 1 to 3 above.

Section 4
JURISDICTION OVER CONSUMER CONTRACTS

Article 13

In proceedings concerning a contract concluded by a person for a purpose which can be regarded as being outside his trade or profession, hereinafter called "the consumer", jurisdiction shall be determined by this Section, without prejudice to the provisions of Article 4 and point 5 of Article 5, if it is–

1. a contract for the sale of goods on instalment credit terms, or

2. a contract for a loan repayable by instalments, or for any other form of credit, made to finance the sale of goods, or

3. any other contract for the supply of goods or a contract for the supply of services, and
   (*a*) in the State of the consumer's domicile the conclusion of the contract was preceded by a specific invitation addressed to him or by advertising; and
   (*b*) the consumer took in that State the steps necessary for the conclusion of the contract

Where a consumer enters into a contract with a party who is not domiciled in a Contracting State but has a branch, agency or other establishment in one of the Contracting States, that party shall, in disputes arising out of the operations of the branch, agency or establishment, be deemed to be domiciled in that State.

This Section shall not apply to contracts of transport.

Article 14

A consumer may bring proceedings against the other party to a contract either in the courts of the Contracting State in which that party is domiciled or in the courts of the Contracting State in which he is himself domiciled.

Proceedings may be brought against a consumer by the other party to the contract only in the courts of the Contracting State in which the consumer is domiciled.

These provisions shall not affect the right to bring a counter-claim in the court in which, in accordance with this Section, the original claim is pending.

Article 15

The provisions of this Section may be departed from only by an agreement–

1. which is entered into after the dispute has arisen, or

2. which allows the consumer to bring proceedings in courts other than those indicated in this Section, or

3. which is entered into by the consumer and the other party to the contract, both of whom are at the time of conclusion of the contract domiciled or habitually resident in the same Contracting State, and which confers jurisdiction on the courts of that State, provided that such an agreement is not contrary to the law of that State.

Section 5
EXCLUSIVE JURISDICTION

Article 16

The following courts shall have exclusive jurisdiction, regardless of domicile:

1. (*a*) in proceedings which have as their object rights *in rem* in immovable property or tenancies of immovable property, the courts of the Contracting State in which the property is situated;
   (*b*) however, in proceedings which have as their object tenancies of immovable property concluded for temporary private use for a maximum period of six consecutive months, the courts of the Contracting State in which the defendant is domiciled shall also have jurisdiction, provided that the landlord and the tenant are natural persons and are domiciled in the same Contracting State.

2. In proceedings which have as their object the validity of the constitution, the nullity or the dissolution of companies or other legal persons or associations of natural or legal persons, or the decisions of their organs, the courts of the Contracting State in which the company, legal person or association has its seat.

3. In proceedings which have as their object the validity of entries in public registers, the courts of the Contracting State in which the register is kept.

4. In proceedings concerned with the registration or validity of patents, trade marks, designs, or other similar rights required to be deposited or registered, the courts of the Contracting State in which the deposit or registration has been applied for, has taken place or is under the terms of an international convention deemed to have taken place.

5. In proceedings concerned with the enforcement of judgments, the courts of the Contracting State in which the judgment has been or is to be enforced.

Section 6
PROROGATION OF JURISDICTION

Article 17

If the parties, one or more of whom is domiciled in a Contracting State, have agreed that a court or the courts of a Contracting State are to have jurisdiction to settle any disputes which have arisen or which may arise in connection with a particular legal relationship, that court or those courts shall have exclusive jurisdiction. Such an agreement conferring jurisdiction shall be either–

(*a*) in writing or evidenced in writing, or

(*b*) in a form which accords with practices which the parties have established between themselves, or

(*c*) in international trade or commerce, in a form which accords with a usage of which the parties are or ought to have been aware and which in such trade or commerce is widely known to, and regularly observed by, parties to contracts of the type involved in the particular trade or commerce concerned.

Where such an agreement is concluded by parties, none of whom is domiciled in a Contracting State, the courts of other Contracting States shall have no jurisdiction over their disputes unless the court or courts chosen have declined jurisdiction.

The court or courts of a Contracting State on which a trust instrument has conferred jurisdiction shall have exclusive jurisdiction in any proceedings brought against a settlor, trustee or beneficiary if relations between these persons or their rights or obligations under the trust are involved.

Agreements or provisions of a trust instrument conferring jurisdiction shall have no legal force if they are contrary to the provisions of Articles 12 or 15, or if the courts whose jurisdiction they purport to exclude have exclusive jurisdiction by virtue of Article 16.

If an agreement conferring jurisdiction was concluded for the benefit of only one of the parties, that party shall retain the right to bring proceedings in any other court which has jurisdiction by virtue of this Convention.

In matters relating to individual contracts of employment an agreement conferring jurisdiction shall have legal force only if it is entered into after the dispute has arisen or if the employee invokes it to seise courts other than those for the defendant's domicile or those specified in Article 5(1).

Article 18

Apart from jurisdiction derived from other provisions of this Convention, a court of a Contracting State before whom a defendant enters an appearance shall have jurisdiction. This rule shall not apply where appearance was entered to contest the jurisdiction, or where another court has exclusive jurisdiction by virtue of Article 16.

Section 7
EXAMINATION AS TO JURISDICTION AND ADMISSIBILITY

Article 19

Where a court of a Contracting State is seised of a claim which is principally concerned with a matter over which the courts of another Contracting State have exclusive jurisdiction by virtue of Article 16, it shall declare of its own motion that it has no jurisdiction.

Article 20

Where a defendant domiciled in one Contracting State is sued in a court of another Contracting State and does not enter an appearance, the court shall declare of its own motion that it has no jurisdiction unless its jurisdiction is derived from the provisions of the Convention.

The court shall stay the proceedings so long as it is not shown that the defendant has been able to receive the document instituting the proceedings or an equivalent document in sufficient time to enable him to arrange for his defence, or that all necessary steps have been taken to this end.

The provisions of the foregoing paragraph shall be replaced by those of Article 15 of the Hague Convention of 15th November 1965 on the service abroad of judicial and extrajudicial documents in civil or commercial matters, if the document instituting the proceedings or notice thereof had to be transmitted abroad in accordance with that Convention.

Section 8
LIS PENDENS — RELATED ACTIONS

Article 21

Where proceedings involving the same cause of action and between the same parties are brought in the courts of different Contracting States, any court other than the court first seised shall of its own motion stay its proceedings until such time as the jurisdiction of the court first seised is established.

Where the jurisdiction of the court first seised is established, any court other than the court first seised shall decline jurisdiction in favour of that court.

Article 22

Where related actions are brought in the courts of different Contracting States, any court other than the court first seised may, while the actions are pending at first instance, stay its proceedings.

A court other than the court first seised may also, on the application of one of the parties decline jurisdiction if the law of that court permits the consolidation of related actions and the court first seised has jurisdiction over both actions.

For the purposes of this Article, actions are deemed to be related where they are so closely connected that it is expedient to hear and determine them together to avoid the risk of irreconcilable judgments resulting from separate proceedings.

Article 23

Where actions come within the exclusive jurisdiction of several courts, any court other than the court first seised shall decline jurisdiction in favour of that court.

Section 9
PROVISIONAL, INCLUDING PROTECTIVE MEASURES

Article 24

Application may be made to the courts of a Contracting State for such provisional, including protective, measures as may be available under the law of that State, even if, under this Convention, the courts of another Contracting State have jurisdiction as to the substance of the matter.

The 1980 Rome Convention on the Law Applicable to Contractual Obligations

The High Contracting Parties to the Treaty establishing the European Economic Community,

Anxious to continue in the field of private international law the work of unification of law which has already been done within the Community, in particular in the field of jurisdiction and enforcement of judgments,

Wishing to establish uniform rules concerning the law applicable to contractual obligations,

Have agreed as follows:

TITLE I
SCOPE OF THE CONVENTION

Article 1
Scope of the Convention

1. The rules of this Convention shall apply to contractual obligations in any situation involving a choice between the laws of different countries.

2. They shall not apply to:

(*a*) questions involving the status or legal capacity of natural persons, without prejudice to Article 11;

(*b*) contractual obligations relating to:
- —wills and succession,
- —rights in property arising out of a matrimonial relationship,
- —rights and duties arising out of a family relationship, parentage, marriage or affinity, including maintenance obligations in respect of children who are not legitimate;

(*c*) obligations arising under bills of exchange, cheques and promissory notes and other negotiable instruments to the extent that the obligations under such other negotiable instruments arise out of their negotiable character;

(*d*) arbitration agreements and agreements on the choice of court;

(*e*) questions governed by the law of companies and other bodies corporate or unincorporate such as the creation, by registration or otherwise, legal capacity, internal organisation or winding up of companies and other bodies corporate or unincorporate and the personal liability of officers and members as such for the obligations of the company or body;

(*f*) the question whether an agent is able to bind a principal, or an organ to bind a company or body corporate or unincorporate, to a third party;

(*g*) the constitution of trusts and the relationship between settlors, trustees and beneficiaries;

(*h*) evidence and procedure, without prejudice to Article 14.

3. The rules of this Convention do not apply to contracts of insurance which cover risks situated in the territories of the Member States of the European Economic Community. In order to determine whether a risk is situated in these territories the court shall apply its internal law.

4. The preceding paragraph does not apply to contracts of re-insurance

Article 2
Application of law of non-contracting States

Any law specified by this Convention shall be applied whether or not it is the law of a Contracting State.

TITLE II
UNIFORM RULES

Article 3
Freedom of choice

1. A contract shall be governed by the law chosen by the parties. The choice must be express or demonstrated with reasonable certainty by the terms of the contract or the circumstances of the case. By their choice the parties can select the law applicable to the whole or a part only of the contract.

2. The parties may at any time agree to subject the contract to a law other than that which previously governed it, whether as a result of an earlier choice under this Article or of other provisions of this Convention. Any variation by the parties of the law to be applied made after the conclusion of the contract shall not prejudice its formal validity under Article 9 or adversely affect the rights of third parties.

3. The fact that the parties have chosen a foreign law, whether or not accompanied by the choice of a foreign tribunal, shall not, where all the other elements relevant to the situation at the time of the choice are connected with one country only, prejudice the application of rules of the law of that country which cannot be derogated from by contract, hereinafter called "mandatory rules".

4. The existence and validity of the consent of the parties as to the choice of the applicable law shall be determined in accordance with the provisions of Articles 8, 9, 11.

Article 4
Applicable law in the absence of choice

1. To the extent that the law applicable to the contract has not been chosen in accordance with Article 3, the contract shall be governed by the law of the country with which it is most closely connected. Nevertheless, a severable part of the contract which has a closer connection with another country may by way of exception be governed by the law of that other country.

2. Subject to the provisions of paragraph 5 of this Article, it shall be presumed that the contract is most closely connected with the country where the party who is to effect the performance which is characteristic of the contract has, at the time of conclusion of the contract, his habitual residence, or, in the case of a body corporate or unincorporate, its central administration. However, if the contract is entered into in the course of that party's trade or profession, that country shall be the country in which the principal place of business is situated or, where under the terms of

the contract the performance is to be effected through a place of business other than the principal place of business, the country in which that other place of business is situated.

3. Notwithstanding the provisions of paragraph 2 of this Article, to the extent that the subject matter of the contract is a right in immovable property or a right to use immovable property it shall be presumed that the contract is most closely connected with the country where the immovable property is situtated.

4. A contract for the carriage of goods shall not be subject to the presumption in paragraph 2. In such a contract if the country in which, at the time the contract is concluded, the carrier has his principal place of business is also the country in which the place of loading or the place of discharge or the principal place of business of the consignor is situated, it shall be presumed that the contract is most closely connected with that country. In applying this paragraph single voyage charter-parties and other contracts the main purpose of which is the carriage of goods shall be treated as contracts for the carriage of goods.

5. Paragraph 2 shall not apply if the characterisic performance cannot be determined, and the presumptions in paragraphs 2, 3 and 4 shall be disregarded if it appears from the cirumstances as a whole that the contract is more closely connected with another country.

Article 5
Certain consumer contracts

1. This Article applies to a contract the object of which is the supply of goods or services to a person ("the consumer") for a purpose which can be regarded as being outside his trade or profession, or a contract for the provision of credit for that object.

2. Notwithstanding the provisions of Article 3, a choice of law made by the parties shall not have the result of depriving the consumer of the protection afforded to him by the mandatory rules of the law of the country in which he has his habitual residence:

—if in that country the conclusion of the contract was preceded by a specific invitation addressed to him by advertising, and he had taken in that country all the steps necessary on his part for the conclusion of the contract, or

—if the other party or his agent received the consumer's order in that country, or

—if the contract is for the sale of goods and the consumer travelled from that country to another country and there gave his order, provided that the consumer's journey was arranged by the seller for the purpose of inducing the consumer to buy.

3. Notwithstanding the provisions of Article 4, a contract to which this Article applies shall, in the absence of choice in accordance with Article 3, be governed by the law of the county in which the consumer has his habitual residence if it is entered into in the circumstances described in paragraph 2 of this Article.

4. The Article shall not apply to:

(*a*) a contract of carriage:
(*b*) a contract for the supply of services where the services are to be supplied to the consumer exclusively in a country other than that in which he has his habitual residence.

5. Notwithstanding the provisions of paragraph 4, this Article shall apply to a contract which, for an inclusive price, provides for a combination of travel and accommodation.

ARTICLE 6
Individual employment contracts

1. Notwithstanding the provisions of Article 3, in a contract of employment a choice of law made by the parties shall not have the result of depriving the employee of the protection afforded to him by the mandatory rules of the law which would be applicable under paragraph 2 in the absence of choice.

2. Notwithstanding the provisions of Article 4, a contract of employment shall, in the absence of choice in accordance with Article 3, be governed:
(*a*) by the law of the country in which the employee habitually carries out his work in performance of the contract, even if he is temporarily employed in another country; or
(*b*) if the employee does not habitually carry out his work in any one country, by the law of the country in which the place of business through which he was engaged is situated;

unless it appears from the circumstances as a whole that the contract is more closely connected with another country, in which case the contract shall be governed by the law of that country.

ARTICLE 7
Mandatory rules

1. When applying under this Convention the law of a country, effect may be given to the mandatory rules of the law of another country with which the situation has a close connection, if and in so far as, under the law of the latter country, those rules must be applied whatever the law applicable to the contract. In considering whether to give effect to these mandatory rules, regard shall be had to their nature and purpose and to the consequences of their application or non-application.*

2. Nothing in this Convention shall restrict the application of the rules of the law of the forum in a situation where they are mandatory irrespective of the law otherwise applicable to the contract.

*Article 7(1) does not have the force of law in the United Kingdom: see Contracts (Applicable Law) Act 1990.

ARTICLE 8
Material validity

1. The existence and validity of a contract, or of any term of a contract, shall be determined by the law which would govern it under this Convention if the contract or term were valid.

2. Nevertheless a party may rely upon the law of the country in which

he has his habitual residence to establish that he did not consent if it appears from the circumstances that it would not be reasonable to determine the effect of his conduct in accordance with the law specified in the preceding paragraph.

ARTICLE 9
Formal validity

1. A contract concluded between persons who are in the same country is formally valid if it satisfies the formal requirements of the law which governs it under this Convention or of the law of the country where it is concluded.

2. A contract concluded between persons who are in different countries is formally valid if it satifies the formal requirements of the law which governs it under this Convention or of the law of one of those countries.

3. Where a contract is concluded by an agent, the country in which the agent acts is the relevant country for the purposes of paragraphs 1 and 2.

4. An act intended to have legal effect relating to an existing or contemplated contract is formally valid if it satisfies the formal requirements of the law which under this Convention governs or would govern the contract or of the law of the country where the act was done.

5. The provisions of the preceding paragraphs shall not apply to a contract to which Article 5 applies, concluded in the circumstances described in paragraph 2 of Article 5. The formal validity of such a contract is governed by the law of the country in which the consumer has his habitual residence.

6. Notwithstanding paragraphs 1 to 4 of this Article, a contract the subject matter of which is a right in immovable property or a right to use immovable property shall be subject to the mandatory requirements of form of the law of the country where the property is situated if by that law those requirements are imposed irrespective of the country where the contract is concluded and irrespective of the law governing the contract.

ARTICLE 10
Scope of the applicable law

1. The law applicable to a contract by virtue of Articles 3 to 6 and 12 of this Convention shall govern in particular:

(*a*) interpretation;
(*b*) performance;
(*c*) within the limits of the powers conferred on the court by its procedural law, the consequences of breach, including the assessment of damages in so far as it is governed by rules of law;
(*d*) the various ways of extinguishing obligations, and prescription and limitation of actions;
(*e*) the consequences of nullity of the contract.*

2. In relation to the manner of performance and the steps to be taken in the event of defective performance regard shall be had to the law of the country in which performance takes place.

*Article 10(1)(*e*) does not have the force of law in the United Kingdom: see Contracts (Applicable Law) Act 1990, s 2(2).

Article 11
Incapacity

In a contract concluded between persons who are in the same country, a natural person who would have capacity under the law of that country may invoke his incapacity resulting from another law only if the other party to the contract was aware of this incapacity at the time of the conclusion of the contract or was not aware thereof as a result of negligence.

Article 12
Voluntary assignment

1. The mutual obligations of assignor and assignee under a voluntary assignment of a right against another person ("the debtor") shall be governed by the law which under this Convention applies to the contract between the assignor and assignee.

2. The law governing the right to which the assignment relates shall determine its assignability, the relationship between the assignee and the debtor, the conditions under which the assignment can be invoked against the debtor and any question whether the debtor's obligations have been discharged.

Article 13
Subrogation

1. Where a person ("the creditor") has a contractual claim upon another ("the debtor"), and a third person has a duty to satisfy the creditor, or has in fact satisfied the creditor in discharge of that duty, the law which governs the third person's duty to satisfy the creditor shall determine whether the third person is entitled to exercise against the debtor the rights which the creditor had against the debtor under the law governing their relationship and, if so, whether he may do so in full or only to a limited extent.

2. The same rule applies where several persons are subject to the same contractual claim and one of them has satisfied the creditor.

Article 14
Burden of proof, etc

1. The law governing the contract under this Convention applies to the extent that it contains, in the law of contract, rules which raise presumptions of law or determine the burden of proof.

2. A contract or an act intended to have legal effect may be proved by any mode of proof recognised by the law of the forum or by any of the laws referred to in Article 9 under which that contract or act is formally valid, provided that such mode of proof can be administered by the forum.

Article 15
Exclusion of renvoi

The application of the law of any country specified by this Convention means the application of the rules of law in force in that country other than its rules of private international law.

ARTICLE 16
"Ordre public"

The application of a rule of the law of any country specified by this Convention may be refused only if such application is manifestly incompatible with the public policy ("ordre public") of the forum.

ARTICLE 17
No retrospective effect

This Convention shall apply in a Contracting State to contracts made after the date on which this Convention has entered into force with respect to that State.

ARTICLE 18
Uniform interpretation

In the interpretation and application of the preceding uniform rules, regard shall be had to their international character and to the desirability of achieving uniformity in their interpretation and application.

ARTICLE 19
States with more than one legal system

1. Where a State comprises several territorial units each of which has its own rules of law in respect of contractual obligations, each territorial unit shall be considered as a country for the purposes of identifying the law applicable under this Convention.

2. A State within which different territorial units have their own rules of law in respect of contractual obligations shall not be bound to apply this Convention to conflicts solely between the laws of such units.

ARTICLE 20
Precedence of Community law

This Convention shall not effect the application of provisions which, in relation to particular matters, lay down choice of law rules relating to contractual obligations and which are or will be contained in acts of the institutions of the European Communities or in national laws harmonised in implementation of such acts.

ARTICLE 21
Relationship with other Conventions

This Convention shall not prejudice the application of international conventions to which a Contracting State is, or becomes, a party.

ARTICLE 22
Reservations

1. Any Contracting State may, at the time of signature, ratification, acceptance or approval, reserve the right not to apply:

(*a*) the provisions of Article 7(1);
(*b*) the provisions of Article 10(1)(*e*).

2. Any Contracting State may also, when notifying an extension of the Covention in accordance with Article 27(2), make one or more of these reservations, with its effect limited to all or some of the territories mentioned in the extension.

3. Any Contracting State may at any time withdraw a reservation which it has made; the reservation shall cease to have effect on the first day of the third calendar month after notification of the withdrawal.

TITLE III
FINAL PROVISIONS
ARTICLE 23

1. If, after the date on which this Convention has entered into force for a Contracting State, that State wishes to adopt any new choice of law rule in regard to any particular category of contract within the scope of this Convention, it shall communicate its intention to the other signatory States through the Secretary-General of the Council of the European Communities.

2. Any signatory State may, within six months from the date of the communications made to the Secretary-General, request him to arrange consultations between signatory States in order to reach agreement.

3. If no signatory State has requested consultations within this period or if within two years following the communication made to the Secretary-General no agreement is reached in the course of consultations, the Contracting State concerned may amend its law in the manner indicated. The measures taken by that State shall be brought to the knowledge of the other signatory States through the Secretary-General of the Council of the European Communities.

ARTICLE 24

1. If, after the date on which this Convention has entered into force with respect to a Contracting State, that State wishes to become a party to a multilateral convention whose principal aim or one of whose principal aims is to lay down rules of private international law concerning any of the matters governed by this Convention, the procedure set out in Article 23 shall apply. However, the period of two years, referred to in paragraph 3 of that Article, shall be reduced to one year.

2. The procedure referred to in the preceding paragraph need not be followed if a Contracting State or one of the European Communities is already a party to the multilateral convention, or if its object is to revise a convention to which the State concerned is already a party, or if it is

a convention concluded within the framework of the Treaties establishing the European Communities.

Article 25

If a Contracting State considers that the unification achieved by this Convention is prejudiced by the conclusion of agreements not covered by Article 24(1), that State may request the Secretary-General of the Council of the European Communities to arrange consultations between the signatory States of this Convention.

Article 26

Any Contracting State may request the revision of this Convention. In this event a revision conference shall be convened by the President of the Council of the European Communities.

Article 27

1. This Convention shall apply to the European territories of the Contracting States, including Greenland, and to the entire territory of the French Republic.

2. Notwithstanding paragraph 1:

(*a*) this Convention shall not apply to the Faroe Islands, unless the Kingdom of Denmark makes a declaration to the contrary;

(*b*) this Convention shall not apply to any European territory situated outside the United Kingdom for the international relations of which the United Kingdom is responsible, unless the United Kingdom makes a declaration to the contrary in respect of any such territory;

(*c*) this Convention shall apply to the Netherlands Antilles, if the Kingdom of the Netherlands makes a declaration to that effect.

3. Such declarations may be made at any time by notifying the Secretary-General of the Council of the European Communities.

4. Proceedings brought in the United Kingdom on appeal from courts in one of the territories referred to in paragraph 2(*b*) shall be deemed to be proceedings taking place in those courts.

Article 28

1. This Convention shall be open from 19 June 1980 for signature by the States party to the Treaty establishing the European Economic Community.

2. This Convention shall be subject to ratification, acceptance or approval by the signatory States. The instruments of ratification, acceptance or approval shall be deposited with the Secretary-General of the Council of the European Communities.

ARTICLE 29

1. This Convention shall enter into force on the first day of the third month following the deposit of the seventh instrument of ratification, acceptance or approval.

2. This Convention shall enter into force for each signatory State ratifying, accepting or approving at a later date on the first day of the third month following the deposit of its instrument of ratification, acceptance or approval.

ARTICLE 30

1. This Convention shall remain in force for 10 years from the date of its entry into force in accordance with Article 29(1), even for States for which it enters into force at a later date.

2. If there has been no denunciation it shall be renewed tacitly every five years.

3. A Contracting State which wishes to denounce shall, not less than six months before the expiration of the period of 10 or five years, as the case may be, give notice to the Secretary-General of the Council of the European Communities. Denunciation may be limited to any territory to which the Convention has been extended by a declaration under Article 27(2).

4. The denunciation shall have effect only in relation to the State which has notified it. The Convention will remain in force as between all other Contracting States.

ARTICLE 31

The Secretary-General of the Council of the European Communities shall notify the States party to the Treaty establishing the European Economic Community of:

(*a*) the signatures;
(*b*) the deposit of each instrument of notification, acceptance or approval;
(*c*) the date of entry into force of this Convention;
(*d*) communications made in pursuance of Articles 23, 24, 25, 26, 27 and 30;
(*e*) the reservations and withdrawals of reservations referred to in Article 22.

ARTICLE 32

The Protocol annexed to this Convention shall form an integral part thereof.

ARTICLE 33

This Convention, drawn up in a single original in the Danish, Dutch, English, French, German, Irish and Italian languages, these texts being equally authentic, shall be deposited in the archives of the Secretariat of the Council of the European Communities. The Secretary-General shall transmit a certified copy thereof to the Government of each signatory State.

PROTOCOL

The High Contracting Parties have agreed upon the following provision which shall be annexed to the Convention:

Notwithstanding the provisions of the Convention, Denmark may retain the rules contained in Søloven (State on Maritime Law) paragraph 169 concerning the applicable law in matters relating to carriage of goods by sea and may revise these rules without following the procedure prescribed in Article 23 of the Convention.

The 1988 Lugano Convention on Jurisdiction and the Enforcement of Judgments in Civil and Commercial Matters

PREAMBLE

The High Contracting Parties to this Convention,

Anxious to strengthen in their territories the legal protection of persons therein established,

Considering that it is necessary for this purpose to determine the international jurisdiction of their courts, to facilitate recognition and to introduce an expeditious procedure for securing the enforcement of judgments, authentic instruments and court settlements,

Aware of the links between them, which have been sanctioned in the economic field by the free trade agreements concluded between the European Economic Community and the States members of the European Free Trade Association,

Taking into account the Brussels Convention of 27 September 1968 on jurisdiction and the enforcement of judgments in civil and commercial matters, as amended by the Accession Conventions under the successive enlargements of the European Communities,

Persuaded that the extension of the principles of that Convention to the States parties to this instrument will strengthen legal and economic co-operation in Europe,

Desiring to ensure as uniform an interpretation as possible of this instrument,

Have in this spirit decided to conclude this Convention and

Have agreed as follows:

TITLE I
SCOPE

ARTICLE 1

This Convention shall apply in civil and commercial matters whatever the nature of the court or tribunal. It shall not extend, in particular, to revenue, customs or administrative matters.

The Convention shall not apply to:

1. the status or legal capacity of natural persons, rights in property arising out of a matrimonial relationship, wills and succession;

2. bankruptcy, proceedings relating to the winding-up of insolvent companies or other legal persons, judicial arrangements, compositions and analogous proceedings;

3. social security;

4. arbitration.

TITLE II
JURISDICTION
SECTION 1
GENERAL PROVISIONS

ARTICLE 2

Subject to the provisions of this Convention, persons domiciled in a Contracting State shall, whatever their nationality, be sued in the courts of that State.

Persons who are not nationals of the State in which they are domiciled shall be governed by the rules of jurisdiction applicable to nationals of that State.

ARTICLE 3

Persons domiciled in a Contracting State may be sued in the courts of another Contracting State only by virtue of the rules set out in Section 2 to 6 of this Title.

In particular the following provisions shall not be applicable as against them:

— in Belgium: Article 15 of the civil code (Code civil - Burgerlijk Wetboek) and Article 638 of the judicial code (Code judiciaire - Gerechtelijk Wetboek),

— in Denmark: Article 246(2) and (3) of the law on civil procedure (Lov om rettens pleje),

— in the Federal Republic of Germany: Article 23 of the code of civil procedure (Zivilprozeßordnung),

— in Greece: Article 40 of the code of civil procedure (Λῶδικας πολιτικῆs δικουομιαs),

— in France: Articles 14 and 15 of the civil code (Code civil),

— in Ireland: the rules which enable jurisdiction to be founded on the document instituting the proceedings having been served on the defendant during his temporary presence in Ireland,

— in Iceland: Article 77 of the Civil Proceedings Act (lög um meðferð einkamála î héraði),

— in Italy: Articles 2 and 4, Nos 1 and 2 of the code of civil procedure (Codice di procedura civile),

— in Luxembourg: Articles 14 and 15 of the civil code (Code civil),

— in the Netherlands: Articles 126(3) and 127 of the code of civil procedure (Wetboek van Burgerlijke Rechtsvordering),

— in Norway: Section 32 of the Civil Proceedings Act (tvistemålsloven),

— in Austria: Article 99 of the Law on Court Jurisdiction (Jurisdiktionsnorm),

— in Portugal: Articles 65(1)(c), 65(2) and 65A(c) of the code civil procedure (Código de Processo Civil) and Article 11 of the code of labour procedure (Código de Processo de Trabalho),

— in Switzerland: le for du lieu du séquestre/Gerichtsstand des Arrestortes/foro del luogo del sequestro within the meaning of Article 4 of the loi fédérale sur le droit international privé/Bundesgesetz über das internationale Privatrecht/legge federale sul diritto internazionale privato,

— in Finland: the second, third and fourth sentences of Section 1 of Chapter 10 of the Code of Judicial Procedure (oikeudenkäymiskaari/rättegångsbalken),

— in Sweden: the first sentence of Section 3 of Chapter 10 of the Code of Judicial Procedure (Rättegångsbalken),

— in the United Kingdom: the rules which enable jurisdiction to be founded on:

(*a*) the document instituting the proceedings having been served on the defendant during his temporary presence in the United Kingdom; or

(*b*) the presence within the United Kingdom of property belonging to the defendant; or

(*c*) the seizure by the plaintiff of property situated in the United Kingdom.

ARTICLE 4

If the defendant is not domiciled in a Contracting State, the jurisdiction of the courts of each Contracting State shall, subject to the provisions of Article 16, be determined by the law of that State.

As against such a defendant, any person domiciled in a Contracting State may, whatever his nationality, avail himself in that State of the rules of jurisdiction there in force, and in particular those specified in the second paragraph of Article 3, in the same way as the nationals of that State.

SECTION 2
SPECIAL JURISDICTION

ARTICLE 5

A person domiciled in a Contracting State may, in another Contracting State, be sued:

1. in matters relating to a contract, in the courts for the place of performance of the obligation in question; in matters relating to individual contracts of employment, this place is that where the employee habitually carries out his work, or if the employee does not habitually carry out his work in any one country, this place shall be the place of business through which he was engaged;
2. in matters relating to maintenance, in the courts for the place where the maintenance creditor is domiciled or habitually resident or, if the matter is ancillary to proceedings concerning the status of a person, in the court which, according to its own law, has jurisdiction to entertain those proceedings, unless that jurisdiction is based solely on the nationality of one of the parties;
3. in matters relating to tort, delict or quasi-delict, in the courts for the place where the harmful event occurred;
4. as regards a civil claim for damages or restitution which is based on an act giving rise to criminal proceedings, in the court seised of those proceedings, to the extent that that court has jurisdiction under its own law to entertain civil proceedings;
5. as regards a dispute arising out of the operations of a branch, agency or other establishment, in the courts for the place in which the branch, agency or other establishment is situated;
6. in his capacity as settlor, trustee or beneficiary of a trust created by the operation of a statute, or by a written instrument, or created orally and evidenced in writing, in the courts of the Contracting State in which the trust is domiciled;
7. as regards a dispute concerning the payment of remuneration claimed in respect of the salvage of a cargo or freight, in the court under the authority of which the cargo or freight in question:

   (*a*) has been arrested to secure such payment,

   or

(*b*) could have been so arrested, but bail or other security has been given;

provided that this provision shall apply only if it is claimed that the defendant has an interest in the cargo or freight or had such an interest at the time of salvage.

ARTICLE 6

A person domiciled in a Contracting State may also be sued:

1. where he is one of a number of defendants, in the courts for the place where any one of them is domiciled;

2. as a third party in an action on a warranty or guarantee or in any other third party proceedings, in the court seised of the original proceedings, unless these were instituted solely with the object of removing him from the jurisdiction of the court which would be competent in his case;

3. on a counterclaim arising from the same contract or facts on which the original claim was based, in the court in which the original claim is pending;

4. in matters relating to a contract, if the action may be combined with an action against the same defendant in matters relating to rights *in rem* in immovable property, in the court of the Contracting State in which the property is situated.

ARTICLE 6A

Where by virtue of this Convention a court of a Contracting State has jurisdiction in actions relating to liability arising from the use or operation of a ship, that court, or any other court substituted for this purpose by the internal law of that State, shall also have jurisdiction over claims for limitation of such liability.

SECTION 3

JURISDICTION IN MATTERS RELATING TO INSURANCE

ARTICLE 7

In matters relating to insurance, jurisdiction shall be determined by this Section, without prejudice to the provisions of Articles 4 and 5(5).

ARTICLE 8

An insurer domiciled in a Contracting State may be sued:

1. in the courts of the State where he is domiciled; or

2. in another Contracting State, in the courts for the place where the policy-holder is domiciled; or

3. if he is a co-insurer, in the courts of a Contracting State in which proceedings are brought against the leading insurer.

An insurer who is not domiciled in a Contracting State but has a branch, agency or other establishment in one of the Contracting States shall, in disputes arising out of the operations of the branch, agency or establishment, be deemed to be domiciled in that State.

Article 9

In respect of liability insurance or insurance of immovable property, the insurer may in addition be sued in the courts for the place where the harmful event occurred. The same applies if movable and immovable property are covered by the same insurance policy and both are adversely affected by the same contingency.

Article 10

In respect of liability insurance, the insurer may also, if the law of the court permits it, be joined in proceedings which the injured party has brought against the insured.

The provisions of Articles 7, 8 and 9 shall apply to actions brought by the injured party directly against the insurer, where such direct actions are permitted.

If the law governing such direct actions provides that the policy-holder or the insured may be joined as a party to the action, the same court shall have jurisdiction over them.

Article 11

Without prejudice to the provisions of the third paragraph of Article 10, an insurer may bring proceedings only in the courts of the Contracting State in which the defendant is domiciled, irrespective of whether he is the policy-holder, the insured or a beneficiary.

The provisions of this Section shall not affect the right to bring a counterclaim in the court in which, in accordance with this Section, the original claim is pending.

Article 12

The provisions of this Section may be departed from only by an agreement on jurisdiction:

1. which is entered into after the dispute has arisen; or

2. which allows the policy-holder, the insured or a beneficiary to bring proceedings in courts other than those indicated in this Section; or

3. which is concluded between a policy-holder and an insurer, both

of whom are at the time of conclusion of the contract domiciled or habitually resident in the same Contracting State, and which has the effect of conferring jurisdiction on the courts of that State even if the harmful event were to occur abroad, provided that such an agreement is not contrary to the law of the State; or

4. which is concluded with a policy-holder who is not domiciled in a Contracting State, except in so far as the insurance is compulsory or relates to immovable property in a Contracting State; or

5. which relates to a contract of insurance in so far as it covers one or more of the risks set out in Article 12A.

Article 12A

The following are the risks referred to in Article 12(5):

1. any loss of or damage to:

   (*a*) sea-going ships, installations situated offshore or on the high seas, or aircraft, arising from perils which relate to their use for commercial purposes;

   (*b*) goods in transit other than passengers' baggage where the transit consists of or includes carriage by such ships or aircraft;

2. any liability, other than for bodily injury to passengers or loss of or damage to their baggage;

   (*a*) arising out of the use or operation of ships, installations or aircraft as referred to in (1)(*a*) above in so far as the law of the Contracting State in which such aircraft are registered does not prohibit agreements on jurisdiction regarding insurance of such risks;

   (*b*) for loss or damage caused by goods in transit as described in (1)(*b*) above;

3. any financial loss connected with the use or operation of ships, installations or aircraft as referred to in (1)(*a*) above, in particular loss of freight or charter-hire;

4. any risk or interest connected with any of those referred to in (1) to (3) above.

SECTION 4
JURISDICTION OVER CONSUMER CONTRACTS

ARTICLE 13

In proceedings concerning a contract concluded by a person for a purpose which can be regarded as being outside his trade or profession, hereinafter called 'the consumer', jurisdiction shall be determined by this Section, without prejudice to the provisions of Articles 4 and 5(5), if it is:

1. a contract for the sale of goods on instalment credit terms; or
2. a contract for a loan repayable by instalments, or for any other form of credit, made to finance the sale of goods; or
3. any other contract for the supply of goods or a contract for the supply of services, and
   - (*a*) in the State of the consumer's domicile the conclusion of the contract was preceded by a specific invitation addressed to him or by advertising, and
   - (*b*) the consumer took in that State the steps necessary for the conclusion of the contract.

Where a consumer enters into a contract with a party who is not domiciled in a Contracting State but has a branch, agency or other establishment in one of the Contracting States, that party shall, in disputes arising out of the operations of the branch, agency or establishment, be deemed to be domiciled in that State.

This Section shall not apply to contracts of transport.

ARTICLE 14

A consumer may bring proceedings against the other party to a contract either in the courts of the Contracting State in which that party is domiciled or in the courts of the Contracting State in which he is himself domiciled.

Proceedings may be brought against a consumer by the other party to the contract only in the courts of the Contracting State in which the consumer is domiciled.

These provisions shall not affect the right to bring a counterclaim in the court in which, in accordance with this Section, the original claim is pending.

ARTICLE 15

The provisions of this Section may be departed from only by an agreement:

1. which is entered into after the dispute has arisen; or
2. which allows the consumer to bring proceedings in courts other than those indicated in this Section; or
3. which is entered into by the consumer and the other party to the contract, both of whom are at the time of conclusion of the

contract domiciled or habitually resident in the same Contracting State, and which confers jurisdiction on the courts of that State, provided that such an agreement is not contrary to the law of that State.

Section 5
EXCLUSIVE JURISDICTION

Article 16

The following courts shall have exclusive jurisdiction, regardless of domicile:

1. (*a*) in proceedings which have as their object rights *in rem* in immovable property or tenancies of immovable property, the courts of the Contracting State in which the property is situated;

   (*b*) however, in proceedings which have as their object tenancies of immovable property concluded for temporary private use for a maximum period of six consecutive months, the courts of the Contracting State in which the defendant is domiciled shall also have jurisdiction, provided that the tenant is a natural person and neither party is domiciled in the Contracting State in which the property is situated;
2. in proceedings which have as their object the validity of the constitution, the nullity or the dissolution of companies or other legal persons or associations of natural or legal persons, or the decisions of their organs, the courts of the Contracting State in which the company, legal person or association has its seat;
3. in proceedings which have as their object the validity of entries in public registers, the courts of the Contracting State in which the register is kept;
4. in proceedings concerned with the registration or validity of patents, trade marks, designs, or other similar rights required to be deposited or registered, the courts of the Contracting State in which the deposit or registration has been applied for, has taken place or is under the terms of an international convention deemed to have taken place;
5. in proceedings concerned with the enforcement of judgments, the courts of the Contracting State in which the judgment has been or is to be enforced.

Section 6
PROROGATION OF JURISDICTION

Article 17

1. If the parties, one or more of whom is domiciled in a Contracting State, have agreed that a court or the courts of a Contracting State are to have jurisdiction to settle any disputes which have arisen or which may arise in connection with a particular legal relationship, that court or those courts shall have exclusive jurisdiction. Such an agreement conferring jurisdiction shall be either:

(*a*) in writing or evidenced in writing, or

(*b*) in a form which accords with practices which the parties have established between themselves, or

(*c*) in international trade or commerce, in a form which accords with a usage of which the parties are or ought to have been aware and which in such trade or commerce is widely known to, and regularly observed by, parties to contracts of the type involved in the particular trade or commerce concerned.

Where such an agreement is concluded by parties, none of whom is domiciled in a Contracting State, the courts of other Contracting States shall have no jurisdiction over their disputes unless the court or courts chosen have declined jurisdiction.

2. The court or courts of a Contracting State on which a trust instrument has conferred jurisdiction shall have exclusive jurisdiction in any proceedings brought against a settlor, trustee or beneficiary, if relations between these persons or their rights or obligations under the trust are involved.

3. Agreements or provisions of a trust instrument conferring jurisdiction shall have no legal force if they are contrary to the provisions of Article 12 or 15, or if the courts whose jurisdiction they purport to exclude have exclusive jurisdiction by virtue of Article 16.

4. If an agreement conferring jurisdiction was concluded for the benefit of only one of the parties, that party shall retain the right to bring proceedings in any other court which has jurisdiction by virtue of this Convention.

5. In matters relating to individual contracts of employment an agreement conferring jurisdiction shall have legal force only if it is entered into after the dispute has arisen.

Article 18

Apart from jurisdiction derived from other provisions of this Convention, a court of a Contracting State before whom a defendant enters an appearance shall have jurisdiction. This rule shall not apply where appearance was entered solely to contest the jurisdiction, or where another court has exclusive jurisdiction by virtue of Article 16.

Section 7
EXAMINATION AS TO JURISDICTION AND ADMISSIBILITY

Article 19

Where a court of a Contracting State is seised of a claim which is principally concerned with a matter over which the courts of another Contracting State have exclusive jurisdiction by virtue of Article 16, it shall declare of its own motion that it has no jurisdiction.

Article 20

Where a defendant domiciled in one Contracting State is sued in a court of another Contracting State and does not enter an appearance, the court shall declare of its own motion that it has no jurisdiction unless its jurisdiction is derived from the provisions of this Convention.

The court shall stay the proceedings so long as it is not shown that the defendant has been able to receive the document instituting the proceedings or an equivalent document in sufficient time to enable him to arrange for his defence, or that all necessary steps have been taken to this end.

The provisions of the foregoing paragraph shall be replaced by those of Article 15 of the Hague Convention of 15 November 1965 on the service abroad of judicial and extrajudicial documents in civil or commercial matters, if the document instituting the proceedings or notice thereof had to be transmitted abroad in accordance with that Convention.

SECTION 8
LIS PENDENS — RELATED ACTIONS

ARTICLE 21

Where proceedings involving the same cause of action and between the same parties are brought in the courts of different Contracting States, any court other than the court first seised shall of its own motion stay its proceedings until such time as the jurisdiction of the court first seised is established.

Where the jurisdiction of the court first seised is established, any court other than the court first seised shall decline jurisdiction in favour of that court.

ARTICLE 22

Where related actions are brought in the courts of different Contracting States, any court other than the court first seised may, while the actions are pending at first instance, stay its proceedings.

A court other than the court first seised may also, on the application of one of the parties, decline jurisdiction if the law of that court permits the consolidation of related actions and the court first seised has jurisdiction over both actions.

For the purposes of this Article, actions are deemed to be related where they are so closely connected that it is expedient to hear and determine them together to avoid the risk of irreconcilable judgments resulting from separate proceedings.

ARTICLE 23

Where actions come within the exclusive jurisdiction of several courts, any court other than the court first seised shall decline jurisdiction in favour of that court.

SECTION 9
PROVISIONAL, INCLUDING PROTECTIVE, MEASURES

ARTICLE 24

Application may be made to the courts of a Contracting State for such provisional, including protective, measures as may be available under the law of that State, even if, under this Convention, the courts of another Contracting State have jurisdiction as to the substance of the matter.

Title VII
RELATIONSHIP TO THE BRUSSELS CONVENTION AND TO OTHER CONVENTIONS

Article 54B

1. This Convention shall not prejudice the application by the Member States of the European Communities of the Convention on Jurisdiction and the Enforcement of Judgments in Civil and Commercial Matters, signed at Brussels on 27 September 1968 and of the Protocol on interpretation of that Convention by the Court of Justice, signed at Luxembourg on 3 June 1971, as amended by the Conventions of Accession to the said Convention and the said Protocol by the States acceding to the European Communities, all of these Conventions and the Protocol being hereinafter referred to as the 'Brussels Convention'.

2. However, this Convention shall in any event be applied:

(*a*) in matters of jurisdiction, where the defendant is domiciled in the territory of a Contracting State which is not a member of the European Communities, or where Article 16 or 17 of this Convention confers a jurisdiction on the courts of such a Contracting State;

(*b*) in relation to a *lis pendens* or to related actions as provided for in Articles 21 and 22, when proceedings are instituted in a Contracting State which is not a member of the European Communities and in a Contracting State which is a member of the European Communities;

(*c*) in matters of recognition and enforcement, where either the State of origin or the State addressed is not a member of the European Communities.

3. In addition to the grounds provided for in Title III recognition or enforcement may be refused if the ground of jurisdiction on which the judgment has been based differs from that resulting from this Convention and recognition or enforcement is sought against a party who is domiciled in a Contracting State which is not a member of the European Communities, unless the judgment may otherwise be recognized or enforced under any rule of law in the State addressed.

APPENDIX 2

JUDGMENT OF CARDOZO, J IN *THE UTICA CITY NATIONAL BANK (RESPONDENT) v JOHN K GUNN (APPELLANT)*

Court of Appeals of New York
(222 NY 204; 118 NE 607)

Held — The order of the Appellate Division in *Utica City National Bank v Gunn* 169 App Div 295 was affirmed. 8 January 1918 the following judgment was delivered.

CARDOZO, J. This action is brought upon a guaranty signed by the defendant and others in the following form:

Articles of Agreement this 12th day of December, 1912, between the Utica City National Bank of Utica, Oneida county, state of New York, party of the first part, and the Utica Pipe Foundry Company, party of the second part.

Witnesseth: Whereas the Utica Pipe Foundry Company requires from time to time loans and discounts from the said party of the first part, and the said party of the first part requires security and guaranty for the payment of such loans and discounts so made, now we, John A Kernan, and John K Gunn, of Utica, NY, and Chas G Wagner of Binghamton, NY, do jointly and severally bind ourselves and our representatives to pay all loans and discounts or renewals, or part renewals thereof, made by the said party of the first part to said Utica Pipe Foundry Company, on its failure to pay the same; so promising on the consideration that the said party of the first part shall and does make such loans and discounts in consideration of the execution and delivery of this agreement by us and each of us. The liability of the guarantors whose names are hereunto subscribed, shall not exceed in amount the sum of one hundred and fifteen thousand dollars ($115,000) on account of this guaranty, with interest on the amounts borrowed.

Dated, Utica, NY

JOHN A KERNAN [LS]

JOHN K GUNN [LS]

CHAS G WAGNER [LS]

At the date of this guaranty the plaintiff held the notes of the Utica Pipe Foundry Company for loans and discounts already made. There were no new loans or discounts after the delivery of the bond. There were, however, some renewals of previous loans and discounts. The old notes were surrendered, and new notes delivered. The question is whether the defendant's obligation under the bond extends to such renewals.

To ascertain the meaning of this contract, we must recall the surrounding circumstances. The limit of liability stated in the bond, $115,000, is the exact sum then due for previous loans and discounts. The bank examiner had suggested that the loans ought to be secured. The bank prepared this bond to silence the examiner's criticism. It filled in a printed form. A letter to the treasurer of the Utica Pipe Foundry Company explained the situation. The explanation was coupled with a statement that the notes would be renewed. There is evidence justifying the inference that these things were known to the defendant. He was a director of the corporation; he had knowledge of the state of its finances; he was told that the bank required the bond of the directors; he knew that some had refused to sign; and he and the treasurer talked of their refusal. The conversation is not stated fully or precisely, but the purpose of the transaction can hardly have been unknown. The slightest inquiry would have revealed it. One does not commonly put one's hand to a bond for $115,000 without some appreciation of the needs of the occasion. The defendant does not say that he was guilty of such folly. There was no thought of a new loan. The sole end to be attained was the safety of the old loan. This the defendant must have understood. A jury could fairly draw the inference that he had knowledge of the circumstances leading to the exaction of the bond.

In the light of those circumstances, therefore, the bond must be construed. The rule of construction is not changed because the defendant is a surety (*Ulster Co Savings Inst v Young* 161 NY 23; *Gates v McKee* 13 NY 232, 237). We may concede that the words, when viewed alone, apart from the setting of the occasion, give support to the defense. The promise is made 'on the consideration that the party of the first part shall and does make such loans and discounts in consideration of the execution and delivery of this agreement by us and each of us.' This looks to the future. It excludes the past. Unless loans or discounts have been made on the faith of the bond, the consideration for the promise fails. But loans and discounts in their proper legal meaning do not include renewals. A renewal is not a loan. It is an extension of the time of payment (*Brown v Marion National Bank* 169 US 416). The loan is made but once, and that is when the first note of the series is given. For like reasons a renewal is not in the strict sense a discount. A discount is a loan coupled with a deduction of the interest (*National Bank v Johnson* 104 US 271, 276). There can be no deduction of interest when no money is paid by the lender from which interest can be deducted.

The proper legal meaning, however, is not always the meaning of the parties. Surrounding circumstances may stamp upon a contract a popular or looser meaning. The words 'loans' and 'discounts' are not so clear and certain that circumstances may not broaden them to include renewals. They often have that meaning in the language of business life. In the thought of business men, to renew a loan or discount is to make it over again, but none the less to make it. Especially is that so where, as here, a new note is given at each renewal, and interest paid. The triers of the facts must fix the sense in which the words were used in the contract now before us (*Kenyon v Knights Templars & MM Aid Assn* 122 NY 247; *Lamb v Norcross Bros Co* 208 NY 427; *Rankin v Fidelity Ins, Trust & SD Co* 189 US 242, 253). To take the primary or strict meaning is to make the whole transaction futile. To take the secondary or loose meaning, is to give it efficacy and purpose. In such a situation, the genesis and aim of the transaction may rightly guide our choice (4 Wigmore on Ev § 2470; Stephen, Digest of Law of Ev, art 91, subds 5 and 6).

The point is made that earlier clauses of the bond exclude the broader meaning. It is said that the parties have themselves distinguished between loans or discounts and renewals. The defendant is to pay 'all loans and discounts or renewals or part renewals thereof'; in consideration of this payment, the plaintiff is to make 'loans and discounts' on the faith of the bond. If renewals or part renewals were to be consideration, they should have been mentioned again. The failure to repeat them means that the only renewals which the defendant is to pay are renewals of new loans and discounts. That is the defendant's argument. Its force, we think, is not controlling. The mention of renewals and part renewals in other clauses of the bond does not of necessity exclude them from the definition of loans and discounts. On the contrary, it may indicate a purpose to include them. The words may have been added, not to point a contrast or a distinction, but to amplify and explain. They have been used for greater certainty, to show the comprehensive sense in which loans and discounts were to be taken. 'Or' may then be read as equivalent to 'including'. If that was the thought, it was unnecessary to repeat the definition. The gloss, once placed upon the words, would hold good throughout the contract. Renewals had already been stated to be included. It might be taken for granted that they would not thereafter be excluded. What weight would be given to the failure to repeat the admonition was for the triers of the facts (*Kenyon v Knights Templar & MM Aid Assn*, supra; *Lamb v Norcross Bros Co*, supra). Verbal niceties might yield in their minds to the overmastering consideration that unless related to past loans, the obligation of the bond was a vain and empty form. It is easier to give a new shade of meaning to a word than to give no meaning to a whole transaction.

The order of the Appellate Division should be affirmed, and judgment absolute ordered against the appellant upon the stipulation with costs in all courts.

CHASE, CUDDEBACK and POUND, JJ, concurring

COLLIN, CRANE and ANDREWS, JJ, dissenting.

APPENDIX 3

LORD THRING: *PRACTICAL LEGISLATION*

The following is from *Practical Legislation* by Lord Thring (London, 1902), who had been parliamentary draftsman during both Disraeli's and Gladstone's administrations.

It may be interesting to the reader to learn something of the mode in which a Government Bill is constructed. The best course will be to take the example of an important Bill such as the Irish Land Act 1870.

The instructions given me were as usual, to a great extent, verbal ones, conveyed during a series of conferences with Mr Gladstone. I used to attend him at his house generally by myself. I never hesitated to tell him my mind, 'This will not do'; he would then stand up with his back to the fire and make me a little speech urging his view of the case; I then replied shortly till the point was settled. I recollect on one occasion his manner was so vehement that I thought I must have gone beyond bounds in contradiction and began to apologise. His reply was, 'Go on as you always have done and make no apologies; if my manner has led you to think that I am offended, I am sorry for it.'

One limit, however, I imposed on myself; I observed that he objected strongly to what sportsmen call hunting heel. When a question had been fully argued and decided he, above all things, disliked to have it reopened, and I never ventured to do so unless I could bring forward some fresh evidence on the subject.

Mr Gladstone was as economical of his time as he was of the public finances. I used to sit on one side of the table whilst he sat on the other side with a letter before him. When a difficult point occurred I would say, 'Wait a moment and I will look at my papers.' Whilst I was searching for the solution Mr Gladstone would go on with his letter, and when he saw me look up he would again give his attention to the Bill. This would occur in a Bill involving the most intricate problems, as, for instance, in the Irish Land Act of 1881, and he seemed to be able to turn his mind from one subject to another without the slightest difficulty or confusion.

Mr Gladstone's was the most constructive intellect with which I ever was brought in contact and also was the most untiring in devotion to its object. He understood and revised every word of a Bill and even settled the marginal notes. Once only had we any discussion as to the arrangement of a Bill, and this arose on the Irish Disestablishment Bill. I wished to put in one short clause at the very commencement, a sentence disestablishing the Irish Church. Mr Gladstone disapproved and I was about to accept his instructions to postpone the provision when Lord Granville interfered, saying, 'Had you not better pay attention to the draftsman's suggestions?' Whereupon Mr Gladstone gave way and the proposed clause appeared at the beginning of the Bill.

A strange contrast to Mr Gladstone's management of Bills was that of Mr Disraeli. He seemed to have an intuitive perception of what would pass the House of Commons, but he cared nothing for the details of a Bill, and once satisfied with the principle of a Bill, he troubled comparatively little about its arrangement or its construction. It was in course of preparing the Reform Bill of 1867 and watching every night its passage through Parliament that I had ample means for the first and last time of judging of Mr Disraeli's characteristics.

I was constantly struck by his great skill in overcoming difficulties as they arose in Parliament, and his tact in meeting by judicious compromises the objections of his opponents. His courtesy to me never failed even under the most trying circumstances. My first introduction to him was so curious that it may be worth telling. I think it was on Wednesday, November 13, 1867, that Mr Walpole, then Home Secretary, gave me to read a copy of the Reform Bill which had been prepared by a parliamentary agent.[1] I expressed to him an opinion unfavourable to the Bill as drawn. This opinion was repeated to Lord Derby who sent for me to the House of Lords on Thursday 14th. I told him in substance what I had told Mr Walpole. Lord Derby said it was too late to take any steps to alter the Bill to the extent which I wished, and I undertook at his request to communicate with the draftsman and to tell him to proceed with his work. I returned to my office and was actually engaged in writing the letter when Mr Disraeli's secretary now Lord Rowton came in and told me as an instruction from Mr Disraeli to entirely redraft the Bill, and added that the Bill must be ready on Saturday, 16th. Accordingly, next day I took the Bill in hand, and working with two shorthand-writers from ten till six, I completed it. The Bill was printed during the night and was laid before the Cabinet on Saturday. It was considered on Monday by Mr Disraeli; he personally instructed me in the matter and the Bill was circulated to the House of Commons on Tuesday.

1 This was Mr Dudley Baxter, a partner of Sir Philip Rose, Disraeli's solicitor; a slightly different account of this incident is given by Lord Blake in *Disraeli* at p 463.

APPENDIX 4

POWER OF ATTORNEY

THIS POWER OF ATTORNEY made the day
of 199 by
[full name of the company] ('the Company') which is incorporated under the law of England and has its registered office at
[ ]
WITNESSETH as follows:–

Appointment of attorneys

1. The Company appoints each of the persons named below ('an Attorney') separately and individually to be an attorney of the Company until and including 199#
on behalf of the Company–

(a) to sign any Relevant Documents (as defined below); and
(b) to do anything which he considers appropriate in relation to a Relevant Document (whether signed by him or another Attorney); and
(c) to exercise the other powers given below.

The following are the Attorneys: (a) ;
; and (c) .

Interpretation

2. In this Deed–

'document' has the meaning given in clause 10 below.
'Final Date' means the date mentioned in clause 1 above;
'Relevant Document' means any document which an Attorney considers necessary or appropriate to be signed and/or delivered on behalf of the Company in connection with–

(i) [here insert a brief general description of the transaction]; or
(ii) any transaction, matter or occurrence related or relevant to the transaction referred to in sub-paragraph (i) above or any aspect of it;

including a document which contains a power of attorney or other powers to act on behalf of the Company or in relation to its assets;

'Relevant Persons' means [here name or identity the other parties, or main parties, to the transaction];
'sign' shall be construed in accordance with clause 10 below.

Irrevocability until Final Date

3. All the powers conferred by this Deed are irrevocable until and including the Final Date.

Attorney's powers

4. Each Attorney–
   (a) has absolute and independent discretion about the exercise of his powers, including the terms of any Relevant Document which he signs or approves; and
   (b) may act under this Deed in England or any other country or both in England and another country;

and some Relevant Documents may be signed and some things done by one Attorney and others by another Attorney.

Sub-delegation

5. Each Attorney may authorise any other person or persons–
   (a) to sign or initial an amendment approved by the Attorney to a Relevant Document previously signed by him or another Attorney or to sign a separate document making such an amendment;
   (b) to deliver or forward (by post or otherwise) a Relevant Document or to authorise another person to do so;
   (c) to transmit (by telex, fax or otherwise) a Relevant Document (or its text) or to authorise another person to do so;
   (d) to hold a Relevant Document in escrow or to the order of the Company or another person or on any other terms;

and each Attorney may also subsequently ratify any action covered by paragraph (a), (b), (c) or (d) above which is taken by a person without such prior authorisation and release him from any liability which he may have incurred to the Company as a result of having acted without prior authorisation.

Method of execution

6. Each Attorney and any person acting under clause 5 above may sign a Relevant Document in the Company's name or (at his option) in his own name on behalf of the Company.

Protection of Relevant Persons

7. In favour of a Relevant Person, it shall be conclusively presumed that an Attorney (and any person purporting to act under the clause 5 above) had full power to sign every Relevant Document and to do everything which he may have purported to sign or do under this Deed on or before the Final Date.

Ratification

8. Without derogating from the previous clause, the Company covenants with each Relevant Person, that it will, forthwith on written request (including a request made after the Final Date), sign any document or do anything which that Relevant Person states is in his or its opinion desirable for the purposes of confirming or conferring validity on any Relevant Document or thing which an Attorney (and any person purporting to act under clause 5 above) purported to sign or do under this Deed on or before the Final Date.

Applicable law and jurisdiction

*9. English law is the law applicable to this Deed; and, for the exclusive benefit of the Relevant Persons, the Company agrees that the courts of England shall have exclusive jurisdiction to settle any disputes which may arise out of or in connection with this Deed.

Meaning of 'document' and 'sign'

10. In this Deed 'document' means every description of document, whether or not governed by English law, including any deed, any notarial act (whether in public or private form) and any document required for the purposes of an official authority or registry; and references to signing a document include references to—

(a) sealing or otherwise executing a deed;

(b) signing, executing or formalising a document in accordance with the law of or practice in a country other than England;

(c) drawing, accepting, making, issuing, endorsing or avalising any bill, note or similar instrument;

(d) initialling or authenticating a document;

(e) signing or initialling an amendment to a document; and

(f) doing anything similar, analogous or related to any of the foregoing.

IN WITNESS whereof the Company has, in accordance with its constitution and a resolution of its directors duly passed on 199#, executed this Power of Attorney as a deed on the day and year first before written.

Signed as a Deed	)
by [full name of Company]	)
Acting by	)
	)
Director	)
	)
Director/Secretary	)

*The first half of clause 9 is only necessary if there is a significant non-English element; and the second half is only necessary where the principal is domiciled outside England.

APPENDIX 5

COMPANY SECRETARY'S CERTIFICATE AS TO BOARD RESOLUTION

To: Compagnie Racine S.A.

This Certificate is given under clause 2(1)(*c*) of the agreement dated today between yourselves and ABC plc ("the Company") for the sale to you of the issued share capital of XYZ Limited ("the Agreement").

I certify as follows:

1. I have been the secretary of the Company since 1 July 1990.

2. On 14 March 1991 the directors of the Company passed the following resolutions:

(1) That the proposed sale of XYZ Limited to Compagnie Racine S.A. is approved in principle.

(2) That Mr A. B. Black, Mr C. D. Brown, Mr E. F. Smith and Mr G. H. White are constituted a committee of the directors with full power and discretion—

(*a*) to agree the terms of the sale, including the consideration, which may wholly or partly consist of shares, loan stock or other securities issued by Compagnie Racine S.A.;
(*b*) to authorise the execution by or on behalf of the Company of any deed, agreement and other document relating to the sale or any matter connected with it;
(*c*) generally, to settle any matter arising in relation to the sale or any matter connected with it.

(3) That the committee may delegate to any director (whether a member of the committee or not) the power to execute any such deed, agreement or other document in a form substantially as approved by the committee but with any minor modifications which he considers appropriate.

(4) That the quorum at any meeting of the committee shall be two.

3. On 25 April 1991 the committee referred to above passed the following resolutions:

(1) That the Company enter into—

(*a*) an agreement with Compagnie Racine S.A., substantially in the terms of the draft produced to the meeting and initialled for identification by the chairman, for the sale to Compagnie Racine S.A. of the entire issued share capital of XYZ Limited for a consideration of £5.5 million to be satisfied, as to £1 million, in cash payable on completion and, as to £4.5 million, by the issue of floating rate notes 1994 of Compagnie Racine S.A.; and

(*b*) the deed of indemnity regarding tax liabilities substantially in the form set out on Schedule 3 to that draft agreement.

(2) That any director is authorised to sign the agreement substantially in the form of the initialled draft, but with any minor modifications which he thinks appropriate; and any two directors are authorised to execute the deed of indemnity substantially in the form of Schedule 3 in the initialled draft, but with any minor modifications which they think appropriate.

4. Under the Company's memorandum and articles of association the board and the committee respectively had power to pass these resolutions; the resolutions were properly passed at meetings of the board and the committee which were duly convened and held and throughout which there was present a quorum of directors or committee members entitled to vote; to the best of my knowledge, any declaration of an interest by a director which was required by section 317 of the Companies Act 1985 or the Company's articles of association was properly made; in accordance with section 382 of the Companies Act 1985, I have entered in the minute books of the Company minutes of the proceedings at both those meetings; and those minutes record the passing of the resolutions referred to above and have been signed by the respective chairmen of those meetings.

5. The Agreement, as signed on behalf of the Company by Mr C. D. Brown, is in the same terms as the draft initialled by the chairman of the committee, except that in clause 4(1) the date of Completion has been changed from 2 May 1991 to 9 May 1991 and the deed of indemnity executed on behalf of the Company by Mr C. D. Brown and E. F. Smith is in the same terms as Schedule 3 in that draft.

As Witness my hand this 26th day of April 1991.

Francis Vesey

Secretary

NOTE

Five points need comment. It is assumed that the articles of association of ABC Limited contain an article in the usual form which authorises the directors to delegate any of their powers to a committee. Second, it is assumed that the sale of XYZ Limited is within the scope of the relevant article: see Guinness plc v Saunders [1990] 2 AC 663, [1990] 1 All ER 652, HL for a transaction which could not be authorised by a committee. Third, the usual form of article contains no express power for a committee to sub-delegate; (see, for example regulation 72 in Table A in the Companies (Table A to F) Regulations 1985 (SI 1985 No 805)). Accordingly, the maxim 'delegatus non potest delegare' applies, although it is thought that a board committee has a limited implied power to sub-delegate the formality of executing a document in a form authorised by the committee and, probably, the approval of minor modifications. Fourth, the language about a quorum of directors 'entitled to vote' reflects that fact that many companies' articles of association disqualify a director from being counted towards a quorum and voting in relation to a contract in which he is interested. Fifth, the reason for certificate's mentioning directors' declarations of interest is that a failure to make such a declaration can make a contract voidable by the company concerned, provided that the court can restore the parties to their pre-contract positions: see the speech of Lord Goff of Chieveley in Guinness v Saunders.

APPENDIX 6

COMMISSION NOTICE C(88) 1696 CONCERNING '*FORCE MAJEURE* IN EUROPEAN AGRICULTURAL LAW' (88/C 259/07)

The aim of this notice is to ensure greater transparency and consistency in the application of the *force majeure* clause in European law, and particularly in agriculture. This is all the more necessary in that this clause appears frequently in Community legislation, the fulfilment of various requirements being expressed to be 'subject to cases of *force majeure*'.[1]

What is more, the attempt to set out in such legislation an exhaustive list of circumstances constituting *force majeure* has long since been abandoned.[2]

This notice is accordingly divided into three chapters: definition of the concept (I), details of its application (II), and requisite proof (III).

The conclusion is that the *force majeure* should be interpreted restrictively.

I. Definition of the concept of *force majeure*

1. The Court of Justice was called upon to interpret the concept of *force majeure* as early as 1968.[3] In the course of subsequent years, its interpretation has varied only very slightly; the definition given in Case 11/70 (Internationale Handelsgesellschaft[4] is still, in substance, valid:

> 'the concept of *force majeure* "is not limited to absolute impossibility but must be understood in the sense of unusual circumstances, outside

1 Commission Regulation (EEC) No 3183/80 laying down common detailed rules for the application of the system of import and export licences and advance fixing certificates for agricultural products (OJ No L 338, 13.12.80, p 1) contains a whole section (Articles 36 and 37) on *force majeure*. Although this Regulation contains detailed rules on the effects of a case of *force majeure*, it does not set out the conditions which must be met if a case of *force majeure* is to be recognised as such.

2 See Article 8(2) of Regulation No 87, OJ No 66, 28.7.1962, p 1895/62. As a first example, see Article 3 of Regulation No 111/63/EEC (amending Article 8 of the abovementioned Commission Regulation No 87), OJ No 147, 14.10.1963, p 2490.

3 Case 4/68 *Schwarzwaldmilch* [1968] ECR 38.

4 1970/ECR 1125.

the control of the trader, the consequences of which, in spite of the exercise of all due care, could not have been avoided except at the cost of excessive sacrifice. This definition has been repeated by the Court on numerous occasions in a large number of Judgments, not only concerning agriculture[5] but also other spheres.'[6]

2. According to a consistent line of Decisions of the Court, the concept of *force majeure* accordingly comprises an objective element (the unusual circumstance, outside the control of the trader) and a subjective element (consequences which could not have been avoided in spite of the exercise of all due care).

(a) With regard to the objective element, it is important to establish the definition of an 'unusual' circumstance which is 'outside the control of the trader'. The Court has not as yet been required to give a very precise ruling; nevertheless, it makes a distinction between normal commercial risks (inherent in each transaction of the same type) and those which are abnormal.[7]

1. An abnormal circumstance is one which is to be regarded as unforseeable or, at least, so improbable that a businessman exercising all due care may consider the risk to be negligible[8] (e.g. a stroke of lightning, ice-bound waterways,[9] an avalanche blocking roads which are normally open in winter, etc.)

2. A circumstance which is 'outside the control of the trader' is one which is beyond his control in the broad sense (a natural disaster, a soveriegn act, a wildcat strike, etc); acts which are not beyond the trader's control are those which, even if fraudulent, are committed by those with whom he has contractual relations[10] since it is the trader's responsibility to select his trading partners with care and to place them under an obligation in the contract, in a way that is sufficiently binding on them, to comply with the terms thereof (where appropriate by making provision for penalties in the event of failure to fulfil contractual obligations).

(b) The subjective element entails the obligation to guard against the consequences of the abnormal occurrence by taking all appropriate measures (with the exception of those involving excessive sacrifices). In particular, the trader must carefully monitor the progress of the operation and take action, without delay, should he detect an

5 See most recently, Case 266/84 *Denkavit* [1986] ECR 149 ground 27.

6 See the recent judgment in Case 209/83 *Ferriera Valsabbia* [1984] ECR 3089. The varying forms of words used by the Court in its Decision must be regarded as resulting from the specific characteristics of the cases in question e.g. See Case 42/79 *Eierkontor* [1979] ECR 3703 ground 10.

7 See, in particular, Case 38/79 *Nordmark* [1980] ECR 655 ground 9; Case 808/79 *Pardini* [1980] ECR 2122 ground 21.

8 See Case 4/68 *Schwarzwaldmilch* [1968] ECR 386.

9 See, in this connection Case 71/82 *BALM v. Brüggen* [1982] ECR 4654 ground 3.

10 See, in this connection, Case 42/79 *Eierkontor* [1979] ECR 3716 ground 10.

anomaly,[11] he must, where appropriate, obtain supplies elsewhere or deal with the goods in another way; he must protect himself in an appropriate manner from the loss of important documents[12], he must exercise all due care in order to comply with the time limits prescribed in the rules.

II. Applicability of the *force majeure* clause

1. In specialised articles on Community law, writers are divided on the question of whether the *force majeure* clause should be recognised as a general principle of Community law (which applies even in the absence of a specific legislation provision)[13].

(a) In this regard, however, it is common ground that the Court of Justice has never ruled explicitly that the *force majeure* clause constitutes one of the general principles of Community law, while the Advocates General have expressed divergent views on this question[14]. In the absence of case law which is clear and unambiguous, it is prudent to take the view that, at present, the *force majeure* clause does not indisputably constitute one of the general principles of Community law which apply even in the absence of an express provision. It constitutes, rather, an exception to the general rule of scrupulous compliance with legislative provisions. Accordingly, as an exception, *the force majeure clause must be interpreted and applied strictly, which immediately circumscribes the manner in which it is dealt with by the Commission and the national authorities*[15].

(b) This conclusion must be drawn, in particular, because the Court of Justice has, in a number of cases[16], declined to apply a *force majeure* clause in the absence of an express provision to that effect and because the purpose of certain provisions of Community law does not, in all cases, allow account to be taken of situations involving an occurrence which may be considered to be a case of *force majeure*. This is so, in particular, in the case of conditions which must be scrupulously met because failure to fulfil them would frustrate normal operation of the rules. An example of this is compliance with the

11 See Case 266/84 *Denkavit v FORMA* [1986] ECR 149 (not yet reported) ground 28.
12 See Case 808/79 *Pardini* [1980] ECR 2122, ground 21; Case 158/73 *Kampffmeyer v EVS Getreide* [1974] ECR 100 grounds 11 and 12.
13 See, in particular, Gilsdorf, 'La force majeure dans le droit de la CEE', Cahiers de driot européen, 1982, p/137 (in particular, p/141), setting out the negative view; Flynn, '*Force Majeure Pleas*' European Law Review, 1981 p 102 (in particular, p 114), setting out the affirmative view.
14 See, setting out the negative view, Advocate-General Capotorti in Case 68/77 *IFG* [1978] ECR 353, in particular 380, and Case 38/79 *Nordmark* [1980] ECR 643, in particular 358; setting out the affirmative view, Advocate General Mayras in Case 32/72 *Wasaknäcke* [1972] ECR 1197.
15 Similarly, See JE Thomson, *Force Majeure:* the contextual approach to the Court of Justice; CMLR 24, 1987, pp 259–271.
16 Eg, Case 38/79 *Nordmark* [1980] 643.

time limit prescribed for the submission of tenders in connection with a procedure for the award of a contract. Such time limit must be respected absolutely and there can be no question of taking account of a situation possibly constituting *force majeure* since otherwise it would be impossible to ensure equal treatment as regards comparing tenders. It is possible to conceive of other exclusionary time limits the non-observance of which necessarily entails the loss of a right or a benefit, even where the delay is due to a case of *force majeure*, although it is not possible to set out an exhaustive list here. In any event, it has to be recognised that every administrative authority has an overriding need of exclusionary time limits since they constitute the only means whereby a particular case may be definitively closed. In the absence of such exclusionary time limits, all cases would have to remain unresolved for an indefinite period since, in theory, a case of *force majeure* could always be invoked in order to justify the delay.

(c) A practice has recently been observed whereby private individuals include in their contracts, on their own initiative, a *force majeure* clause which they undertake to interpret on an informal basis. They claim that they are thereby doing two things simultaneously: in the first place, remedying the deficiencies in Community law governing the matter and, on the other hand, judging themselves the question of the applicability of such clause.

It must be emphasised straightaway that such a course of action cannot produce the results which are anticipated from the standpoint of Community public law. *The concept of force majeure, as applied in the context of Community law, is an autonomous concept which is specific to that law.* It cannot be interpreted in the light of the national legal order governing the contract nor, *a fortiori*, according to the wishes of the contracting parties. The latter may, of course, by reason of their freedom of contract, include whatever clauses they choose, but they must recognise that such clauses govern their bilateral relations exclusively and they can in no event be relied on as against the Community.

(d) It is on those grounds that it is expedient not to take the view that the *force majeure* clause constitutes one of the general principles of Community law which apply even in the absence of an express provision. In accordance with that approach, the Commission will endeavour to make proposals, wherever it proves advisable, for the inclusion of a *force majeure* clause in instruments which do not currently contain one[17].

2. Nevertheless, the view may be taken that the *force majeure* clause simply gives expression, in a practical form, to the principle of proportionality which is undeniably one of the general principles of Community law[18].

The Court has, on a number of occasions, ruled that the inclusion of a *force majeure* clause could protect a Regulation providing for stringent

17 An example would be the recent amendement of Regulation (EEC) No 2220/85 by Regulation (EEC) No 1181/87 (OJ No L 113, 30.4.1987, p 31).

18 See, on these lines, Case 25/70 *Köster* [1970] ECR 1161 ground 22.

obligations accompanied by penalties for their non-fulfilment from criticisms based on an alleged breach of the principle of proportionality[19].

The Court has, moreover, recognised as exceptional cases that, even where the relevant rules do not contain any explicit reference to *force majeure*, it may be justified, in order to avoid excessive inequality of treatment, to relieve a trader of certain obligations imposed by the rules (e.g. observance of certain time limits) if his failure to fulfil those obligations was caused by circumstances that can be treated as *force majeure*, provided such relief is not incompatible with the essential objectives of the rules concerned[20].

This approach appears to rest, at least implicitly, on the link between the principle of proportionality (a superior principle of Community law applicable even in the absence of any written legal basis) and the applicability of a *force majeure* clause[1].

Thus, the possibility that observance of the principle of proportionality may, in certain exceptional cases, require the application of an unwritten *force majeure* clause cannot be wholly excluded. As a general rule, however, the wording of the rules must be strictly adhered to, since in many cases the application by analogy of an unwritten *force majeure* clause might impair the proper operation and the purpose of the rules, and hence would not be covered by the principle of proportionality. The subject must therefore be approached with great caution, and the national authorities are invited, in any case of doubt, to contact the Commission's departments.

III. Questions of evidence

Community rules (like national legislation) do not lay down specifically how *force majeure* is to be proved. It should be noted, however, that the use of the expression 'except in case of *force majeure*' has the effect of imposing the burden of proving that such a case exists on the traders who rely on it.

Since cases of *force majeure* are an exception to the legal rules, the standard of proof required must be at least as high as that required by the rules on the modes of proof that the obligation has been fulfilled. Consequently, incontrovertible documentary evidence must generally be required. Nevertheless, it is not easy to determine precisely the type of evidence that may be accepted in each situation. In case of doubt, it would be prudent to arrange consultations on individual cases presenting special features, to avoid equalities of treatment depending on which Member State is responsible for the authorities who have to evaluate the evidence.

19 Case 11/70 *Internationale Handelesgesellschaft* [1970] ECR 1125 ground 25;
Case 25/79 *Köster* [1970] ECR 1161 ground 31 and 40;
Case 147/81 *Merkur* [1982] ECR 1389 ground 11 *et seq.*

20 See Case 64/74 *Reich* [1975] ECR 261 ground of judgment 3; Case 6/79 *Union française des céréals* [1978] ECR 1675 ground 4; Case 71/87 *Inter-KOM*, judgment of 19.4.1988, not yet reported.

1 However, the Court has consistently held that the principle of proportionality does not preclude the total loss of benefit conferred in the case of failure to observe a principal obligation; see in particular Case 66/82 *Fromançais* [1983] ECR 395 and Case 272/81 *RUMI* [1982] ECR 4167.

IV. Conclusion

The principles involved in the foregoing analysis may be summarised as follows:

1. *Force majeure* is an exception to the general rule that the rules in force must be strictly observed; hence, it must be interpreted and applied restrictively.
2. *Force majeure* is not a general principle of law, but can be regarded, in exceptional cases, as an embodiment of the principle of proportionality, in the strict conditions laid down by the Court's Decisions.
3. The proof required of traders who rely on *force majeure* must be incontrovertible.

This means in practice that the national administration responsible for applying the *force majeure* clause in specific cases must approach the matter with the utmost caution, in evaluating both the facts relied on and the evidence adduced in support of the application. In case of doubt, they are invited to contact the Commission's departments.

INDEX